NEW STATES FOR A NEW INDIA

Centre de Sciences Humaines (Centre for Human Sciences): Created in 1990, the CSH is part of the network of 27 research centres of the French Ministry of Foreign Affairs. In 2007 it became UMIFRE 20 CNRS-MAEE, that is, a financially autonomous research institution under the dual tutelage of the French Ministry of Foreign and European Affairs (MAEE) and the French National Centre for Scientific Research (CNRS). The Centre's research work is primarily oriented towards the study of contemporary issues in the development of India and South Asia. The activities of the Centre are focused on four main areas, namely: Economic reforms and sustainable development; Politics and social change; Regional dynamics in South Asia and international relations; and Urban dynamics.

Centre de Sciences Humaines,
2 Aurangzeb Road,
New Delhi 110 011, India
Tel: (91 11) 3041 00 70
Fax: (91 11) 3041 00 79
Email: infos@csh-delhi.com
Website: http://www.csh-delhi.com

Institut Français de Pondichéry (French Institute of Pondicherry): Created in 1955 under the terms agreed to in the Treaty of Cession between the Indian and French governments, the IFP (UMIFRE 21 CNRS-MAEE) is a financially autonomous research institution under the dual tutelage of the French Ministry of Foreign and European Affairs (MAEE) and the French National Centre for Scientific Research (CNRS).

It fulfils its mission of research, expertise and training in human and social sciences, and ecology, in South and South-East Asia. Major research works focus on Indian cultural knowledge and heritage (Sanskrit language and literature, history of religions, Tamil studies, etc.), contemporary social dynamics (in the areas of health, economics and environment) and the natural ecosystems of south India (sustainable management of biodiversity).

Institut Français de Pondichéry
11 Saint Louis Street, PB 33,
Pondicherry 605 001, India
Tel: (91) 413 2334 168
Fax: (91) 413 2339 534
Website: http://www.ifpindia.org

NEW STATES FOR A NEW INDIA

Federalism and Decentralization in the States of Jharkhand and Chhattisgarh

Edited by

SAMUEL BERTHET
GIRISH KUMAR

MANOHAR

CSH
UMIFRE 20
CNRS-MAEE

CENTRE DE SCIENCES HUMAINES
2011

First published 2011

ISBN 978-81-7304-915-6

Published by
Ajay Kumar Jain *for*
Manohar Publishers & Distributors
4753/23 Ansari Road, Daryaganj
New Delhi 110 002

Typeset by
Kohli Print
Delhi 110 051

Printed at
Salasar Imaging Systems
Delhi 110 035

Contents

Preface

Does each significant turn taken by India find its translation into the federal setting of the country, such as the creation of new states? In the last one decade or so, there has been a persisting idea of an upcoming new India. Though a link has rarely been pointed out, one cannot ignore that an integral feature of a *new India* is the creation of three new states just at the turn of the present century: Uttaranchal (now Uttarakhand), Jharkhand and Chhattisgarh. What light do these creations shed on 'new India'? The contributions of the various scholars in this volume provide extremely valuable insights on the nature of the *new* state in the making. If India emerges more and more on the international stage as a key player, the internal setting of the country is also prone to fast changes. Many changes in the pattern of the country, whether social, political, economic or environmental, support this emergence on the international stage.

The present volume is the result of a shift in my area of study from modern and contemporary history of India to the latest evolution of Indian federal and local polity. It was inspired by academicians in India, who were more interested in contemporary issues linked to federalism, while the European Union was seemingly in a crucial phase of its construction (during 2002–5). Nevertheless, from cultural dynamics in modern India[1] to federalism and decentralization in India, one can see a thread and common issues such as the constructive and conflicting relationship between organic diversity and the continuous homogenizing trend, the defining feature of the modern state.

Nevertheless, the modern state does not have an even effect, politically and economically, on the territorial organization. It is characterized by centres with extremely high degree of concentration of power. There the political conflicts are publicly and ritually staged. These centres are supported by margins, essential to their survival, where conflicts between the same parties are solved in the backstage. The existence of those margins allows this extraordinary concentration of power. This dual and complementary relationship between the official stage, displayed in the centres, and the backstage or the political and geographical margins had been depicted in the early modern context, during the sixteenth century in Italy, by French writer Stendhal in his *Chroniques italiennes* (1836–9) or the *Italian Chronicles.*[2] This relationship between the centre and the margin is constantly reinvented or renegotiated along the line of the changes of a modern state always asking for more political and economic concentration against a more organic territorial organization, an important feature in pre-modern and early South Asian societies.

The impressive figure of diverse entities gradually accommodated into what has become the Union of India and the Republic of India is striking for any social scientist. Any European witnessing the changing fortunes of European federalism in the making is naturally impressed by federal arrangements in India which has helped a continent-sized country to negotiate its great diversities.

My study was initially aimed at outlining common elements in the two federal systems: Europe and India. While much enthusiasm was expressed for such a study from the Indian side, I had to face skepticism from the French side. Indeed, in 2003 the French jury in charge of screening my application for a comparative study between Indian and European federalism was not convinced by the very reality of European federalism. As a matter of fact, this skepticism was shared by a majority of French voters as well as by a majority of Dutch ones. The latest development of Indian federalism through a case study received more attention. As a matter of fact, the issue of Indian federalism and smaller states was being debated once again, following the creation of three new states and the Telengana Rashtra Samiti's claim for a separate state of Telengana in Andhra Pradesh. To the historian, this claim for statehood looked as a very significant evolution, since the movement for the creation of the state of Andhra Pradesh—resulting of territories carved out from the state of Madras adjoined to the state of Hyderabad—had played an instrumental role in defining the guiding principles for the creation of states contained in the recommendation made by the State Reorganization Commission in 1955.

But to come back to the comparative approach, one among the many common issues between the very different cases of European and Indian federalism is the 'federal-local' debate. In the first place, is the empowerment of federal states contradictory or necessary to decentralization? In the European Union, hopes were rising high in the regional parties that European federalism would take the shape of a federation or a union of regions and free them from the stranglehold of modern nation states. Regional entities would therefore witness a revival after centuries of a tightening hold of nation states on them, which had just started to loosen in the 1970s. This was particularly the case in highly centralized countries such as France or Spain. Nevertheless, in the first decade of the twenty-first century the debate shifted to the idea of the 'global' as against the 'national', the European Union being increasingly perceived as an agency of the free market and global economy against the pre-1989 nation states' protective social systems.

In the Union of India, the creation of smaller states only few years after the passing of the 73rd and 74th amendments gave the issue of federalism *versus* decentralization a renewed relevance, and created a new dynamic. This constitutional enactment came after decades of efforts pursued in order to strengthen the third tier of Indian democracy. Though it is often described as one of the 'traditional' basis of the Indian political organization, the local administration had been by far the worst-off among the three levels of the administrative apparatus. Compared to the state and central level, it had very little decision-making and financial power to really become an important component of Indian political life. The issue of federalism *versus* decentralization is of particular relevance in the two states we are dealing with, two of the most rural ones of peninsular India. The 73rd and 74th amendments were meant to boost rural development, provide resources and political empowerment at the local level, but also foster industrial progress in two of the three states richest in mineral resources. A contradiction between the interests of a new elite in these states, main beneficiary of the new global economy and inclined towards fast industrial development, and the villagers concerned with the social and environmental impact of such development would arise soon. Promoting development through the federal state or through local decentralization has different meanings and implications. A new balance between the two perspectives of development may have to be found in the new political entities.

Assessing the impact of federalism *vis-à-vis* decentralization is certainly a key issue to understand the latest evolution of modern states in the contemporary context, particularly in an ever encompassing global economy.

My interest in this issue took me to Prof. Balveer Arora (JNU), a political scientist of great repute well known for his in-depth understanding of Indian federalism. My affiliation to the Centre de Sciences Humaines in New Delhi brought me in touch with Dr. Girish Kumar, an established scholar in the field of decentralization, who eventually agreed to co-edit this volume. His thoughtful remarks and demands for rigorous scholarship have been a great stimulation for me to enter into this new field of academic studies. My discussion with both of them propelled me to go further on the subject. My general approach was complemented by visits to Chhattisgarh for a case-study, meeting with local activists, administrators, politicians, and scholars, such as Dr. Savyasaachi who had extensively surveyed the political systems in the tribal areas and Dr. Ilina Sen who had contributed to Chhattisgarh Mukti Morcha. These various approaches were brought together within a seminar where different specialists in the field shared their experiences of the region. This volume is the outcome of an international seminar 'Federalism and Decentralized Governance in the Union of India: A Comparative Study of Jharkhand, Chhattisgarh and Andhra Pradesh', organized by the Centre de Sciences Humaines (CSH) and held on 14–15 October 2004 at the IIC, New Delhi. It aimed at understanding the grounds for the creation of the states of Chhattisgarh and Jharkhand in the context of the possible creation of Telangana.

The seminar was the outcome of a team effort in which the CSH was involved at every step in various capacities—right from awarding me a fellowship to mobilizing its network of scholars working in the area. A special thanks to Prof. Joël Ruet and Dr. Véronique Dupont, directors of the CSH, for supporting my draft proposal on the study of federal dynamics. The initial ambition of my proposal on a comparison between Indian and European federalisms was refocused in due course on an assessment of the evolution of Indian federalism through a case-study of latest developments in the creation of new states. India being what it is, a comprehensive study of any one state, even supposedly 'small'—which is neither really the case with Jharkhand nor with Chhattisgarh—is sufficient to engage one for a lifetime.

Interactions with Dr. Stéphanie Tawa Lama-Rewal at CSH contributed greatly to my efforts at understanding the fast changing reality of the Indian political scene, especially at the local level. So were interactions with Dr. Cyril Robin and Bertrand Lefebvre, researchers, whose friendly support and lively thoughts were invaluable. Of course, the continuous exchanges and the contribution by another colleague at CSH, Prof. Dipankar Sengupta deserves a special mention. His choice to move towards new academic and geographical heights crippled our efforts to include him in the editorial team, but he remained associated with this project.

I must also thank Dr. Amit Prakash, who, in spite of an overburdened schedule, accepted to go back to his data and update them for the sake of the seminar and then for the publication of this volume. Prof. Virginius Xaxa has also very kindly accepted to deal once more with the tribal issues for the purpose of this academic venture. The inputs and participation of Pravir Krishn, an IAS officer of Madhya Pradesh cadre, posted in Delhi at that time, have been extremely insightful. Last but not the least, I would like to thank M.A. Iqbal and Kalawati, who participated to the seminar sharing their experience of almost thirty years of rural development in tribal regions in all its beauty and contradictions, trying to maintain at a distance all the possible political bias in a particularly complex context.

Thanks also to Attreyee Roy Chowdhury, Rupa Sengupta and Arpita Mitra, the magic trio of Publications in-charges at the CSH who survived the undulated roadmap of an edited volume, its various avatars and the changes of locations of its authors with foremost focus and tenacity. And finally thanks to Dr. Basudeb Chaudhuri, Director of CSH, for giving the final touch in concretizing this collective work.

Chittagong
May 2009

SAMUEL BERTHET

NOTES

1. Samuel Berthet, *Cultural Dynamics of the Indian Elite: Indo-French Relations during the Raj (1870–1947)*, Delhi: Manohar, 2006.
2. Interestingly, under the Realistic writer's pen, the scores between the Roman aristocracies were also settled in the neighbouring forest areas. A selection of those chronicles are published in English: Stendhal, *Three Italian Chronicles*, New York: New Direction Publishing Corporation, 1991.

CHAPTER ONE

Introduction: Federalism and Decentralization in India at the turn of the Twentieth Century—The Case of Chhattisgarh and Jharkhand

SAMUEL BERTHET

Creation of new and smaller states has been an enduring theme in the political history of the Indian Union. Each redrawing of boundaries has been a step towards the integration of the regions concerned. The process can be traced back to the integration of the princely states in the aftermath of Indian Independence and, again, in 1954–6 with the creation of the States' Reorganization Commission. Various re-adjustments were subsequently made to accommodate the demands within the Indian Republic's federal polity: bifurcation of a unilingual Bombay state into Maharashtra and Gujarat in 1960, Haryana and Punjab in 1966, elevation to statehood of Nagaland in 1963, Himachal Pradesh in 1971, Manipur, Meghalaya, Tripura and Mizoram in 1972, integration into the Indian Union of Sikkim in 1975. India has therefore undergone a long spell of states' reorganization leading to the formation of new entities. While the coming into being of Uttaranchal, Jharkhand and Chhattisgarh during the months of November and December 2000 did not go altogether unnoticed. It did not provoke any major political, economic or administrative questioning either.

Without any significant outbreak of militancy or challenge to the centre's authority emanating from any corner preceding bifurcation, the coming into being of these new entities, particularly

Chhattisgarh, has sometimes been termed 'quiet'. In fact, their creation has thrown up two questions: first, was it a step taken by a mature federal polity acknowledging the ability of the regional forces to provide improved governance and accelerate the process of decentralization? Second, which is more a corollary to the first question, was it a move to placate growing regional elites which are truly supportive of national parties and national interests? In the latter case, strengthening of the decentralization process would not necessarily be a consequence of the creation of these new states. Their formation—and indeed the larger issue of yielding to statehood demands—may therefore seem to herald a significant shift in the evolution of Indian federalism.

These two questions can help in assessing the evolution of Indian federalism, usually seen as oscillating between two contradictory trends: on the one hand, over-centralization supported by the state bureaucracy and, on the other, inevitable regional assertion, marked by varying degrees of regional autonomy. There is hardly a case for the latter with regard to the new states created in 2000 since, except for Jharkhand, the most protracted regional movements, Vidarbha and Telengana, have not managed to achieve statehood. The birth of Chhattisgarh and Jharkhand can even be looked at through an opposite perspective: the State tightening its hold over under-administered regions with the prospect of gaining high returns from the exploitation of their rich natural resources, one of the consequences of reforms pursued by successive central governments since 1991. In other words, the creation of new states would be an initiative of the central government in the context of liberal reforms and globalization.

The debate on political issues and development policies is struggling to find room in the context of new states where the utilitarian philosophy of governance tends to dilute ideological contradictions. Till 2000, movements for the creation of states were generally supported by strong cultural claims, based on the linguistic factor. In the case of Chhattisgarh, the language issue was at best peripheral. Indeed, it seems to have been addressed to a greater degree in undivided Madhya Pradesh.[1] The unexpected coming into being of these states seems thus to have been triggered by the imperatives of the global economy, supported by an elite at the regional level, but not necessarily an elite with a regionalist agenda.

Before considering general issues of governance and decentralization, we will first discuss the commonly accepted idea that Chhattisgarh and Jharkhand are 'tribal' states. It is important to re-evaluate this notion since backwardness, a term inherited from the colonial administration and at the very core of the definition of the Scheduled Tribes (ST) category, is used as the basis of political discourse and as a justification for economic and industrial policies furthering ultra-liberal conceptions of development both at the state and local levels.

TRIBAL STATES, BACKWARD AREAS AND REFORMS

The creation of Jharkhand and Chhattisgarh could appear to be part of an evolving federal framework with relation to the politico-administrative recognition given to the tribal population by the Constitution, through the Fifth Schedule, in the very first years of the Indian Republic. This recognition of the specificity of tribal regions was further strengthened by the tribal sub-plans from the fifth to the eighth plan, between 1974 and 1997.[2] Even within the discourse concerning promotion of ST rights, resources were prioritized over political empowerment: 'As the tribal areas are very big depositories of natural resources, its exploitation in both national and tribal interest is quite necessary. The tribal areas are under-developed, so also the people, therefore a sensitized development administration is also necessary,' says B.D. Sharma.[3]

The steps foreseen were again administrative rather than political, and based on the distinctiveness of the geographical units where STs accounted for more than 50 per cent of the total population. Schemes under the Integrated Tribal Development Project were set up in these units. From 1980 onwards, the remaining tribal areas were covered by the Modified Areas Development Approach. The project implementation committee was chaired by the collector and included as members the heads of various development departments as well as a project administrator as secretary. Representatives were only members of the advisory committees along with the above-mentioned bureaucrats. One pitfall was the use yet again of administrative channels disconnected from the representative process, making it difficult to spur a much needed political leadership. The benevolent approach of tribal cause promoter, B.D. Sharma itself did not exclude paternalistic bias: 'The administrative system should be holistic, responsible for all aspects of life.' Attempts to develop tribal areas as separate administrative enclaves are symptomatic of the difficulties in creating a participative and organic developmental pattern with regard to the regions concerned.

In the modern context, the expression 'tribal states' is a contradiction in terms. Our understanding of the word 'tribal' is a colonial legacy: it denotes backward communities deprived of modern technology as well as fully functioning political structures as per the modern conception of a state.

During the nineteenth century, the hinterland of the Indian peninsula underwent a transformation. As a reservoir of raw materials and subdued manpower, it sustained the development of the British Empire and the prosperity of the new administrative and industrial elites. The stress on natural resources has not decreased since; rather, resource extraction has gained new momentum since the 1990s.

The new politico-economic order set up the practical apparatus for the segregation of tribal communities by a special administrative regime. The objectives of the creation of the Excluded Tracks and later the Scheduled Areas were two-fold. One, giving the modern state the opportunity to manage resource-rich forest areas which could anyway not come under the same administrative regime, such as the 'areas under the Permanent Settlement' for instance. Two, preventing tribal communities from falling prey to middlemen. While the first objective was fulfilled, the second was not, and a nexus between the administration and the middlemen/business communities became one of the major factors preventing the development of tribal areas.

In areas under direct British rule, the sociological pattern underwent important structural changes and political bargaining and communal assertion, two fundamentals for the development of a majoritarian democracy, were already in play for decades together.

When tribal movements took place before 1947, they were on the margins of the political scene and often clashed with the new Indian political elite's interests. Therefore, they were less reflected in the agenda of the nationalist movement in structuring the new State. When merged into the Indian Republic, tribal areas under princely rule did not bring with them a legacy of political negotiation according to the new representative system's rules.

The ST population has been assigned a fixed identity, serving administrative purposes. While its sociological relevance remains highly debatable, this categorization is the result of modern state-building, a process in which room to accommodate social diversity tends to be reduced and is gradually replaced by homogeneity, and by which porous borders are rigidified. This holds good for ecological borders as underlined by Rangarajan[4] as well as for human borders. It would not be possible to understand the tribal communities' lack of unity in asserting and defending their own rights if the heterogeneity of the ST category were not taken into account. The same could be said of the OBC or SC categories, but in the STs' case one has to consider yet another crucial historical factor: lesser degree of insertion into normative politico-administrative structures.

The usual depictions of ST communities have a few common points: a 'primitive' state of economy—or backwardness—location in the forest and a symbiotic relation with nature and ancestral traditions. But more than being a scientific appraisal of the actual situation and legacy of hundreds of communities spread over the peninsula, these depictions reflect the political, administrative and economic consequences of modern state-building. The communities in question have been pushed to and maintained at the margins by a modern state that condemns nomadic, non-agrarian and craft communities, as well as agrarian communities with non-settled practices or which defy modern socio-economic labels.

Qualifying tribal communities as 'primitive' and asking for their integration into the mainstream, a common aspiration among political leaders, is a convenient way to justify intensive and large-scale exploitation of natural resources and the consequent eviction of a population declared unfit for modern conditions of life.

Colonization had been carried out by describing the native

population as incapable of making the most of the natural wealth required for liberal economic development. After becoming independent, many states re-appropriated this ideological notion in order to justify their hold on land or regions for exploitation without any involvement of the local community, regardless of its interest or the sustainability of such extraction.[5] Policies related to colonization were by and large designed by financial and industrial lobbies, which are today again the prime benefactors of state privatization in the world economy. As Béatrice Hibou has underlined, privatization of the state does not mean weakening of the state, but an evolution that can eventually lead to the tightening of its grasp on territory. Similarly, a regional guerrilla and anti-guerrilla situation can lead to a reinforcement of the state.[6] The politics of identity merely justified the politics of resources. The projection of Chhattisgarh and Jharkhand as tribal states serves mainly as a logo for an industrial development policy for which the local population and biodiversity may have to pay a heavy price. It is revealing that in the Jharkhand government's six-page document on development focusing on ten aspects of socio-economic policy, forest and environment find no mention.[7] Karat (1999) equally underlines the fact that the breakdown of national barriers due to the economic consequences of globalization is not contrary to tighter control of the centre over territory. The same analysis could be applied to the creation of the three new states in 2000.

During the Raj and in the aftermath of Independence, tribal assertion for legal rights was often intertwined with the princes' demand for the defence of their estates against state encroachment. The tribal communities therefore inherited the conflict-ridden relations between the princes of small hilly states and the central government. The last two decades have witnessed the dissolution of the tribals' distinctive political bargaining power in Jharkhand, courtesy their leaders' absorption into or alliance with national political parties and the concomitant of their growing dependence on the latter. It is noticeable that in Chhattisgarh, the ST community does not represent any specific political force. The powers vested in political and judicial policies are unreachable for a population whose self-governance culture was oral-based, and whose languages were officially unrecognized. Due to the extremely poor quality of infrastructure resulting from minimal investment by state and central governments as well as high corruption, no significant change in terms of literacy, skill formation, capacity building could take place.

Left out of the industrial and commercial development issuing from the economic pattern set up by the colonial administration, the ST communities' livelihood became more than ever linked to their natural environment. With the diversity and historical legacy of their socio-geographic situation obliterated and the focus mainly on the concentration of tribal population in the hilly-forest region, STs remained associated with forests and backwardness. The notion of the hinterland as India's back-office is rooted in the mindset of the country's modern economic and administrative centres. How could the creation of new states reverse this process of disempowerment that began taking a dramatic turn under the colonial regime and with the development of the modern industrial economy? If anything, the major risk of creating new states was to centralize even greater powers at the state level in the hands of a regional and national elite which alone would be in a position to seize the new opportunities.

In the aftermath of the creation of Chhattisgarh and Jharkhand, there were mixed feelings of fulfilment, justified by the 'small is beautiful' philosophy and the room apparently given to tribal identity, as well as of surprise (in the case of Chhattisgarh) and of anxiety regarding their future. If India's unity has not been weakened by the emergence of these states, the arguments in support of their formation and subsequent evolution bring several crucial issues to the forefront. As early as 2000, in the context of the new global economy concerns were raised about supposed 'good governance' in regions where people are considered the prime victims of disempowerment—particularly the STs—under the modern economy.

The Jharkhand Mukti Morcha and the Chhattisgarh Mukti Morcha, though differing in their objectives, history and nature, were two socio-regionalist movements demanding better governance in a decentralized framework and suggesting that the agenda of the Indian freedom movement remained unfulfilled for some communities. The continuing projection of the STs as backward and the perpetuation of their exclusion from decision-making processes have been underlined by Amit Prakash (2001) in his study of Jharkhand.

SMALLER STATES, REGIONALIZATION OF POLITICS IN INDIA AND POLITICAL MOBILIZATION

Sociologists have underlined that, while the 1980s were rich in mass movements such as the Narmada Bachao Andolan or the Chhattisgarh Mukti Morcha, the 1990s saw a decline in political mobilization. Moreover, even these movements addressed regional issues and did not become national movements. In the new millennium, it seems more and more difficult for social activists to define political mobilization since the emphasis has shifted from a political balance of power and confrontation to the more politically neutral concept of governance, *good governance* being the new motto.

Civil society, NGOs and self-help groups have acted with a more targeted approach, not always on neutral political grounds if we refer to the social activism of outfits affiliated to political parties. Activism in the name of empowerment came to be channellized through civil society frameworks (sometimes achieving spectacular results as in the case of the Tarun Bharat Sangh of Rajendra Singh in Alwar, Rajasthan), and less and less through political mass movements oriented towards economic issues. The extension of the 73rd Amendement Act to Scheduled Areas (1996) was aimed at giving a legal framework to rural and local empowerment. Nevertheless, civil society organizations have sometimes been perceived as counterweights to rural empowerment, bypassing local institutions due to direct funding by international or national agencies, even as the third tier of Indian democracy still struggles for significant devolution of functions, funds and functionaries as many studies have reported (Jayal 2006; Kumar 2006).

This is particularly important in a context where the politics of resources—whether it concerns forest products, water or mining—is the main issue whether in Jharkhand or Chhattisgarh and especially in regions inhabited mainly by the STs.

With the end of the Cold War and the relocation of the political debate at the centre-right of the political spectrum, the left parties have gradually been integrated into a new political mainstream dominated by the liberal economic ideology. No longer are there the two diametrically opposed blocs of the 'normal' political arena which alternatively determine and direct mode of governance. This is where the notion of 'governance' re-emerges, concealing the adversarial forces engaged in the political game. Consecutively, the political forces opposing the liberal economic regime—increasingly characterized as global—started to grow at the margins of the official political scene. With the expansion of the naxal-maoist movement in India, this 'margin' has eventually assumed significant scale. The extreme left's sway has been very significant in the two new states of the tribal belt. And the Chhattisgarh government has added some fuel to the fire by raising and supporting armed civilian groups, called Salwa Judum, further pushing away the problem from the civil and legal debate. The question is: Have new platforms been created in the new states for political debates corresponding to their specific issues? Democratic empowerment of tribal and other marginalized communities would depend on the capacity of the governments of the two new states to create such space.

Associating better governance with smaller states would also mean linking the creation of states with decentralization. The first years of Chhattisgarh and Jharkhand show that the decentralization process, which seemed to gain momentum in the 1990s, is being challenged despite the creation of smaller states, and some time due to these very entities.

DECENTRALIZATION, POLITICS OF RESOURCES (GOVERNANCE) AND EMPOWERMENT

The consensus between the two major national parties regarding the creation of new states in 2000 is in line with the continuity they have provided in relation to reforms since 1991. As a matter of fact, the creation of the three new states in the name of better governance can itself be assessed as being as much a part of the economic reforms process as of the regionalization of political parties.

Regarding the decentralization process in relation to local governance and the Indian context, Niraja Gopal Jayal (2006) underlines its political nature, describing it as a 'normative-political project of greater inclusion, and the representation of historically disadvantaged and marginalized groups constitutes the truly exciting part of the Indian experiment'. Kumar (2006) also avers that if for nothing else, the 73rd Amendment deserves appreciation for bringing legitimacy to the open democratic system in the country. However, for a variety of reasons, he feels that the project of local democracy has gone on vascillating between elected autocracy and shared democracy. This therefore corresponds to the overall project of the population of the two new smaller states of Jharkhand and Chhattisgarh dominated by OBCs, STs and SCs. Better access to decision-making of the historically deprived and marginalized communities at large, as well as the movement they have articulated in the case of Jharkhand has been discussed by Amit Prakash and Cyril Robin, and by Samuel Berthet in the case of Chhattisgarh.[8] Jayal also specifies that 'communities that have historically negotiated their social relationships through indigenously evolved reasonably egalitarian mechanisms become fractious and conflict ridden as decentralization brings with it development funds and new opportunities for the concentration of power'. She argues that the administrative set up of decentralization has perhaps received less attention than it would require for efficient functioning. If political representation at the local level is undergoing changes via reservation for women and marginalized communities, devolution of power through administrative and financial decentralization is, in many cases, yet to take place.

In the 1990s, the 73rd and 74th Amendements aimed at providing safeguards for actual implementation of democratic decentralization at the district, block and village levels. Soon after the Panchayati Raj Institutions were set up and extended to Scheduled Areas, conflicts arose between state representatives and communities at the village level. A notable case in Chhattisgarh was Nagarnar. Also affected were neighbouring states such as Orissa, in the tribal region of Kashinagar, for instance. The government of Jharkhand proved reluctant to implement the provisions concerning the panchayat's institutions.[9] The two-child norm proved another way of preventing mass participation. The politics of identity revealed itself as not easy to reconcile with democracy at the local level. Another instance was the attitude of Tamil Nadu, a state at the forefront of the defence of federal prerogatives but reluctant to give free rein to the third tier of the Indian democratic polity. Jammu & Kashmir, bestowed with special status where its own autonomy is concerned, also proved unwilling to share power and resources with constituent regions, districts or villages.

As Nayyar (1998) and Mooij (2005) have observed, there is an ever-widening discrepancy between the growing political representation of the economically deprived and their actual influence on the framing of economic policies. The prevailing idea, therefore, is that no major political change follows the integration of the STs and other economically disadvantaged groups into the political mainstream and the democratic process. Virginius Xaxa (2005) draws a similar conclusion on the effect of reservation on the political representation of the STs. Special rule in tribal-dominated Bastar and the need felt by the Chhattisgarh government to prevent information from freely circulating show that a certain degree of control is sought prior to eventual integration into the mainstream and normal political functioning.

In regions like Chhattisgarh, where identity politics has not led to mass mobilization at the state level what are the means for the average population mobilization revolves around resource management: mine workers' condition, minor forest produce, water, mineral resources, etc. Identification between different layers of the social body within a particular region, and the solidarity to emerge from this regional citizenry, are preconditions for efficient use of local resources and redistribution of the benefits of their exploitation.

Another way of looking at the issue would be to consider the creation of a new state as a step towards engaging in the process of decentralization and of implementing measures to reverse the top-down decision-making process in order to empower the marginalized masses. That would mean equating the creation of states with decentralization, which is what the notion of good governance seems to suggest. Creation of new states has been justified by pointing to the vast distances and the consequent mismatch between the interests of the elite in the capital and those of people of the regions to whom statehood is granted. How could politicians from Bhopal have any grasp over the situation in remote Chhattisgarh and Bastar? Were the interests of the elite in Patna linked to the tribal-dominated districts of Santhal Paraganas? Negligible devolution of funds to regions where colossal benefits accrued from the exploitation of natural resources was claimed to be the main justification for the creation of new states, in the case of both Jharkhand and Chhattisgarh. Both regions were known to provide huge income to the former undivided states, revenues in which they did not have any substantial share in return in the form of investment and infrastructure. Hence carving out those regions from the administrative units they belonged to was projected as an obvious solution and immediate remedy.

During the 1990s, reforms came to be accepted by politicians and state officials who found a new way to accommodate and even to augment their own interests. Reforms facilitated by the creation of new states in 2000 opened up new ways to bargain for benefits for the white collar class, politicians and state officials. The support for intensified exploitation of natural resources in the new states given by both politicians and state officials is an illustration of this new solidarity of interests between this class and MNCs. Chronologies are often revealing and, if we accept S.K. Das' (Mooij 2005) analysis that by 1997–8 the IAS had become 'reforms-minded', the smooth coming into being of the new states in 2000 as part of the reform of the Indian economy, seems all the more logical.

THE VOLUME

This volume looks at various aspects of the tribal situation, the question of small states and political evolution in the context of Chhattisgarh and Jharkhand, as well as issues related to decentralization.

Understanding the identity and history of the new states is necessary since popular and well-articulated movements, through political organizations and trade unions as also public forums such as newspapers and other media, can contribute to creating a political force with the ability to check policies implemented by the elite at the state level. Without such a movement, who can act as a countervailing power?

Resources are the issue on which conflicts arise between the state and the locals in Jharkhand as well as in Chhattisgarh, particularly in the tribal regions. The three states were carved out from less culturally homogeneous states as indicated by their names: Uttar Pradesh, Madhya Pradesh, and Bihar, none of them associated with a dominant language. As a matter of fact, there have been semantic controversies: Jharkhand *versus* Vananchal and Uttarakhand *versus* Uttaranchal, translating in the first case different projects, but whose name refers to a geographical rather than a cultural pattern unlike, for instance, Santhal Parganas. The state of Chhattisgarh, on its part, extends well beyond the 36 forts it refers to, overlapping with regions with little links to Chhattisgarhi culture such as Bastar, or the northern tribal districts of Ambikapur or Surguja.

Nevertheless, the tribal factor is at the forefront in the two recently created states studied here, Jharkhand and Chhattisgarh, first as old strongholds of tribal culture in Indian history and, second, as units with a high ratio of STs. Amit Prakash in 'Identity and Development in Jharkhand: Electoral Politics, 1991–2004' and Cyril Robin in 'The Creation of Vananchal: Reassessment of the Jharkhand State' underline how the movement for statehood really gained momentum when the non-tribal population joined it, and especially the elite who were associated with the exploitation of natural resources. As Amit Prakash emphasizes, it is still difficult to predict the political outcome of Jharkhand's emergence from the overlapping of the politics of development and the politics of identity, as a state where many political parties have been successively voted in and out. What is therefore stressed is how, after almost a century of political mobilization in Jharkhand, the political scene remains very fragmented. In this regard, the political landscapes of Jharkhand and Chhattisgarh differ widely, the latter having no comparable records of mass mobilization despite the Chhattisgarh Mukti Morcha and other social movements, and being dominated by a bipolar opposition between the two main national parties, the Congress and the BJP.

The two studies also corroborate the fact that acceptance of the creation of states in tribal regions came after a shift from 'social class'/economic demands—a configuration which never took the shape of long-standing mass movements—to 'communal'/socio-cultural demands. This transition went along with the rise of the BJP in the 1990s and the building of a Hindutva bastion in the tribal regions.

The results of the elections in both Chhattisgarh and Jharkhand attracted attention on a phenomenon rooted in the post-Independence history of the Indian Republic. With the weakening of the struggle of deprived social categories, identifying themselves as tribal communities against 'non-tribals', outsiders or *dikku*, to use the popular Jharkhandi expression, the notion of 'tribal states' lost its significance. It was reassessed in a communal context in terms of the notion of *vanvasi* (Sundar 1997), integrating the ST community into an organic vision of the nation as defined by Hindu nationalists.

What does the designation 'tribal states' refer to? In his paper 'Mapping the Scheduled Tribes: Questioning the Creation of New States in India', geographer Bertrand Lefebvre connects census data to India's geographical pattern to asses how far the concept is relevant. Unlike the states' names or the socio-cultural definition tend to show there are no natural design for internal border in the tribal belt. Far from strengthening the inner coherence of the geographical distribution of the ST population, the creation of the two states might have further divided an already heterogeneous and fractured community. One could argue that any attempt to construct states on ethnic grounds is against the very idea of the nation. Moreover, the notion of linguistic states has been questioned long back by Bernard Cohn (1987). But the lack of flexibility of modern borders, even at the federal level, can also have certain disintegrative effects—such as exclusion, division and overall weakening—on minorities and, in this case, the social environment of ST communities.

India has a long experience in dealing with federalism in general and with separatist movements, for instance, in the tribal areas of the north-east. The context is, however, rather different in the peninsula. Here, such movements did not really take shape, the feeling of belonging to the country was not questioned and sometimes even strongly reassessed as with the term *adivasi.* Is there a specific explanation for this, corresponding to a specific regional pattern of tribal presence within the peninsula as compared to that in the north-eastern states of India? Virginius Xaxa in 'Tribal Movements and Articulation of Autonomy' examines different forms of movements seeking autonomy for tribals in the north-eastern region and in mainland India with special reference to the Jharkhand movement. Xaxa has observed that demand for autonomy was more focused in the north-eastern region as compared to Jharkhand where the demand for a separate state got enmeshed with a host of other issues, including land, forest, displacement and discrimination in public sector employment. The paper also highlights the lessons drawn from the implementation of the Sixth Schedule Areas. As a matter of fact, the tribal regions have remained far behind the rest of India in the development index, as well in the health indicators, as among the poorest in the world. They are also the most affected by land displacement (45 per cent of the persons affected by displacement are tribal, though they account for 8 per cent of the total population of the country). Again, the creation of Chhattisgarh has not put an end to the STs' demand for statehood in central India. If Christian conversions played a significant role in giving momentum to a certain tribal consciousness in the early twentieth century, the inroads of missionaries and religious competition have also played a role in the fragmentation of the tribal community in the north-eastern states and Jharkhand, as more recently in Bastar, and often led to new and harsher communal lines of division.

The very idea that the creation of a new state would help bridge the gap between the people and their elected leaders besides accelerating the pace of development has been questioned by Girish Kumar. In 'Smaller States, Federalism and Decentralization: Implications for Governance in Chhattisgarh' he shows that development strategies of the new state contradict this perception. Kumar, in fact, argues that structural problems of under-development cannot be tackled with the traditional development approach; they call for an alternative vision of development. This would entail providing access to education and skill formation to people. The neo-regional elites have no patience for this painstaking and obviously, time consuming process.

Decentralization, as Savyasaachi has underlined in this volume, also means in the present economic context better and more direct access to the global market for the citizen/consumer at the local level and vice versa, but not better and more direct access to decision-making at the global level. In the face of this changed relationship of the citizen/consumer as compared to the economic protectionism that predominated before the era of reforms, what are the new forums for negotiation for the citizen/consumer? What political reform would ensure that the latter has the means to influence decision-making at the global level? While the question is left open, the consequences of a more decentralized system (PESA) are seen as two-sided, opening a direct gateway for international actors to enter the Scheduled Areas. The notion of the hinterland as India's back-office, mentioned and analysed in its present context by Savyasaachi, is rooted in the country's modern economic and administrative structure. And it calls for a reconsideration of the geo-economic development pattern of the *new India* and its new states, whether tribal or not. What is required is a new developmental blueprint encompassing the needs and realities of the diversity of the country's population and environment, based on a more organic and less rigid concept of interdependence between different natural and human milieus. Savyasaachi argues that unless a new approach towards land is sanctioned by law, sustainable economic development might be jeopardized. A very similar conclusion has been drawn by a prominent Indian bureaucrat, Gopal Krishna Gandhi, former governor of Bengal, with reference to the struggle for land traced from the Indigo revolt to recent events in Nandigram.[10] The urgent need to reassess the value of land (and water), from a commodity to a sustainable resource, might be the most crucial issue concerning the future politics of development. Introducing reforms for resource management not only concerns political functioning but is also a prerequisite for socio-economic profitability, as Dipankar Sengupta highlights in his study of community participative natural resources management, 'Decentralization, Local Knowledge and Labour Absorption: The Case of

Chhattisgarh'. Sengupta compares different experiences with the case of Chhattisgarh, providing an update on all the practical ideas that contributed to the crystallization of the 'small is beautiful' concept. The concept was based on local community participation and use of local knowledge that takes into account the specificities of the natural environment. The *modus operandi* M.K. Gandhi and Schumacher promoted for sustainable development of rural regions seems to apply fully to Chhattisgarh and Jharkhand, but appear in none of the guidelines of the economic policies of both governments. The recent economic and industrial transformation of the two states, along with the corresponding displacement, bring to the fore the issue of labour absorption.

Ilina Sen, in her article, 'Distorted Development and Possibilities of Alternatives in Chhattisgarh', shows how the original ideas of alternative development which inspired the trade union movement, Chhattisgarh Mukti Morcha, did not percolate to the decision-making apparatus of the new state and how even the very first steps taken by the new government were quite opposed to Gandhi's and Schumacher's notion of *smallness*. Several decisions of the Chhattisgarh government (Chhattisgarh Information Act, mining policy)[11] are new political and economic instruments prioritizing the interests of MNCs over the pre-2000 ideas of development worked on by regional forums.

Finally, it is more continuity, through a gradual and consensual shift monitored by the decision makers, than ruptures which prevails. As a matter of fact, privatization of natural resources had started before the creation of the new states. One may recall, for instance, the famous case in undivided Madhya Pradesh of the 22 km-stretch of the Seonath River being sold in 1998 to the private sector through a local entrepreneur, Water Radius Limited. Similar selling of river water is foreseen in Maharashtra.

How did the link between tribal and non-tribal communities break up, and how did mutual influences turn unilateral, with non-tribal culture being overtly acknowledged as superior and tribal culture as backward and unfit? The conflict is therefore not only political and economic but also cultural. This is one of the issues addressed by Samuel Berthet in 'Chhattisgarh: Redefining the Role of the State?'. Beyond dealing with the question of the further exclusion of the STs, this paper is a general reassessment of the redefined relationship between the citizen and the state, at both the central and federal levels. Such a reassessment seems necessary in the context of the reforms under way since the early 1990s.

NOTES

1. In Chhattisgarh, the implementation of the use of school books written in the main regional languages has slowed down after the creation of the state.
2. See Divya Srivastava, *The Developement of Scheduled Tribes in Madhya Pradesh*, Delhi: Gyan Publishing House, 2000. Amit Prakash, *Jharkhand, Politics of Development and Identity*, Delhi: Orient Longman, 2001.
3. Quoted in Srivastava, op. cit., pp. 109–10,
4. Mahesh Rangarajan, *Fencing the Forest: Conservation and Ecological Change in India's Central Provinces 1860–1914*, Delhi: Oxford University Press, 1996.
5. George Monbiot, 'Who's Stone Age, U.K. Politicians or Bushmen?', *The Hindu*, 22 March 2006.
6. Béatrice Hibou, *La privatisation des Etats*, Paris: CERI, Karthala, 1999.
7. Government of Jharkhand, 'A Vision for Better Future', op. cit.
8. Cyril Robin, 'Jharkhand: Between Tribal Mobilisation and the Rise of the OBC', and Samuel Berthet, 'Tribals, OBC, Reformist Movements and Mainstream Politics in the State of Chhattisgarh', in Christophe Jaffrelot and Sanjay Kumar, *Rise of the Plebeians? The Changing Face of Indian Legislative Assemblies*, CSH-CSDS-CERI, Delhi: Routledge, 2009.
9. D.P. Sharan, 'Jharkhand Government Told to Hold Local Elections in April', *The Hindu*, 14 December 2004.
10. Opening address for the Seminar 'The Culture of Indigo: Exploring the Asian Panorama—Aspects of Plant, Product and Power' held from 29 November to 1 December 2008, organized by Kapila Vatsyayan, India International Centre.
11. Government of Chhattisgarh Industrial Policy (2004–9), Commerce and Industries Department Industrial Policy (2004–9), see *A Critique of Chhattisgarh Industrial Policy 2004–9* by Sanjeev Ghotge, NCAS, Pune, http://www.cgnet.in/Min/

REFERENCES

Arnold, David, 1982: 'Rebellious Hillmen: The Gudem-Rampa Risings, 1839–1924', in Ranajit Guha (ed.), *Subaltern Studies I*, Delhi: Oxford University Press.

Asian Development Bank, 2002: 'Preliminary Indigenous People Development Program', in *Chhattisgarh State Road Development*, Supplementary Appendix N.

Bates, C., 1995: 'Race, Caste and Tribe in Central India: The Early Origins of Indian Anthropometry', in *Edinburgh Paper in South Asian Studies*, no. 3.

Bhuimali, Anil, 'Relevance of M.K. Gandhi's Ideal of Self-Sufficient Village Economy in the 21st Century', http://www.mkgandhi.org/articles/bhuimali.htm

Chaudhuri, Ranjit, 'Towards Understanding Gandhian Economics', Institute of Gandhian Studies, Wardha, http://www.mkgandhi.org/articles/Eco_ranjit.htm

Cohn, Bernard S., 1987: *An Anthropologist among the Historians and Other Essays*, Delhi: Oxford University Press.

Commonwealth Human Rights Initiative, 2006: *The Right to Information and Panchayat Raj Institution: Chhattisgarh as a Case Study*, Delhi.

Frankel, Francine R., Balveer Arora, Rajeev Bhargava , Zoya Hasan (eds.), 2000: *Transforming India: Social and Political Dynamics of Democracy*, Delhi: Oxford University Press.

Government of Chhattisgarh, 2001: *Chhattisgarh State Forest Policy*, Resolution No. F 7-42/2001/F.C 22nd October 2001, Raipur: Forest and Culture Department, Mantralaya.

———, 2005: *Human Development Report: Chhattisgarh.*

Govindu, Venu Madhav, Deepak Malghan, 2005: 'Building a Creative Freedom: J.C. Kumarappa and His Economic Philosophy', *Economic and Political Weekly*, 24 December, vol. XL, no. 52, pp. 5477–85.

Guerin, Isabelle and Jane Palier, 2004; 'Les Self-Help Groups en Inde du Sud en tant qu'espaces de discussions et d'actions collectives permettent-ils un accès a plus de "pouvoirs" (empowerment)?', *XXèmes journées ATM-CREDES*, Nancy.

Guha, Sumit, 1999: *Environment and Ethnicity, 1200–1991*, Cambridge: Cambridge University Press.

Jaffrelot, Christophe and Sanjay Kumar, 2009: *The Rise of the Plebeians? The Changing Face of Indian Legislative Assemblies*, CSH-CSDS-CERI, Delhi: Routledge.

Jay, Edward J., 1970: *A Tribal Village of Middle India*, Calcutta: Anthropological Survey of India.

Jayal, Niraja Gopal, Amit Prakash and Pradeep S. Sharma, 2006: *Local Governance in India, Decentralization and Beyond*, Delhi: Oxford University Press.

Karat, Prakash, 1999: 'Liberalization and Hindutva: The New Threat to National Unity', *Social Scientist*, vol. 27, nos. 9–10, September–October, pp. 42–50.

Kumar, Girish, 2006: *Local Democracy in India: Interprating Decentralisation*, Delhi: Sage Publication.

Miri, Mrinal, 1993: *Continuity and Change in Tribal Society*, Shimla: Indian Institute for Advanced Studies.

Mooij, Jos (ed.), 2005: *Economic Reforms in India*, Delhi: Sage.

Mukharji, Nirmal, Balveer arora (eds.), 1992: *Federalism in India: Origins and Development*, Delhi: Vikas Publishers.

Nayyar, Deepak, 1998: 'Economic Development and Political Democracy: Interaction of Economics and Politics in Independent India', *Economic and Political Weekly*, 33(49): 3121–31.

Prakash, Amit, 2001: *Jharkhand: Politics of Development and Identity*, Delhi: Orient Longman.

PIB, 2006: 'Forest Rights Bill: A Historic Step', 24 January, Indlaw.com, Inputs from Ministry of Tribal Affairs.

Rajagopalan, Shashi, 2002: Study on Tribal Cooperatives in India: A Situation Analysis Report with Recommendations for Future Actions, March 2002, Indisco Programme, International Labour Organization.

Ramnath, Madhu and Arjun Nag, 2004: *Crossing Boundaries, Adivasi Women and Forest Produce: A Story from Central Bastar, Chhattisgarh, India* (Sinva Tcho Hunapath, Adivasi Meharar Man Attar Ran, Jinish Mandjar Batsar, Chhattisgarh Tcho Gothok Kahani), Jagdalpur.

Rangarajan, Mahesh, 1996: *Feming the Forest: Conservation and Ecological Change in India's Central Provinces 1860–1914*, Delhi: Oxford University Press.

Sarin, Madhu, 2005: 'Scheduled Tribes Bill 2005: A Comment', *Economic and Political Weekly*, 40(21): 2131–34.

Sarin, Madhu, Neera M. Singh, Nandini Sundar, Ranu K. Bhogal, 2003: 'Devolution as a Threat to Democratic Decision-making in Forestry? Findings in Three States in India', Working Paper 197, Overseas Development Institute, London.

Schumacher, E.F., 1993: *Small is Beautiful: A Study of Economics as if People Mattered*, Delhi: Vintage.

Srivastava, Divya, 2000: *The Development of Scheduled Tribes in Madhya Pradesh*, Delhi: Gyan Publishing House.

Sundar, Nandini, 1997: *Sovereigns and Subalterns: Anthropological History of Bastar 1854–1996*, Delhi: Oxford University Press.

Xaxa, Virginius, 2005: 'Electoral Reservations for the Scheduled Tribes: The Legitimation of Domination', in S. Tawa Lama-Rewal, *Political Representation and Social Change: The Working of Electoral Reservations in the Indian Democracy*, Delhi: Manohar.

CHAPTER TWO

Identity and Development in Jharkhand: Electoral Politics, 1991–2004

AMIT PRAKASH

In contemporary India, much of the political contestation seems to take the shape and form of politics of identity. The premises, boundaries, self-definitions, modes of articulation, and so on, of such politics of identity may vary across space and time but the basic argument stands that there is almost no serious contestation of the political space (with the state as well as with other similarly politically-articulate groups) that is not rooted in (and often articulated through) the politics of identity.[1]

The range of politics of identity in India is wide: linguistic movements in many parts of India during the late 1950s–70s; the numerous ethnic identities in the north-eastern parts of the country; the Dalit assertion of north India; various 'development-deficit'-oriented articulations across the country (such as Telangana, Ladakh, erstwhile Uttar Pradesh hills or Uttaranchal, north West Bengal, tribal south Gujarat and erstwhile tribal Madhya Pradesh or Chhattisgarh, etc.); the Coorg issue in Karnataka, communal mobilization of 1980s and 1990s; and so on. With the exception of the communal identity politics and Dalit assertion, all other articulations of identity demand various degrees and forms of autonomy.

However, there is no consensus about what is the meaning and content of 'autonomy'. Articulations of visions of autonomy are as varied as the groups and political actors demanding it. Many groups in Nagaland view autonomy as a sovereign state, while many of the other articulations would be happy with a state within the Indian Union. Still others wish to see the creation of a sub-state 'development' council while yet others have a vision of a regional, multi-state structure.[2]

The case of Jharkhand, which is the focus of this paper, is one of the articulations of such a vision of autonomy—one which has successfully managed to largely, if not wholly, realize this vision. Demand for autonomy for the Jharkhand region,[3] premised on tribal heritage and culture of the region in erstwhile Bihar, is one of the oldest such demands in the country. The first recorded articulation of a proto-Jharkhandi identity demanding autonomy in the form of a governor's province is to be found in the 1920s before the Simon Commission.[4] However, the Commission did not advocate this course of action. Hence, although the province of Orissa was created under the constitutional reforms of 1935, the practice of exclusion of the region of Jharkhand from normal administration was continued.

Further, the demand for autonomy made by the Jharkhand movement did not attain any significant success on account of the fact that the movement was perhaps the only such movement which began with a serious demographic handicap in terms of socio-cultural heterogeneity of the population of the region. Only about a third of the population of the region was of tribal origin in the 1950s. This forced the elite in Jharkhand to grapple with the rules of exclusion rather early. By late 1940s, the Jharkhandi identity which was demanding autonomy was already balancing the tribal heritage and culture argument with a region-oriented 'development deficit' self-description. This had an important impact on the articulation of the demand for autonomy.

After Independence, the issue of autonomy surfaced once again. Jaipal Singh and the Jharkhand Party (JHP) continued to try to persuade the various official fora of the need to create a state of Jharkhand premised on the tribal way of life and its separate heritage and culture. These efforts did not meet with any noticeable success till the 1990s when the question of a separate administrative structure for the region was taken seriously and the Jharkhand Area Autonomous Council (JAAC) was created, followed by a separate state in 2000.

Owing to the rejection of the demand for a separate state by various official and representative fora and their insistence that the issue in Jharkhand was essentially about 'development-deficit', the self-definition and articulation of the identity also underwent a re-alignment. The articulation of Jharkhandi identity soon took on board this 'development-deficit' analysis of their mobilization offered by the various state agencies as additional grounds for demanding a separate state. The 'internal colony' argument—much of which was supported by development indicators—started to become one of the central premises for mobilization. Over a period of time, these issues of identity and development became inextricably linked to electoral politics of the region.[5]

This paper seeks to analyse the changing electoral dynamics of the region in relation to the demand for autonomy during the decade of the 1990s in the context of socio-economic change in the region.

I. OVERVIEW OF THE POLITICS OF DEVELOPMENT AND IDENTITY: 1950s TO 1990s

By the time India gained Independence in 1947, the Jharkhandi leaders had succeeded in the creation of a political community in south Bihar with the hope of engaging with the independent Indian state in a manner similar to the nationalist's engagement with the colonial state (Prakash 1999). However, the nationalistic, socialistic credentials of the Indian state gave it a degree of political legitimacy and support which the JHP was not able to undermine, which was also assisted by the overwhelming control of the state over the economic and information resources. The Jharkhandi community was clearly the recipient of the largesse which the state chose to allocate to them. Owing to their weak political position in the legislatures, the Jharkhandi leaders were unable to effectively lobby for a better resource allocation and development investment in the Jharkhand region. Hence, the Jharkhandi population was constrained to depend on the plans that the state drew up for them instead of having a meaningful role in the development planning for the region.

The politics of development and identity in Jharkhand in the period 1947–91 is complex and is marked by overall poor growth of development indicators and multifarious political articulations and contests. A fuller discussion of the patterns during this period is precluded by the focus of this paper and space constraints.[6] However, a brief delineation of the main characteristics of the politics and development during 1947–91 is crucial in order to locate the later discussion for the period 1991–2004 in its historical and politico-economic context.

As far as the development profile of the Jharkhand region in the 1950s is concerned, Figures 2.2–2.10[7] indicate that the development profile of the Jharkhand region in 1951 was quite poor but it was so in most parts of India. However, socio-economic development indicators (such as death, birth and infant mortality rates, agricultural and industrial production, employment patterns and literacy and education rates) were better in the Jharkhand region than that of Bihar as a whole in 1951. However, even in 1951, Jharkhand region was contributing a disproportionate share of revenue to the coffers of Bihar while receiving only a miniscule proportion of developmental investment. This pattern continued over the next five decades, lending credence to the Jharkhandi argument that the region was an internal colony of Bihar.

Indicators of socio-economic development during 1951–91 tell a similar story (Figures 2.2–2.10). Admittedly, most indicators of social and economic development show a substantial improvement over the four decades 1951–91, but the rate of improvement in Bihar as a whole far outstripped the improvements in the Jharkhand region. This differential is true in most indicators with two important exceptions. The first exception to the rule of a more sluggish developmental effort is the growth in literacy and education in Jharkhand. On this front, the improvements in the Jharkhand region were better than Bihar as a whole. This factor has an important role to play in the intensification of the Jharkhand movement and the central role that All Jharkhand Students' Union (AJSU) came to play in the movement in the 1980s.

The second major factor that contributed to the sharpening of the Jharkhand movement was a disproportionate growth in the proportion of tax revenues collected from the Jharkhand region in Bihar. This further intensified the alienation of the Jharkhandi population from the state government of Bihar.

While the developmental patterns of Bihar were marked by the lack of substantial change, the politics of the region was anything but staid (Prakash 2001: 85–131). In the 1950s, the JHP's agenda of autonomy and statehood for the Jharkhand region had found enthusiastic support amongst the electorate of the region. The JHP not only performed exceedingly well in the 1952 election (JHP won three of the eight seats—seven of twelve, if the multi-member constituencies[8] are included) and the 1957 election (winning eight of twelve seats). During this decade the JHP virtually laid down the law for the region but gradually lost popular support. JHP, despite enthusiastic popular support, failed to convince the States Reorganisation Commission to recommend the creation of a separate state and increasingly started depending on tribal premises for mobilization (in a demographic context of declining tribal component in the population of Jharkhand). To this was added the factor of sluggishness in the growth of developmental profile of the region. All three factors ensured that JHP was increasingly marginalized in the decades to come.

Between 1961 and 1991, the electorate experimented with a wide spectrum of political formations—from the Congress party (INC) to the extreme Left, without much avail. Neither development effort saw an acceleration nor did the issue of autonomy and statehood make any headway. The political process during the decades of the 1960s, 1970s and much of 1980s was fractured across various political formations active in the region. The failure of the JHP to secure a separate state led the electorate to adopt the developmental vision of the INC. While the issue of autonomy and statehood never quite lost its appeal amongst the people, they swiftly realized the political impediments to its realization leading to their support ebbing away from Jharkhandi parties. Further, the numerous Jharkhandi parties that emerged—all claiming to be the true inheritors of the JHP—went into almost complete disarray.

The phase of national parties was truly underway in Jharkhandi politics. The INC performed well in the 1962 elections and even better in the 1967 election (partly due to the fact that JHP had merged with the INC in 1963) and 1971 elections. The 1977 election found the national pattern being repeated in Jharkhand with the Bharatiya Lok Dal (BLD) leading the way and Jharkhandi parties being more or less absent from any serious contest.

Despite two decades of support to the INC's development vision, the rate of growth of the development profile of Jharkhand did not show any significant improvement. The electorate therefore discarded the INC and the 1980 election again saw support for a wide variety of political formations, from INC to Janata Party to the rejuvenated JHP. However, the INC was back in favour in the 1984 election[9] winning all the Lok Sabha seats from the region. This election marks a break in the political process in Jharkhand. The 1989 saw the entry of a new actor—the Bharatiya Janata Party (BJP)—on the political horizon of Jharkhand, which brought back the issue of autonomy and statehood onto the political agenda of the region with its proposal for smaller states.[10]

Another feature of the political process of Jharkhand in the 1980s was the three-pronged strategy articulated by the electorate. On the one hand, electoral support was extended to national parties, particularly the INC and BJP, which would form the government at the Union level and could legislate for a separate state. On the other hand, electoral support at the state level was extended to the regional parties likely to form the government at the state level in the hope of influencing a better developmental response. Simultaneously, sizeable political support was extended to the agitational politics of AJSU and Jharkhand Coordination Committee (JCC). Blockade of mineral transportation from the region was a part of this strategy which served the purpose of bringing the issue onto the national agenda, owing to which the Committee of Jharkhand Matters was appointed in 1990.[11]

The 1990s is therefore a crucial decade in the politics of development and identity in Jharkhand which will be taken up in detail in the next section.

II. THE POLITICS OF DEVELOPMENT AND IDENTITY IN THE 1990s AND BEYOND

The pattern of growth in the development profile of the Jharkhand region did not change significantly in the decade 1981–91. The demographic balance altered during this decade to make politics on tribal lines even more difficult since by 1991, only 27.66 per cent of the population were of tribal origin. Literacy continued to represent the successful component of public policy in the region. By 1991, more than 33 per cent of the population of the region was literate. This growth in literacy was matched by a growth in further education as well. The Jharkhand region continued to outperform Bihar as a whole as far as literacy and education was concerned.

There was a decline in employment, with just about 32 per cent of the population being employed in 1991 (over 36 per cent in 1981). There was an increased percentage of population depending on agriculture and a decline in the percentage of population employed in the non-agricultural sector (Figure 2.4). Despite a rise in the number of persons employed in agricultural activities, there had been a decline in the irrigation potential of the region during the decade 1981–91. This decline can also be noticed in land irrigated by government canals (Figure 2.7). The overall development profile of the Jharkhand region had declined over the past two decades.

In such a developmental scenario, the elections to the Lok Sabha were held in 1991. This election while continuing some of the facets of the 1989 election in terms of BJP with its promise of a separate state winning five of the fourteen seats (with more than 30 per cent of average votes), also marked the virtual exclusion of the INC from any serious electoral contest in the region. In the 1991 election, the INC did not win any parliamentary seats (despite 18 per cent of the average votes in Jharkhand constituencies) while the JMM won six. Faced with a sluggish and inert developmental scenario, electoral support for autonomy was therefore stronger in this election (Table 2.1).

As far as electoral support for the pro-autonomy JMM was con-

TABLE 2.1: PERFORMANCE OF POLITICAL PARTIES IN CONSTITUENCIES OF JHARKHAND IN LOK SABHA ELECTIONS 1991

Constituency Name	Number of Candidates	Winner Party and per cent of Votes Polled	Runner up Party and per cent of Votes Polled	III Party and per cent of Votes Polled	IV Party and per cent of Votes Polled	V Party and per cent of Votes Polled
Chatra	37	JD 38.07 Upendra Nath Verma	BJP 27.74 Dhirendra Agarwal	INC 20.01 Nagmani	JP 4.16 Ajoy Kumar Singh	IND 3.17 Bhuneshwar Yadav
Dhanbad	40	BJP 44.20 Rita Verma (W)	MCOR 25.59 AK Roy	JMM 10.55 Aklu Ram Mahto	INC 9.72 Yogeshwar Prasad Yogesh	IND 0.84 Amtaf Dutta
Dumka	13	JMM 58.28 Shibu Soren	BJP 28.34 Babulal Marandi	INC 9.81 Set Hemraj	IND 0.95 Jonathan Tudu	IND 0.73 Kunjiram Tudu
Giridih	18	JMM 48.21 Binod Bihari Mahto	BJP 31.79 Ramdas Singh	INC 16.24 Sarfaraz Ahmed	IND 0.52 Jaikant Pandey	IND 0.49 Bijay Prasad Singh
Godda	22	JMM 49.12 Suraj Mandal	BJP 29.39 Janaardan Yadav	INC 16.42 Manzarul Haque	JP 1.72 Ashok Kumar Singh	IND 0.63 Manohar Singh
Hazaribagh	26	CPI 34.45 Bhuneshwar Prasad Mehta	BJP 29.50 Yadunath Pandey	IND 12.97 Teklal Mahto	INC 12.36 Gyan Ranjan	IPF 5.67 Tridibesh Ghosh
Jamshedpur	23	JMM 40.22 Silcudra Mahto	BJP 29.29 Amrendra Pratap Singh	INC 17.20 Chandan Bagchi	IND 10.01 Suraj Singh Basera	INC 0.56 Chandra Sekhar Prasad
Khunti (ST)	12	BJP 36.02 Karia Munda	JHP 23.38 N.E. Horo	INC 21.01 Simon Tigga	IND 9.93 Prabhakar Tirkey	JMM 6.93 Ramesh Kumar Munda

Kodarma	26	JD 33.17 Mumtaz Ansari	BJP 30.28 Ritlal Prasad Verma	INC 26.14 Tilakdhari Prasad Singh	IPF 6.49 Mahendra Prasad Singh	JP 0.43 Adibuzama Rizvi
Lohardagga (ST)	17	BJP 37.40 Lalit Oraon	INC 22.80 Sumati Oraon (W)	JD 16.89 Karam Chand Bhagat	IND 16.35 Binod Bhagat	JKP 1.95 Asha Roa (W)
Palamau (SC)	20	BJP 37.95 Ram Deo Ram	JD 32.08 Jorawar Ram	INC 13.64 Kamala Kumari (W)	SKD 6.49 Jawahir Ram	IPF 2.81 Kishore Kumar
Rajmahal	14	JMM 38.21 Simon Marandi	INC 31.13 Thomas Hansda	BJP 27.40 Santlal Marandi	IND 0.74 Kasan Soren	IND 0.62 Kisan Murmu
Ranchi	46	BJP 48.47 Ram Tahal Choudhary	JD 22.57 Awadhesh Kumar Singh	INC 17.29 Sheo Prasad Sahu	JP 4.33 Subodh Kant Sahay	IND 2.85 Ram Dayal Munda
Singhbhum (ST)	24	JMM 36.10 Krishna Marandi	INC 22.34 Bijay Singh Soy	BJP 20.56 Munda Radhey Sambrui	JP 4.76 Bagum Sambrui	JD 4.12 Mangal Singh Lamaye

Note: *ST Constituency, # SC Constituency

Source: *Statistical Report on General Election, 1991 to the Tenth Lok Sabha*, vol. I (National and State Abstracts & Detailed Results), Election Commission of India, New Delhi, n.d.

cerned, they fared poorly in 1991 compared with the 1989 election in terms of vote share but won six of the fourteen seats in the region. JMM's average vote percentage in the seats they won declined to 36.79 per cent (almost 49 per cent in 1989) while they polled an average 29.28 per cent in constituencies where they had presence amongst the first five candidates. JD, by virtue of being the party in a position to influence development policy implementation at the local level, continued to receive some degree of electoral support in the region. However, by 1991, the political process of the region crystallized into a clear support for the BJP, which was promising a separate state[12] and JMM, to ensure that this promise was not forgotten by the BJP in the national parliament (Table 2.2).

BJP's clear articulation of the demand for a separate state has since yielded rich dividends for the party in every election since 1991. The Lok Sabha election in 1996 saw a stronger electoral support for the BJP with JMM once again being relegated to the political backwaters, not to recover for the next three elections. In fact, the BJP, with its national standing and a clear potential of forming the government at the Union level, took the wind out of the sails of the JMM—the only active Jharkhandi party in the region.

In the 1996 elections (Table 2.3), BJP candidates were elected from twelve of the fourteen Lok Sabha constituencies in the region with an average of 33 per cent of the votes (Figures 2.11 and 2.12). The JMM and INC won one seat each. INC thus failed to convert its 16 per cent of the average votes polled in all constituencies in

TABLE 2.2: PERFORMANCE OF JHARKHANDI POLITICAL PARTIES IN LOK SABHA ELECTIONS 1991

Election Year	Average Votes Polled by All Jharkhandi Parties in Constituencies with Electoral Presence	Average Votes Polled by All Jharkhandi Parties in all Constituencies of Jharkhand	Average Percentage of Votes Polled in Seats Won by Jharkhandi Parties	Seat Won Out of Total Seats in Jharkhand
1991	29.28	18.82	36.79	6 out of 14

TABLE 2.3: PERFORMANCE OF POLITICAL PARTIES IN CONSTITUENCIES OF JHARKHAND IN LOK SABHA ELECTIONS 1996

Constituency Name	Number of Candidates	Winner Party and per cent of Votes Polled	Runner up Party and per cent of Votes Polled	III Party and per cent of Votes Polled	IV Party and per cent of Votes Polled	V Party and per cent of Votes Polled
Chatra	33	BJP 42.85 Dheerendra Agarwal	JD 32.10 Krishna Nandan Prasad	INC 7.15 Mumtaj Ansaree	IND 6.90 Mahesh Singh Yadav	CPI (ML)(L) 1.72 Chinta Singh
Dhanbad	54	BJP 33.44 Rita Verma (W)	JD 30.69 Samresh Singh	MCOR 14.17 A K Roy	JMM 6.31 Munir Ahmed Khan	INC 5.97 Bijay Kumar Singh
Dumka*	13	JMM 31.94 Shibu Soren	BJP 30.89 Babulal Marandi	JD 26.31 Basudev Besra	INC 6.67 Thakur Tudu	IND 0.91 Helen Soren (W)
Giridih	28	BJP 36.52 Ravindra Kumar Pandey	JD 21.18 Saba Ahmed	JMM (M) 16.66 Raj Kishor Mahato	INC 13.99 Rajendra Prasad Singh	JMM 8.49 Lal Chand Mahato
Godda	23	BJP 35.88 Jagdambi Prasad Yadav	JD 26.84 Salauddin Ansari	JMM 19.94 Suraj Mandal	INC 10.09 Furkan Ansari	IND 2.57 Panchanand Thakur
Hazaribagh	36	BJP 36.36 Mahabir Lal Viswakarma	CPI 26.84 Bhuneshwar Prasad Mehta	JMM 15.81 Tekalal Mehto	INC 9.07 Chandrashekhar Dubey	CPI (ML)(L) 3.06 Gunni Oraon (W)
Jameshedpur	39	BJP 38.36 Bharadwaj Nitish Janardan	JD 25.07 Inder Singh Namdhari	JMM 19.42 Shilendra Mahato	INC 16.56 K P Singh	AMB 0.67 Nimai Mahato

(Contd.)

TABLE 2.3 Contd.

Constituency Name	Number of Candidates	Winner Party and per cent of Votes Polled	Runner up Party and per cent of Votes Polled	III Party and per cent of Votes Polled	IV Party and per cent of Votes Polled	V Party and per cent of Votes Polled
Khunti*	11	BJP 33.20 Kariya Munda	INC 26.58 Shushila Kerketta (W)	JMM 14.93 Prabhakar Tirkey	JKP 14.79 Nirmal Anom Horo	JD 6.52 Devid Bhangar
Koderma	26	BJP 39.44 Ritlal Prasad Verma	JD 31.83 Ramesh Prasad Yadav	INC 11.22 Umesh Chandra Agarwal	JMM 8.03 Salkhan Soren	CPI(ML)(L) 3.11 Mohan Datta
Lohardagga*	15	BJP 34.01 Lalit Oraon	INC 25.42 Bandi Oraon	JD 18.20 Karam Chand Bhagat	JMM 15.24 Bernard Minj	JKPP 2.58 Binod Kumar Bhagat
. ... #	20	BJP 43.42 Braj Mohan Ram	JD 31.98 Udai Narayan Choudhary	INC 10.78 Radha Krishna Kishore	BSP 3.80 Bhuneshwar Ram	JKP 1.66 Kanhai Ram
Rajmahal*	13	INC 45.22 Thomas Hansda	JMM 19.55 Simon Marandi	BJP 16.65 Jhano Rewati Tudu (W)	JD 15.73 Lobin Hembrom	IND 0.79 Karan Soren
Ranchi	26	BJP 35.94 Ram Tahal Singh	INC 29.38 Keshav Mahato Kamlesh	JD 26.46 Ashok Kumar Singh	JMM 1.92 Bhagwan Prasad Bhagat	IND 1.31 Francis Sarbas
Singhbhum*	27	BJP 20.88 Chitrasen Sinku	IND 18.30 Vijay Singh Soy	JMM (M) 12.94 Krishna Mardi	INC 12.29 Pradeep Kumar Balmuchu	JD 10.89 Hiber Guria

Note: *ST Constituency, # SC Constituency

Source: *Statistical Report on General Election, 1996 to the Eleventh Lok Sabha*, vol. I (National and State Abstracts & Detailed Results), Election Commission of India, New Delhi, n.d.

Jharkhand into seats during this election. Clearly, the inadequate performance of the development machinery over five decades had encouraged re-emergence of popular support for the idea of autonomy. Besides, BJP was the only party with a possibility of forming the Union government which clearly promised the creation of separate state. These factors led to an unprecedented support to the BJP, a relative newcomer to the region.

As far as the JMM was concerned, they seem to be becoming increasingly marginalized in the region. While the demand and mobilization for a separate state was led by Jharkhandi groups such as the JMM, and AJSU, owing to the virtual high-jacking of their agenda for autonomy by the BJP, such political groups have been unable to claim that they alone are the legitimate proponents of the Jharkhandi political opinion. Consequently, since the 1991 elections they have been increasingly marginalized in the electoral politics of Jharkhand.

Likewise, their vote share in the 1996 elections declined further and JMM polled about 32 per cent of the votes in the sole seat it won. Average votes polled by the JMM declined to 14.4 per cent while the average votes polled in the constituencies with a presence amongst first five candidates declined to 15.5 per cent (Table 2.4). This was a far cry from the large electoral support that JMM and other such parties have enjoyed in the past.

The 1998 general elections continued the same electoral pattern with very few significant differences (Table 2.5). While the INC

TABLE 2.4: PERFORMANCE OF JHARKHAND POLITICAL PARTIES IN LOK SABHA ELECTIONS 1996

Election Year	Average Votes Polled by All Jharkhandi Parties in Constituencies with Electoral Presence	Average Votes Polled by All Jharkhandi Parties in all Constituencies of Jharkhand	Average Percentage of Votes Polled in Seats Won by Jharkhandi Parties	Seat Won Out of Total Seats in Jharkhand
1996	15.52	14.41	31.94	1 out of 14

TABLE 2.5: PERFORMANCE OF POLITICAL PARTIES IN CONSTITUENCIES OF JHARKHAND IN LOK SABHA ELECTIONS 1998

Constituency Name	Number of Candidates	Winner Party and per cent of Votes Polled	Runner up Party and per cent of Votes Polled	III Party and per cent of Votes Polled	IV Party and per cent of Votes Polled	V Party and per cent of Votes Polled
Chatra	14	BJP 45.06 Dhirendra Agrawal	RJD 38.38 Nagmani	JD 6.62 Md. Saeed Khan	SSD 2.98 Dwarika Prasad	IND 2.92 Naresh Bhuiyan
Dhanbad	09	BJP 50.60 Rita Verma	MCOR 30.17 A K Roy	RJD 16.83 Aklu Ram Mahato	IND 0.66 Marigendra Kumar Yadav	SP 0.59 Surendra Prasad Roy
Dumka*	06	BJP 47.01 Babu Lal Marandi	JMM 44.88 Shibu Soren	CPI 4.32 Kaleshwar Hembram	JD 2.90 David Murmu	SP 0.69 Lalita Hembram
Giridih	05	BJP 45.50 Rabindra Kumar Pandey	INC 34.54 Rajendra Prasad Singh	JMM (M) 12.13 Raj Kishore Mahto	JD 7.53 Lal Chand Mahto	IND 0.30 Kailas Chandra Mahto
Godda	06	BJP 47.13 Jagdambi Prasad Yadav	JMM 36.45 Suraj Mandal	JD 11.20 Abutalib Ansari	IND 3.70 Enamul Haque	SP 1.19 Faiyaz
Hazaribagh	08	BJP 46.71 Yashwant Sinha	CPI 23.08 Bhuwaneshwar Prasad Mehta	JMM (M) 20.23 Teklal Mahto	CPI (ML) (L) 4.35 Deoki Nandan Vedia	JMM 4.18 Pratima Devi (W)
Jameshedpur	11	BJP 41.50 Abha Mahto (W)	IND 27.87 Russi Modi	CPI 13.42 Tika Ram Majhi	IND 9.79 Sudhir Mahato	RJD 5.69 Onkarnath Jaiswal

Khunti	04	BJP 43.29 Kariya Munda	INC 34.66 Sushila Kerketta (W)	JMM 12.65 Ram Dayal Munda	JKP 9.41 N E Horo	–
Koderma	07	BJP 42.06 Ritlal Prasad Verma	RJD 27.39 Avid Hussain	INC 18.36 Tilakdhari Prasad Singh	JD 7.06 Gauttam Sagar Rana	CPI (ML) (L) 4.47 Mahendra Prasad Singh
Lohardagga*	07	INC 45.66 Indra Nath Bhagat	BJP 41.87 Lalit Oraon	JMM 4.90 Prabhat Tirkey	JD 3.17 Bhubaneswar Lohra	JKP 2.27 K D Jojo
Palamau#	05	BJP 53.72 Braj Mohan Ram	RJD 40.05 Uday Narayan Chaudhary	CPI (ML) (L) 3.73 Kishore Koomar	BJC 1.71 Suren Ram	IND 0.79 Ram Chandra Das
Rajmahal*	11	BJP 34.03 Som Marandi	INC 34.02 Thomas Hansda	JMM 25.68 Simon Marandi	CPM 3.83 Jyotin Soren	IND 0.98 Ramshil Murmu
Ranchi	12	BJP 58.12 Ram Tahal Choudhary	INC 37.16 Keshav Mahto Kamlesh	FBL 1.32 Napendra Krishna Mahto	CPI (ML) (L) 0.74 Shubhendu Sen	JMM 0.67 Bahadur Singh
Singhbhum*	04	INC 36.44 Vijay Kumar Soy	BJP 34.33 Chitrasen Sinku	JMM 24.39 Mangal Singh Bobonga	JMM (M) 4.84 Krishna Mardi	—

Note: *ST Constituency, # SC Constituency

Source: Statistical Report on General Election, 1998 to the Twelfth Lok Sabha, vol. I (National and State Abstracts & Detailed Results), Election Commission of India, New Delhi, n.d.

slightly improved its presence in the region by winning two seats with 17 per cent of the average vote, BJP was the undisputed winner in the electoral contest of 1998. BJP candidates were elected in 12 of the 14 constituencies in the region more than 45 per cent of the votes (Figures 2.11 and 2.12). It must be noted that by this time, all major political actors in the Jharkhand region had come around to supporting the idea of a separate state (which could also be a partial factor in the marginal recovery of INC's electoral fortunes). However, the BJP with its astute mix of small states agenda, tribal mobilization and fielding of candidates with a tribal background created a situation in which the JMM increasingly became politically marginalized. Further, since it was increasingly becoming clear that the electorate had by now decided to fully support the autonomy agenda, only national parties with significant numbers in the Lok Sabha would be relevant. This is exactly what the results of the 1998 elections underline.

Consequently, the JMM was unable to win even a single seat in the region in the 1998 elections. Besides, the average votes polled by JMM across all the constituencies declined to 14.4 per cent. However, the vote share of JMM in those constituencies where it had a presence amongst the first five candidates rose significantly to 22.5 per cent. Such rise in the vote share did not translate into a higher number of seats won by the JMM on account of the extreme polarization of the political process of the region during the 1998 election (Table 2.6).

TABLE 2.6: PERFORMANCE OF JHARKHAND POLITICAL PARTIES IN LOK SABHA ELECTIONS 1998

Election Year	Average Votes Polled by All Jharkhandi Parties in Constituencies with Electoral Presence	Average Votes Polled by All Jharkhandi Parties in all Constituencies of Jharkhand	Average Percentage of Votes Polled in Seats Won by Jharkhandi Parties	Seat Won Out of Total Seats in Jharkhand
1998	22.52	14.47	–	0 out of 14

The large mandate given by the Jharkhandi electorate to the BJP did not translate into significant gains for the population of the region. The Union government did not last a full term and elections were called for once again in 1999 wherein, there was hardly any change in the pattern of electoral outcome in the region. The BJP won eleven of the fourteen seats with 45 per cent average votes while the INC won two seats with an average vote share of 23 per cent. The Rashtriya Janta Dal (RJD) won only one seat with an average vote share of 8 per cent (Figures 2.11 and 2.12; Table 2.7). It seems that the BJP's loss of one seat in the region (compared with the 1998 election) may reflect a declining electoral support for the party.

However, a perusal of Tables 2.5 and 2.7, delineating the performance of political parties for the 1998 and 1999 elections, shows that the BJP candidates were elected by a larger proportion of the votes in almost all the seats won by them. The JMM continued to be increasingly marginalized in the electoral contest during the 1999 elections. As in the 1998 elections, the JMM did not win any seat in the 1999 election.[13]

Further, the JMM also faced an all-round decline in the average votes polled. In the constituencies in which the party had an electoral presence amongst the first five candidates, the average votes polled fell to 12.88 per cent from 22.5 per cent in 1998. Besides, the overall average votes polled by the JMM in all the constituencies of Jharkhand region declined to 11.9 per cent from 14.4 per cent in 1998 (Table 2.8).

Clearly, the four elections held in the decade of the 1990s were dominated by the BJP in Jharkhand. Since the major difference between the electoral positions of BJP and other political parties active in Jharkhand region was the promise of a separate state, it is perhaps not wrong to deduce that the electoral support for BJP's clear articulation of a separate state in Jharkhand carried the day for the party. In fact, the attraction of the separate state promised by the BJP held so much of a sway in these elections that the political formations which had led the demand for such a separate state since before Independence were also marginalized. This shift of electoral support from JMM and INC to the BJP in Lok Sabha

TABLE 2.7 PERFORMANCE OF POLITICAL PARTIES IN CONSTITUENCIES OF JHARKHAND IN LOK SABHA ELECTIONS 1999

Constituency Name	Number of Candidates	Winner Party and per cent of Votes Polled	Runner up Party and per cent of Votes Polled	III Party and per cent of Votes Polled	IV Party and per cent of Votes Polled	V Party and per cent of Votes Polled
Chatra	14	RJD 52.73 Nagmani	BJP 39.51 Dhirendra Agrawal	BSP 2.70 Mahavir Prasad Yadav	JMM 1.20 Pooran Chand	NCP 0.83 Kamlesh Kumar Singh
Dhanbad	10	BJP 48.07 Rita Verma (W)	MCOR 46.21 A K Roy	JMM 2.44 Kansari Mandal	CPI (ML) (L) 1.03 Upendra Narayan Singh	JD (S) 0.82 S K Verma
Dumka*	10	BJP 36.87 Babulal Marandi	JMM 36.02 Rupi Soren Kisku (W)	INC 24.68 Ramesh Hembram	AMB 0.78 Ravan Murmu	NCP 0.71 Anand Tudu
Giridih	09	BJP 46.70 Ravindra Kumar Pandey	INC 42.97 Rajendra Prasad Singh	JMM (U) 8.04 Shiva Mahato	JMM 1.18 Kartik Mahato	BSP 0.55 Kamal Das
Godda	08	BJP 34.91 Jagdambi Prasad Yadav	JMM 22.30 Suraj Mandal	INC 17.18 Furkan Ansari	CPI 13.64 Sanjay Kumar	RJD 9.49 Javed Iqbal Ansari
Hazaribagh	13	BJP 47.98 Yashwant Sinha	RJD 17.12 Akalu Ram Mahto	JMM (U) 12.05 Teklal Mahto	CPI 9.40 Ramendra Kumar	INC 6.24 Ishwari Ram Paswan
Jameshedpur	10	BJP 45.40 Abha Mahato (W)	INC 26.06 Ghanshayam Mahato	JMM 12.80 Sunil Kumar Mahato	CPI 8.97 Dulal Munshi	JMM (U) 5.74 Sudhir Mahato

Khunti*	04	BJP 46.31 Karaiya Munda	INC 39.82 Sushila Kerketta	JKP 13.09 N E Horo	FBL 0.78 Ghanshayam Singh Munda	–
Koderma	09	INC 46.02 Tilakdhari Prasad Singh	BJP 44.31 Ritlal Prasad Verma	CPI (ML) (L) 3.55 Nazmul Hasan	NCP 3.29 Dr Mumtaj Ansari	JMM 1.52 Bhagwat Rana
Lohardagga*	09	BJP 45.02 Dukha Bhagat	INC 43.97 Indra Nath Bhagat	JMM 7.77 Bishwasnath Bhagat	CPI (ML) (L) 1.35 Jai Prakash Minj	JD(S) 0.65 Bhubaneswar Lohra
Palamau#	05	BJP 53.37 Braj Mohan Ram	RJD 36.65 Jorawar Ram	BSP 6.84 Rampati Ram	CPI (ML) (L) 2.28 Kishore Kumar	JP 0.86 Renu Devi (W)
Rajmahal*	07	INC 44.68 Thomas Hansda	BJP 33.59 Som Marandi	JMM 20.46 Simon Marandi	IND 0.51 Mahesh Malto	IND 0.47 Kistu Murmu
Ranchi	11	BJP 65.72 Ram Tahal Singh	INC 23.93 K K Tewari	JMM 6.76 Prem Chand Mahto	CPI (ML) (L) 1.09 Anant Prasad Gupta	FBL 0.82 Napendra Krishna Mahto
Singhbhum*	07	BJP 49.04 Laxman Gilua	INC 31.59 Vijay Singh Soy	JMM 15.17 Champai Soren	UGDP 2.37 Lakshman Soy	JMM (U) 0.90 Krishna Mardi

Note: *ST Constituency, # SC Constituency

Source: *Statistical Report on General Election, 1999 to the Thirteenth Lok Sabha*, vol. I (National and State Abstracts & Detailed Results), Election Commission of India, New Delhi, n.d.

TABLE 2.8: PERFORMANCE OF JHARKHAND POLITICAL PARTIES IN LOK SABHA ELECTIONS 1999

Election Year	Average Votes Polled by All Jharkhandi Parties in Constituencies with Electoral Presence	Average Votes Polled by All Jharkhandi Parties in all Constituencies of Jharkhand	Average Percentage of Votes Polled in Seats Won by Jharkhandi Parties	Seat Won Out of Total Seats in Jharkhand
1999	12.88	11.96	–	0 out of 14

election continued in the 2004 election, wherein JMM won four sets, INC six, and the RJD two. The BJP and CPI won one seat each. Also interestingly, BJP's share in the 2004 election stayed at a high 22 per cent but this did not translate into seats for the party while INC with 26.5 per cent of the vote-share won six seats from the state. Clearly, pluralization of the polity, as was emerging in the rest of the country, has also started to mediate the electoral scenario of Jharkhand. The contemporary pattern points to a continuance of this pluralized political state. This conclusion is underscored by the electoral patterns of the 2005 Assembly elections in which no single party was able to secure a complete majority, leading to governmental instability in the state.

Turning attention to the development profile of the erstwhile Jharkhand region of Bihar and the new state of Jharkhand in 2001, some central indicators are available to evaluate the changes in the development profile of Jharkhand between 1991 and 2001.[14]

The population of Jharkhand grew at a decadal rate of 23.19 per cent between 1991 and 2001 (24 per cent during 1981–91) compared with 28.43 per cent decadal growth of Bihar. The sex ratio of Jharkhand in 2001 was 941 compared with 922 in 1991. Literacy rate has performed well in Jharkhand. While literacy rate of Jharkhand in 1991 was 33.65 per cent, it had risen to 54.13 per cent in 2001 (literacy figures for Bihar for 1991 and 2001 were 21.1 per cent and 47.53 per cent, respectively). Similarly, female literacy in Jharkhand rose from 20.8 per cent in 1991 to 39.38 in 2001 while the same figures for Bihar were 18.63 per cent in 1991 and 33.57 in 2001. Clearly, as far as literacy was concerned, Jharkhand far outperformed Bihar during the decade 1991–2001.

Perhaps employment rates in agricultural and non-agricultural sectors are the most crucial indicators as far as economic development is concerned. Jharkhand continued the patterns of earlier decades with much higher non-agricultural employment levels compared with Bihar. While 22.22 per cent of Jharkhand's population was employed in agricultural activities in 1991, the same figure in 2001 was 25.16 per cent.

A similar growth was also noticed in agricultural employment in Bihar with 23.95 per cent of the population being employed in agriculture-related activities in 1991, rising to 26.21 per cent in 2001. However, the most significant difference can be noted in non-agricultural employment. In Jharkhand, 9.12 per cent of the population was employed in non-agricultural activities in 1991 (in Bihar it was 5.75 per cent), by 2001, the figure was 25.16 per cent (Bihar: 7.67 per cent). Thus, overall employment in Jharkhand had grown at a much higher rate than Bihar.

This overall positive trend in the socio-economic development of Jharkhand during the period 1991–2001 formed the backdrop of the parliamentary elections of 2004. This election was important for being the first election in the new state of Jharkhand and also for the significant political re-configurations that seem to emerge from the result of this election.

By the time the general elections were held in 2004, the new state of Jharkhand had been in existence for over three years and BJP, the party which was the largest beneficiary of the pattern of electoral support in the 1999 election, was in power at the state level[15] (as at the Union level as a part of the National Democratic Alliance). However, the trends and patterns of electoral support for the BJP noticed in the 1999 elections did not continue in the 2004 elections (Table 2.9). A BJP candidate was elected only from one constituency in Jharkhand, that of Koderma from which Babulal Marandi, the former chief minister, was elected with 44 per cent of the votes polled. BJP polled less than half of the 1999 average vote share at 22 per cent (Figures 2.11 and 2.12).

Further, JMM and other Jharkhandi political groups[16] re-emerged

TABLE 2.9 PERFORMANCE OF POLITICAL PARTIES IN CONSTITUENCIES OF JHARKHAND IN LOK SABHA ELECTIONS 2004

Constituency Name	Number of Candidates	Winner Party and per cent of Votes Polled	Runner up Party and per cent of Votes Polled	III Party and per cent of Votes Polled	IV Party and per cent of Votes Polled	V Party and per cent of Votes Polled
Chatra	16	RJD 27.89 Dhirendra Agarwal	JD (U) 23.56 Inder Singh Namdhari	BJP 22.88 Nagmani	IND 11.92 Ramlal Oraon	SP 3.29 Suresh Yadav
Dhanbad	19	INC 37.76 Chandra Shekhar Dubey	BJP 25.08 Rita Verma (W)	MCO 15.66 A.K. Roy	IND 11.28 Samresh Singh	SLP (L) 1.98 Dina Bandu Singh
Dumka*	10	JMM 54.32 Shibu Soren	BJP 35.92 Sone Lal Hembrom	BSP 2.16 Baijnath Manjhi	AJSU 1.97 Jonathan Tudu	IND 1.46 Sona Murmu (W)
Giridih	12	JMM 49.03 Tek Lal Mahto	BJP 28.06 Ravindra Kumar Pandey	JD (U) 11.44 Inderdeo Mahato	AJSU 4.52 Raj Kishore Mahato	BSP 1.91 Kamal Sahu
Godda	12	INC 44.88 Furkan Ansari	BJP 41.66 Pradeep Yadav	JD (U) 5.27 Suraj Mandal	BSP 2.75 Jai Prakash Yadav	IND 1.33 Shamim Akhtar
Hazaribagh	14	CPI 50.47 Bhubneshwar Prasad Mehta	BJP 35.54 Yashwant Sinha	AJSU 5.20 Chandra Prakash Choudhary	CPI (ML) (L) 2.06 Heera Gope	IND 1.59 Snehlata Devi (W)
Jamshedpur	16	JMM 51.00 Sunil Kumar Mahato	BJP 37.40 Abha Mahto (W)	SP 2.24 Omkar Nath Jaiswal	NPF 1.42 Surya Singh Besra	IND 1.42 Sitaram Tudu

Khunti*	11	INC 44.54 Sushila Kerketta (W)	BJP 34.00 Kariya Munda	JKP 6.50 Niral Enem Horo	JD (U) 4.32 Dr. Ram Dayal Munda	BSP 4.21 Ajit Kiro
Koderma	10	BJP 44.40 Babulal Marandi	JMM 25.64 Champa Verma (W)	CPI (ML) (L) 16.54 Raj Kumar Yadav	INC 6.52 Tilakdhari Prasad Singh	BSP 2.06 Mahesh Ram
Lohardagga*	13	INC 48.00 Rameshwar Oraon	BJP 28.65 Dukha Bhagat	IND 12.64 Chamra Linda	IND 2.08 Sukhdeo Lohra	BSP 1.53 Bhupendra Nath Ram
Palamau#	14	RJD 32.22 Manoj Kumar	BJP 23.63 Braj Mohan Ram	JD (U) 16.64 Radha Krishn Kishore	BSP 9.49 Jitendra Kumar	INC 8.42 Vijay Kumar
Rajmahal*	8	JMM 32.76 Hemlal Murmu	INC 32.33 Thomas Hansda	BJP 27.85 Som Marandi	BSP 2.11 Chunda Tudu	IND 1.67 Dilip Hembrom
Ranchi	19	INC 40.82 Subodh Kant Sahay	BJP 38.61 Ram Tahal Choudhary	IND 7.53 Bandhu Tirky	CPM 5.42 Rajendra Singh Munda	IND 1.67 Rajesh Kumar
Singhbhum*	8	INC 42.55 Bagun Sumbrai	BJP 31.17 Laxman Gilua	AJSU 13.96 Sukhram Oraon	JDP 6.31 Salkhan Murmu	IND 2.60 Dimple Lamay (W)

Note: *ST Constituency, # SC Constituency

Source : Statistical Report on General Election, 2004 to the 14th Lok Sabha, vol. II, Election Commission of India, New Delhi, n.d.

on the electoral horizon of Jharkhand after more than a decade of dismal performance verging on the point of political irrelevance. Although a number of Jharkhandi political formations were in the fray, only the JMM was able to win seats in the region. JMM candidates were elected from four of the fourteen Lok Sabha seats in the region—a splendid performance considering more than a decade of electoral debacle for the party. Further, the JMM polled an average of almost 47 per cent of the votes polled in the seats won by its candidates, which was quite respectable. However, this performance by the JMM in 2004 election does not reflect a rise in popular support for the Jharkhandi political opinion in the state. In fact, the average electoral support for all the Jharkhandi parties in constituencies in which they had a presence amongst the first five candidates declined to 8.24 per cent in the 2004 election from 12.88 per cent in 1999 (Table 2.10).

Since Independence, this is the lowest level of electoral support for Jharkhandi political parties in constituencies in which they had a presence amongst the first five candidates. Further, the overall electoral support to Jharkhandi political parties in all the constituencies of Jharkhand declined to 4.12 per cent in the 2004 election from 11.96 per cent in the 1999 elections. This poor level of electoral support for Jharkhandi political groups was the second-lowest in all the general elections since 1952. Clearly, all is not well with Jharkhandi political groups in the state.

The largest beneficiary in the shifting patterns of electoral support

TABLE 2.10: PERFORMANCE OF JHARKHANDI POLITICAL PARTIES IN LOK SABHA ELECTIONS 2004

Election Year	Average Votes Polled by All Jharkhandi Parties in Constituencies with Electoral Presence	Average Votes Polled by All Jharkhandi Parties in all Constituencies of Jharkhand	Average Percentage of Votes Polled in Seats Won by Jharkhandi Parties	Seat Won Out of Total Seats in Jharkhand
2004	8.24	4.12	46.77	4 out of 14

in the new state of Jharkhand in the 2004 general election was the INC, which was elected from six of the fourteen constituencies with an average vote of about 26 per cent (Figures 2.11 and 2.12). In fact, a study of Table 2.9 indicates that the Jharkhand political dynamics seems to have reverted to that of early 1970s and early 1980s when the INC used to dominate the elections in the region.

III. IMPLICATIONS OF THE DEVELOPMENTAL AND POLITICAL PATTERNS

Changes in the development profile have been the central factor in the dynamics of the political process of the Jharkhand region. However, this relationship is not one of a direct correlation but is a contingent and complex variable. Development policy makers in the early 1950s had hoped that a vigorous development policy would weaken demands for autonomy on cultural lines. However, the poor implementation of the policy and inadequate improvements in the development profile had encouraged the electorate to demand an autonomous state precisely for the reason of a non-functional development policy under the existing arrangements. Under these circumstances, the issues of Jharkhandi identity were raised to augment the political resources controlled by the electorate. The fortunes of the Jharkhandi groups that have stood for a separate state of Jharkhand reflect these dynamics.

The INC had been partially successful in focusing attention on the development needs of the region (as opposed to the identity issue) and had gained significant electoral support for such a policy in the late 1960s, 1970s and early 1980s. However, the INC lost its legitimacy and support, which was generated by its pro-poor rhetoric and some concrete efforts at improving development, due to the developmental inertia in the region leading to inadequate socio-economic development. Hence, in the late 1980s and 1990s, the population and the electorate of Jharkhand were willing to once again experiment with the various political parties that were present in the region, including the Jharkhandi political groups.

The BJP entered the electoral horizon of the Jharkhand region precisely at this time and the reasons which led to the decline of the INC also partially explain the success of the BJP. The BJP projected itself with the slogan *sab ko dekha baar baar, hamko dekho ek baar* [You (the electorate) have tried all parties time and again, try us once] to appeal to the electorate of the region that had been let down by all political groups in the region too many times as far as their developmental requirements were concerned. Further, the BJP also stole the thunder of the Jharkhandi political opinion by offering its own concept of a separate state in Jharkhand under the name of *Vananchal* (Forest State) to appeal to a cross-section of the electorate in the region—something which actually saw fruition in 2000.

The failure of the political parties in the Jharkhand region to offer avenues for the exchange of resources between the electorate and the state and the consequent decline in the development profile added another dimension to the relationship of dependence in the region. In the 1990s, the electorate was splitting the political resources which they controlled into three components. The 1991 and 1996 elections have shown that the state-level electoral support was extended to Janata Dal (or RJD) which was in office at the state-level[17] and could have influenced public policy implementation. In the Lok Sabha elections, this political support was extended to the BJP as it was the only national party that was promising the creation of a separate state of Jharkhand. The third component of the strategic use of political resources by the public at large consisted of avenues to force the two parties to remember their promises during the term of office. This was manifested in the support for the agitational politics of the JMM, the JCC and the AJSU consisting of economic blockades and general strikes. This kind of agitational politics forced the state to take cognisance of the Jharkhandi electorate, since these agitations often required coercion by the state in order to keep the mineral lifeline of the country running. Such violence undermines the legitimacy of the state and the regime. Consequently, the regime in office is forced to take urgent policy measures to contain future strife.

This three-pronged approach in the late 1980s and the 1990s

has yielded better profits for the people of the Jharkhand region than all others. Such strategic use of political resources has led the state to engage in a more meaningful exchange of resources with the population of the Jharkhand region. As a result, a Committee on Jharkhand Matters (COJM) was appointed (see Section II) and by 1995, the Bihar Vidhan Sabha had legislated to create the Jharkhand Area Autonomous Council (JAAC)[18] and finally a separate state of Jharkhand was created in 2000. The splitting of political resources at the command of the electorate has thus forced the state to respond with better policy measures.

The Lok Sabha election of 2004 underlines the continuation of the pattern of strategic use of the political resources at their command by the electorate. Once the state had been created in 2000, the electorate saw little use for the BJP, not least due to the policy shortcomings of the BJP government at the state level. Further, issues such as the domicile policy for government employment did not help the BJP in seeking a larger electoral support. The improvements in socio-economic profile in the period 1991-2001 notwithstanding, the BJP was unable to offer a roadmap for the development of the state. The Jharkhandi political parties on the other hand were also not a very attractive political choice for the electorate on account of the fact that the rationale for their existence (creation of a separate state of Jharkhand) had disappeared and they had never actually offered an alternative vision for the development of the state. Further, the RJD, which was in power at the state level when Jharkhand was a part of Bihar did not offer a viable alternative on account of their inability to contribute to the development of Jharkhand despite being in power for almost a decade. The INC therefore emerged as a dominant player in the new state.

Thus, overall, any predictions that may have been made about electoral support to BJP's *Vanvasi* ideology in Jharkhand have been belied. BJP's appeal to the electorate in Jharkhand was limited to the party's promise for a separate state of Jharkhand. Once that had been realized, the electorate shifted support to the developmental vision of the INC—something which was tried intensively in the 1960s and 1970s with little success. Conversely, the argument that the ethnic aspects of Jharkhandi identity—which had formed the basic premise for the quest for autonomy—had run itself out will also not be true. Continued support to the JMM is only one aspect of this argument. The large-scale popular support for Birsa Day and Hul celebrations (commemorating 150 years of the Santhal Hul) are facts in point.

The complex intermeshing of identity and development are thus yet to play themselves out in the politics of the new Jharkhand state. The contours of this politics of development are fluid and complex, as demonstrated in the results of the first election for the Jharkhand Vidhan Sabha in 2005. The impact of factors will be clearer in the years to come.

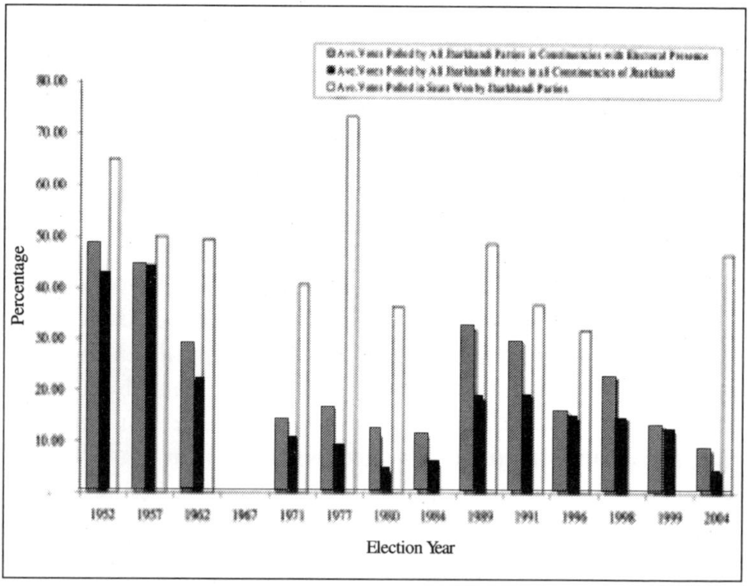

Note: *In the 1967 election, the JHP was a part of the INC. Hence, the performance of the Jharkhandi political formations in this election cannot be calculated.

Figure 2.1: Average Percentage of Votes Polled by Jharkhandi Parties 1952–2004

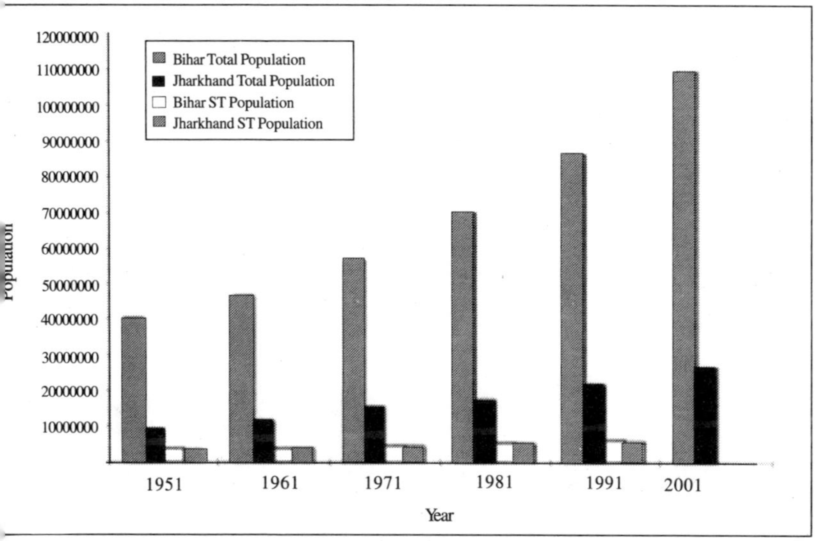

Figure 2.2: Growth in Total and Scheduled Tribes Population in Bihar and Jharkhand 1951–2001

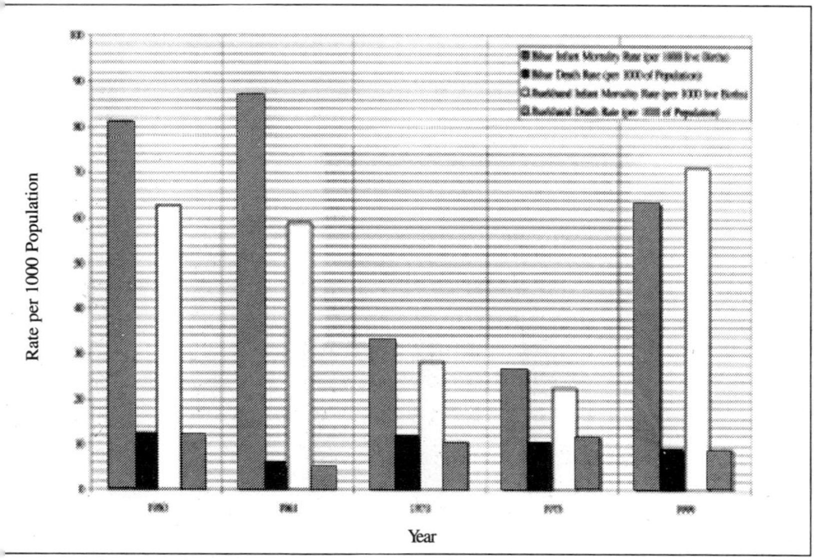

Figure 2.3: Infant Mortality and Death Rates in Bihar and Jharkhand 1950–99

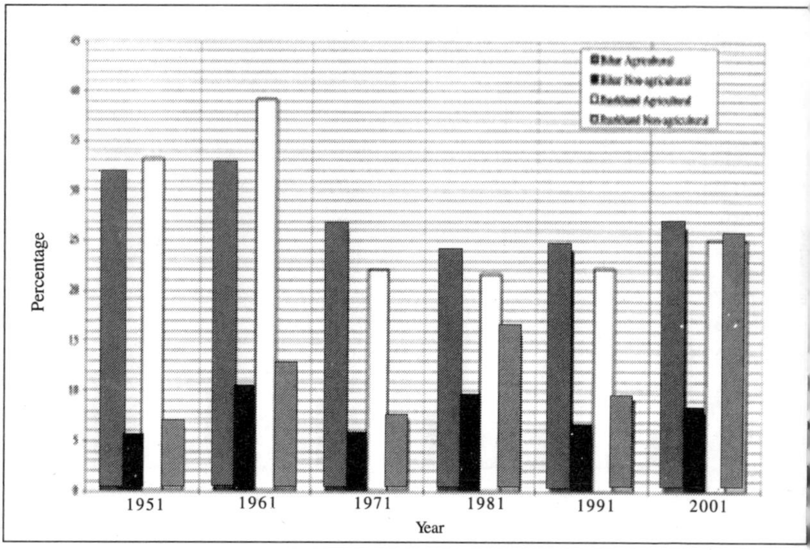

Figure 2.4: Occupational Pattern of Workers in Bihar and Jharkhand 1951–2001

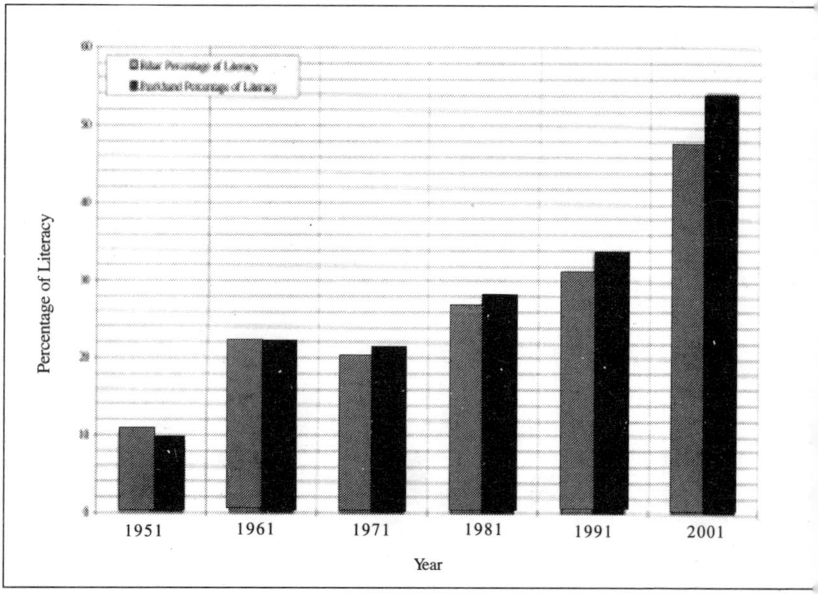

Figure 2.5: Growth of Literacy in Bihar and Jharkhand 1951–2001

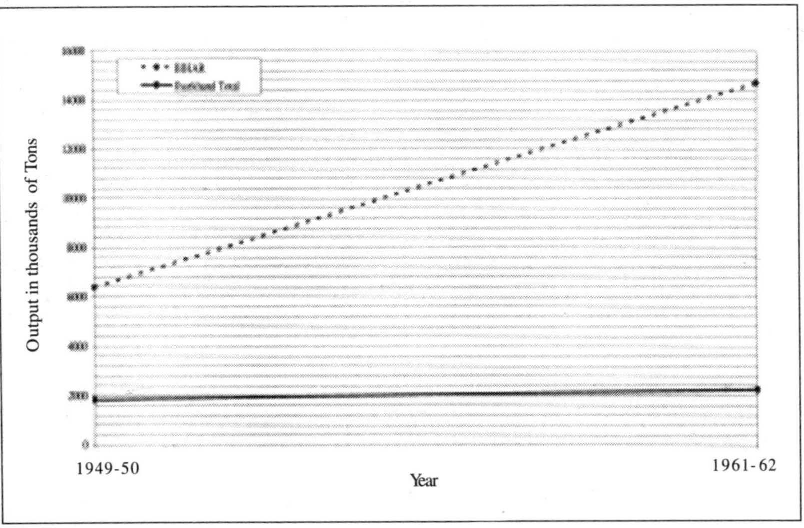

Figure 2.6: Total Agricultural Output of Principal Crops in Bihar and Jharkhand 1949–10 to 1961–2

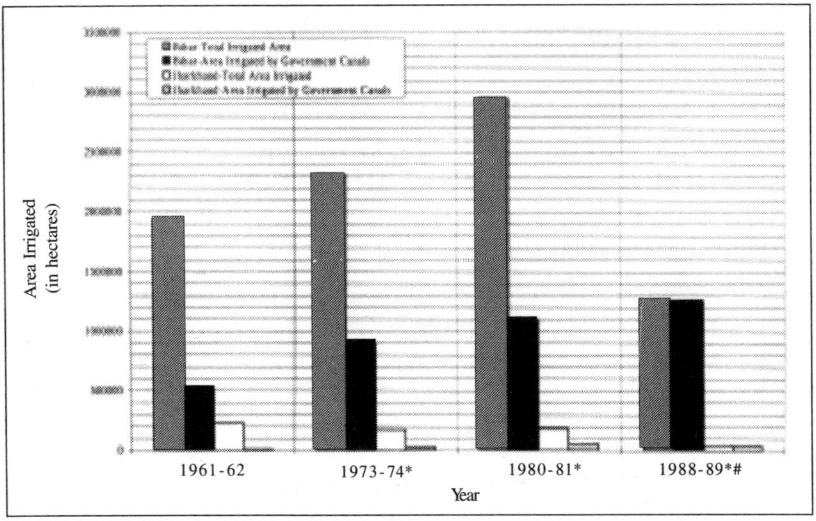

Notes: *Rounded up to the nearest thousand in the source.
Area irrigated by means other than government canals is not available.

Figure 2.7: Source of Irrigation in Bihar and Jharkhand 1961–89

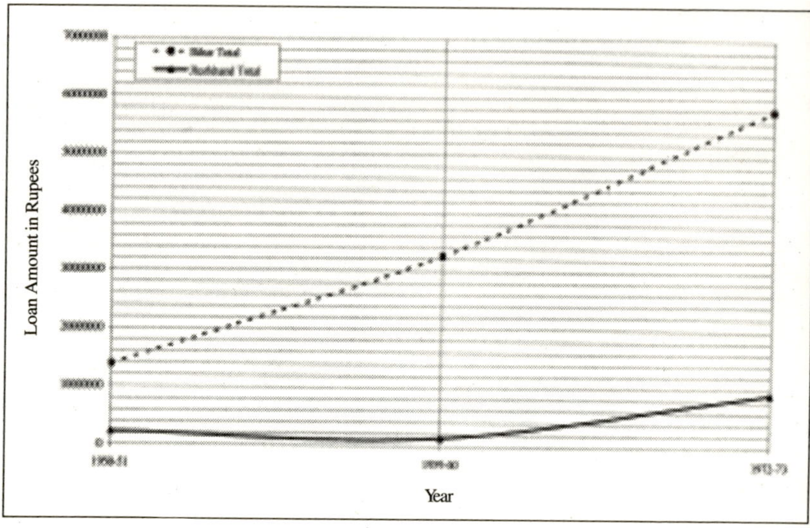

Figure 2.8: Land Improvement Loans Advanced in Bihar and Jharkhand 1950–1 to 1972–3

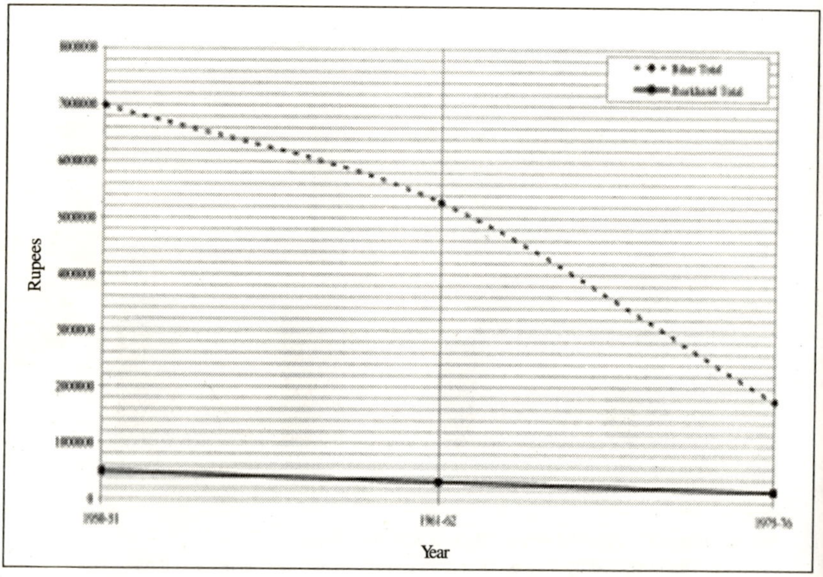

Figure 2.9: Collection of Agricultural Income Tax in Bihar and Jharkhand 1950–1 to 1975–6

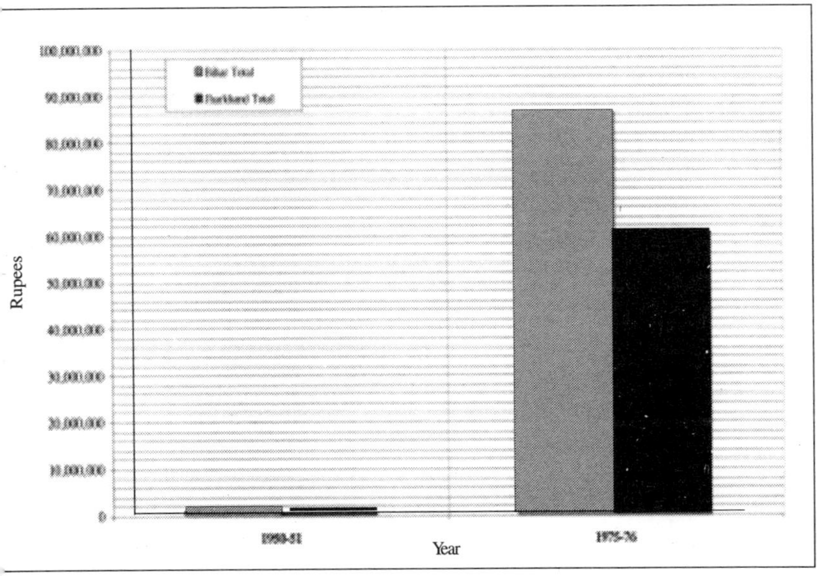

Figure 2.10: Electricity Tax Collected in Bihar and Jharkhand 1950–1 to 1975–6

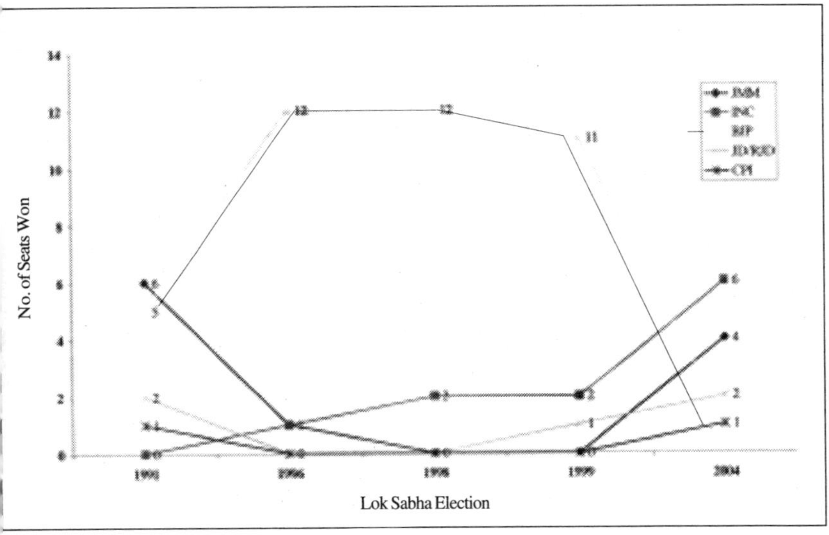

Figure 2.11: Seats Won by Political Parties in Lok Sabha Elections in Jharkhand 1991–2004

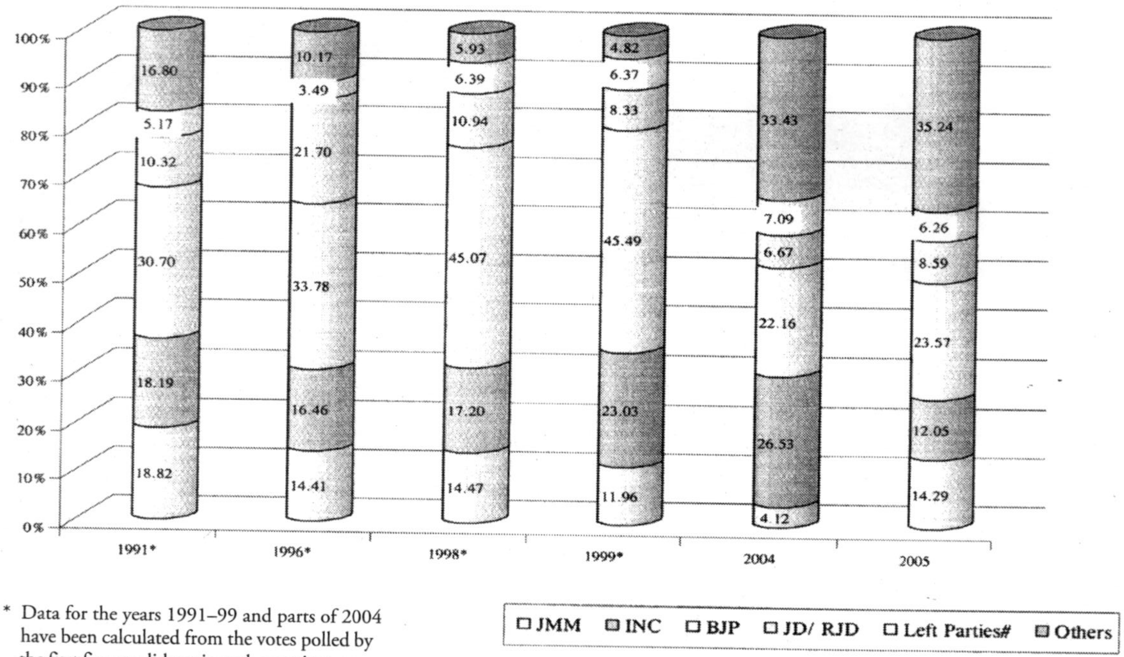

* Data for the years 1991–99 and parts of 2004 have been calculated from the votes polled by the first five candidates in each constituency. May not tally with total.

\# CPI; CPM; MCOR; IPF; CPI(ML); CPI(ML)(L)

Source: Reports of the Election Commissoin

NOTES

1. While some of the Left movements may not qualify for such a description, their being restricted to certain geographical pockets in the country would indicate that the question of identity is not totally irrelevant.
2. The term 'autonomy' is used here in the limited sense to denote political and administrative autonomy and does not seek to discuss or comment upon the autonomy of individuals and social groups.
3. The original demand of a Jharkhand consisted of the 25 districts from tribal regions of four states—Bihar, Madhya Pradesh, West Bengal and Orissa. However, through a series of intricate political negotiations over half a century, the geographical spread of Jharkhand has come to mean the districts of eastwhile south Bihar only (Bokaro, Chatra, Deoghar, Dhanbad, Dumka, East Singhbhum, Garhwa, Giridih, Godda, Gumla, Hazaribagh, Koderma, Lohardagga, Pakur, Palamau, Ranchi, Sahebganj, and West Singhbhum), which form the Jharkhand state today.
4. Chota Nagpur Improvement Society, a political organization active in the Jharkhand region in the 1920s, had sought to invoke the unique culture and heritage as the premise of tribal identity to demand a governor's province, along with an enlightened and progressive administration. 'Memorandum submitted by the Chota Nagpur Improvement Society', *Report of the Indian Statutory Commission*, vol. XVI, part 1, London: HMSO, 1930, p. 435. For full details see Prakash, 2001, pp. 58–60, 95–6.
5. See Prakash (2001) for a full analysis of the inter-linkage of identity and development in the Jharkhand region during 1951–91.
6. See Prakash, 2001, Chapters 4–6, for a full discussion.
7. In the interests of continuity and ease of reference, all the figures have been included at the end of the paper.
8. In 1952, when the Lok Sabha had 489 seats, the country was divided into 314 single-member constituencies, 86 double-member constituencies and one three-member constituency. In 1957, with 494 seats in the Lok Sabha, there were 312 single-member constituencies and 91 double-member constituencies. Reservation of seats for SC/STs was the main reason for the creation of double-member constituencies. In Bihar, Palamu-cum-Hazaribagh-cum-Ranchi, Purnea-cum-Santhal Pargana, Santhal Paragana-cum-Hazaribagh, and Dumka were declared double-member constituencies. The Scheduled Tribes were assured a seat in the double-member constituencies through a special procedure for declaring results. Results of the reserved seats were declared first, wherein the ST candidates polling the highest number of votes from among the ST contestants was declared elected

(for unreserved seats, candidates polling the largest number of votes was declared elected, irrespective of his/her social affiliations). The electorate in such constituencies had two votes, and in the results of these two elections, both winners and runners-up were elected from such constituencies. For details, see Singh and Bose, 1984: 13.

9. The results of the 1984 elections need to be treated with caution as this election was truncated by the assassination of Indira Gandhi. Hence, most parts of the country saw an unprecedented 'sympathy-vote' in favour of the INC leading to the largest majority in the Lok Sabha ever. Thus, this result may not be a part of a long-term electoral trend in the Jharkhand region.
10. The BJP clearly articulated its view of smaller states in its election manifesto for the 1991 Lok Sabha election only and in the *Resolution Regarding Creation of New States of Uttaranchal and Vananchal* tabled on 5 March 1993 in the Lok Sabha. However, politically, the issue was very much alive in the 1989 election.
11. This committee was constituted by the Union Ministry of Home Affairs in an attempt to find a solution to the issue. It comprised all the major political figures of the Jharkhand movement irrespective of their official party affiliation. Besides, there were many other experts ranging from anthropologists to social activists who served on the COJM. The important political figures of the Jharkhand movement who were members of the COJM were Dr. R.D. Munda, Dr. A.K. Singh, N.E. Horo, Shibu Soren, B.B. Mahto, B.P. Kesri, S.S. Besra, Prabhakar Tirkey, Santosh Rana, Suraj Mandal, Shailendra Mahato and Prof. Stephen Marandi. The state was represented by the relevant officials. The joint secretaries to the ministries of Rural Development, Tribal Development and Home Affairs represented the central government while the Government of Bihar was represented by the secretaries in the Ministries of Home Affairs and Tribal Welfare and the Regional Development Commissioner of the Jharkhand region. For full details and the importance of the Committee, see Prakash, 2001, Chapter 7.
12. In the election manifesto for the 1991 Lok Sabha election, BJP promised: 'The BJP recognises that regional imbalances have developed in some states because of their size. The party would appoint a commission to report on formation of smaller states which are economically and democratically viable. Initially, BJP will have Uttaranchal, Vananchal and Union Territory of Delhi as three new states of the Indian Union . . . ', *Manifesto of the Bharatiya Janata Party for Lok Sabha Election 1991*: 3.
13. The JMM did not win any seat in the 1999 elections but Shibu Soren of the JMM won the Dumka parliamentry seat in a by-election after it was

vacated by Babulal Marandi on 8 March 2001 consequent to his swearing in as the first chief minister of the newly created state of Jharkhand.

14. All data used in this paper for the year 2001 has been taken from Census 2001 available at the website of the Census Commissioner of India at http://www.censusindia.net/
15. The Bihar Reorganisation Act 2000 provided that the newly constituted Legislative Assembly of Jharkhand would have a term coterminous with that of the Bihar Legislative Assembly as those MLAs in the Bihar Assembly who had been elected from the Jharkhand region formed the bulk of the MLAs in the Assembly of Jharkhand.
16. Such as the All Jharkhand Students Union (AJSU) and the revived Jharkhand Party (JHP) led by N.E. Horo.
17. The Janata Dal split after charges of corruption were levelled against the then chief minister, Laloo Prasad Yadav. Consequently, he formed a new party called the Rashtriya Janata Dal (RJD) that was in office in Bihar with Rabri Devi as the chief minister until the Vidhan Sabha Elections of 2005.
18. See Prakash, 2001, Ch. 7 for full details and dynamics of the creation and functioning of the Committee on Jharkhand Matters and Jharkhand Autonomous Area Council.

REFERENCES

Kohli, Atul, 1990, *Democracy and Discontent: India's Growing Crisis of Governability*, Cambridge: Cambridge University Press.

Manifesto of the Bharatiya Janata Party for Lok Sabha Election 1991, Delhi: BJP Central Office.

Narayan, S., 1988, *Movements Development: Police and Judiciary in Tribal World*, New Delhi: Inter India Publication.

Prakash, Amit, 1999, 'Contested Discourses: Politics of Ethnic Identity and Autonomy in the Jharkhand Region of India', in *Alternatives: Social Transformation and Humane Governance*, vol. 24, no. 4, pp. 461–96.

——— 2001, *Jharkhand: Politics of Development and Identity*, Delhi: Orient Longman.

Rekhi, Upjit Singh, 1988, *Jharkhand Movement in Bihar*, Delhi: Nunes.

Singh, V.B. and Shankar Bose, 1984, *Elections in India: Data Handbook on Lok Sabha Elections*, London: Sage.

Soren, Sibu, 1992, 'Jharkhand Rajya Ka Sawal [The Question of Jharkhand State]', in S. Narayan (ed.), *Jharkhand Movement: Origin and Evolution*, Delhi: Inter-India Publications.

CHAPTER THREE

The Creation of Vananchal: Reassessment of the Jharkhand State

CYRIL ROBIN

The newly created Jharkhand state was carved out of Bihar and came into being on 15 November 2000. Owing to its mineral-based resources and the available industrial infrastructure, Jharkhand is considered as one of the most financially viable states in the whole country. Though supposedly created to fulfil the aspirations arisen from the movement for a separate Jharkhand, the state that came into existence corresponds to the concept of Vananchal expounded by the Sangh Parivar in the late 1980s to counter the Church-supported Jharkhand movement and not to the concept of Jharkhand developed by those, mainly tribals, who struggled for its formation for almost eight decades. The latter's idea of a Jharkhand state consisted of districts from Bihar, West Bengal, Orissa and Madhya Pradesh. As a consequence, the tribal population represented 'only' 26.3 per cent of the Jharkhand population at the time of the 2001 census, placing this state at the tenth rank in India in terms of the percentage of tribal population, far from the north-eastern states and Chhattisgarh (31.8 per cent).[1] This percentage of the total population of Jharkhand has had a direct impact on the sociology of the MLAs of the state. Indeed, the political scene of Jharkhand is polarized between Scheduled Tribes (ST) and Other Backward Classes (OBC), reassessing within the political field the tribal identity of the state.

The purpose of this paper is to demonstrate, through the analysis of the sociology of the MLAs of the state, that the tribal identity of Jharkhand is challenged by a strong political representation of members of the OBCs resulting from the failure of the so-called Jharkhand movement in favour of a 'Greater Jharkhand' *versus* the youngest and most feasible concept of Vananchal.

THE MOVEMENT FOR THE CREATION OF JHARKHAND: A MOVEMENT WITHOUT UNITY

All through the nineteenth century, the Jharkhand region saw insurgencies against the British, reflecting the grievances, injustices as well as the exploitation of the *Adivasis* in the Chhotanagpur Plateau and the Santhal Pargana region. These revolts for socio-economic and political freedom like the Kol Rebellion in 1831–2, the Santhal insurrection of 1855 or the Birsa movement in 1895–1900[2] contributed to the genesis of the Jharkhand movement and to the formation of several tribal-dominated organizations such as the Shiksha Samiti in 1906, the Chhotanagpur Unnati Samaj in 1915 (CNUS) and the Chhotanagpur Catholic Sabha in 1936. But if these organizations sought to promote the interests and the identity of the tribal population, they separately fought for the rights of the tribals.

In 1928, one of these formal organizations, the CNUS, established with the support of all the major tribal groups,[3] pressed its demand for a separate state for the Adivasis to the Simon Commission.[4] The main objectives of the CNUS were the upliftment of Chhotanagpur from its backwardness and the social, political and economic improvement of the Adivasis' conditions. But, 'in the same age-old British tradition, the demand of the Tribals to separate Chhotanagpur from Bihar was rejected'.[5]

In the elections held in January 1937 under the Government of India Act of 1935, the different organizations struggling for the rights of the Adivasis fought the elections by nominating one candidate against the other; the Chhotanagpur Unnati Samaj, the Kisan Sabha and the Chhotanagpur Catholic Sabha fielded their own candidates for the polls. As a result, 'the Congress swept the polls defeating the candidates fielded by the CNUS and the KS. All the reserved seats were captured by the Congress'.[6] This electoral fragmentation among the Jharkhandi organizations already revealed the divisions that existed within the Jharkhand movement, mainly between the Christian tribals and non-Christian tribals.

Nevertheless, in the aftermath of this political defeat, tribal leaders closed their ranks. In 1938, they united and formed into a single organization called the Adivasi Mahasabha (AM).[7] The AM succeeded in bringing Santhals, Hos, Oraons, Mundas, Kharias and, above all, Christian and non-Christian tribals together. Thus united, the AM did well in the following municipal election in February 1938 with nominees elected in majority. But, Adivasis hadn't still a leader able to speak for them and to represent them to the British authorities. In 1939, Jaipal Singh (a Munda), then a minister in Bikaner princely state and former captain of the Indian hockey team during the ninth Olympics at Amsterdam, presided over a meeting of the AM at the invitation of its leaders. As noted by Tirkey, 'Jaipal Singh was himself interested and keen to take active part in the improvement of *Chhotanagpuri*. [He] stressed that freedom from exploitation demanded that Chhotanagpur and Santhal Pargana should become states within India.'[8] Then, from this meeting, Jaipal Singh was accepted by the Adivasis as their *Marang Gomke* (supreme leader), and appointed the president of the Adivasi Mahasabha. Thereafter, the primary goal of the AM leaders became the achievement of a separate state of Jharkhand. In order to strengthen their demand, the AM needed to obtain more support from the *Sadaans*[9] who had settled in Jharkhand permanently. Finally, it was decided in 1950 to rename the Adivasi Mahasabha as the Jharkhand Party in order to extend the membership to non-Adivasi residents of the Chhotanagpur and Santhal Pargana regions.[10] As a consequence of the formation of the Jharkhand Party, the Jharkhand movement achieved stronger political dimensions.

On the eve of the general elections of 1952, the Jharkhand Party and its leader, Jaipal Singh were both highly popular. As a result, the tribal-dominated party won 32 seats of which 5 seats were from the general and 2 from the Scheduled Castes (SC) reserved constituencies. The Jharkhand Party then represented the second largest party in the first Bihar Vidhan Sabha (Legislative Assembly) and the leader of the opposition. For the first time, the movement for a separate Jharkhand state was strongly represented by a political party gathering Christian and non-Christian tribals together.

In 1953, with the appointment of the States Reorganization Commission (SRC) by the Government of India, the Jharkhand Party had the opportunity to cash in on its electoral success. The party submitted two memoranda to the SRC for the creation of a Jharkhand state. But the SRC Report (published in 1956) only recommended the constitution of a development board for Chhotanagpur and Santhal Pargana regions. In the opinion of the members of the SRC, as a minority ('only a little more than one-third of the total population of the Chhotanagpur Division and Santhal Pargana'), the Adivasis were not in a position to claim for the creation of a Jharkhand state. Moreover, as the tribal population is divided into several language groups—Santhali, Mundari, Kurukh, Ho, and so on—the linguistic criteria could not be at the root of the formation of Jharkhand, like Telugu for Andhra Pradesh.[11] This decision of the SRC showed the opposition that existed between the logic at the Centre to reorganize the country according to specific criteria and the logic at the regional level for the creation of a 'tribal state'. Thus, the refusal to create a Jharkhand state prevented a strong regional identity from developing and deepening.

As the Jharkhand Party failed in its demand for a separate state, the tribal identity of the region was challenged. Nevertheless, despite the disillusionment of the ST communities, the popularity of the Jharkhand Party did not decline so much. Indeed, despite the setback, the Jharkhand Party maintained its 32 seats in the 1957 Bihar Legislative Assembly elections. Nevertheless, out of these 32 seats, 23 were STs against 26 in 1952. This decrease in the number of ST elected under the Jharkhand Party banner seems to highlight the resentment of the tribal population toward the failure of the Jharkhand Party.

As a result, from the 1957 elections onwards, the Jharkhand movement started eroding and Jaipal Singh, the leader of the Jharkhand Party, already felt that his party was about to split because of the growing struggles between the leaders and the effectiveness of the Congress party's methods against its political opponents.[12] As a result, the share of the Jharkhand Party in the

Bihar Vidhan Sabha declined from 9 to 6 per cent between 1952 and 1962. Mainly due to internal divisions amongst the leadership, this social and political weakening led to its merger with the Congress party in 1963.

THE JHARKHAND MUKTI MORCHA, A NEW PARTY CHAMPIONING THE CREATION OF JHARKHAND?

Till the end of the 1970s, factionalism within the Jharkhand movement prevented it from maintaining a sizeable and homogeneous presence in the Bihar Legislative Assembly. For instance, in the 1972 General Elections, three parties—the Hul Jharkhand headed by Seth Hembron and Justin Richard, the All India Jharkhand Party led by Sumbrai and the Jharkhand Party headed by N.E. Horo—represented the Jharkhand movement and could only secure seven seats out of 318.

From the late 1970s, the Jharkhand Mukti Morcha (JMM) could have appeared as the party able to revitalize the Jharkhand movement. Indeed, the association of the erstwhile Sonot Santhal Samaj (Pure Santhal Society) movement led by Shibu Soren with the Shivaji Samaj led by Binod Bihari Mahato, an organization struggling against the backwardness of the Kurmi/Mahato peasant community, and the Marxist Coordination Committee of A.K. Roy, a militant trade union leader in the colliery of Dhanbad, led to the formation of the JMM and added a new dimension to the Jharkhand movement.[13] As a consequence of the militant activities of these leaders among mine workers in Dhanbad and the Santhal peasants, the party 'gradually gained a stronghold in Singbhum, Santhal Pargana and Dhanbad'[14] and gathered in one organization workers and peasants, tribals and non-tribals.

However, as a result of this geographical presence, the electoral support of the Jharkhand Mukti Morcha was smaller than it was in the early 1950s for the Jharkhand Party. Till 2000, the votes polled by the JMM in the Bihar elections never went above 4 per cent whereas the Jharkhand Party had obtained in 1952 and 1957 elections more than 7 per cent. Besides, unlike the Jharkhand Party in which Mundas, Oraons and Hos were significantly represented in spite of the Santhal presence, the representation of the tribes within the JMM was largely dominated by the Santhals as evident from Table 3.1.

In addition, although the JMM is characterized by a definite tribal identity, with 62.4 per cent of ST MLAs, the share of the non-tribals is more significant than in the Jharkhand Party, as it is evident from Table 3.1. It is noteworthy to notice that this larger representativeness, in terms of castes and communities, has not enabled the JMM to increase the electorate of the Jharkhand movement and the number of the MLAs as compared to the Jharkhand Party: the JMM never won more than 19 seats in the Bihar Assembly against 30 for the Jharkhand Party and the JMM never got

TABLE 3.1: CASTE AND COMMUNITY OF THE MLAS OF THE TWO MAIN JHARKHANDI PARTIES, 1952–2005

(*in per cent*)

Castes and Communities	Jharkhand Party (1952–62)	JMM (1980–2005)	Total
Upper Castes	2.6	1.2	1.9
Brahmin	1.3	–	0.6
Rajput	1.3	–	0.6
Kayastha	–	1.2	0.6
Backward Castes	6.5	22.4	14.2
Kurmi	2.6	14.1	8.6
Koeri	2.6	–	1.2
Bania	1.3	8.2	4.9
Eextremely Backward Castes	–	1.2	0.6
Scheduled Castes	6.5	8.2	7.4
Scheduled Tribes	88.0	62.4	74.7
Santhal	37.7	42.4	40.1
Munda	10.4	1.2	5.6
Oraon	14.3	4.7	9.3
Ho	5	–	2.5
Others	16.9	14.1	15.4
Muslims	–	3.5	1.9
Unidentified	–	1.2	0.6
Total	100 N=77	100 N=85	100 N=165

Source: Survey by Cyril Robin.

more than 4 per cent of the total votes polled when the Jharkhand Party obtained more than 7 per cent in the 1952 and 1957 state elections. Moreover, a scandal in the early 1990s[15] and the BJP's political rise in the region, saw the JMM lose ground among the tribal people.

JHARKHAND: A NEW STRONGHOLD OF TRIBAL POLITICS?

From the late 1980s, the leaders of the Congress at the Centre became aware of the Jharkhand issue after the All Jharkhand Students Union (AJSU)[16] emerged as the leading force of the Jharkhand movement from the mid-1980s and launched a series of agitations in the region between 1986 and 1989. The negotiations with the state and the central government from 1986 to 1994 led to the Constitution in September 1994 of the Jharkhand Area Autonomous Council (JAAC) which granted a measure of autonomy to the region but fell far short of the demand for statehood. Besides, due to the creation of the JAAC and the constant rivalries among the tribal leaders of the Jharkhandi parties—each accusing the others of being 'agents of one national party or the other—the Jharkhand movement lost much of its momentum. Undoubtedly, the Jharkhand parties failed to build-up a strong and united movement for statehood to Jharkhand and their political credibility eroded, thereby creating a leadership vacuum which the BJP filled. In 1988, 'the Bihar unit of the BJP adopted for the first time a resolution demanding a Vananchal[17] state comprising 18 districts'.[18]

From the end of the 1980s, two streams came in conflict: one was concerned with the tribal population, the struggle for their rights over land and their cultural identity; the other, BJP-led, campaigned for better administration and management of the mineral resources, which often leads to the expropriation of the tribal population inhabiting the land.

As the Bihar legislative elections had been held in February 2000—year of the creation of Jharkhand—the first and new Jharkhand Legislative Assembly did not cause new elections.

In the new assembly, due to the ST reserved constituencies, the

ST represented 35.8 per cent of the total MLAs. As a consequence, the political identity of the new Jharkhand state seemed to be dominated by the tribals. But this political identity was challenged by the OBC (Backward Castes + Extremely Backward Castes) representatives who constituted 27.2 per cent of the Vidhan Sabha.

With regard to the political parties, the STs represented the largest group in all the main organizations, except for the Lalu Prasad Yadav led-RJD. But parties, or pre-poll alliance, that won the biggest number of ST seats is not a Jharkhandi party. Indeed, the BJP-led alliance (NDA) won 15 out of the 28 ST reserved seats whereas the candidates of the Jharkhand Mukti Morcha-tribal-dominated leader of the Jharkhand movement—only gained in seven ST reserved constituencies. Besides, unlike the JMM MLAs over-dominated by the Santhals, the ST candidates of the NDA came from the Santhal and two other tribes: Munda and Oraon. As a consequence, the NDA was more represented in the ST-reserved constituencies than the pro-tribal Jharkhandi parties, as evident from Table 3.2. However, unlike the INC and the JMM, the BJP-led NDA was not characterized by an overwhelming number of STs as the OBC representatives constituted 33 per cent and the upper caste 20 per cent against 38 per cent for the ST. Moreover, in the Babulal Marandi government, 40 per cent of the ministers belonged to the STs and 30 per cent to the OBCs.

For the first state elections in Jharkhand in 2005, the JMM, allied with the INC and succeeded in adding 5 seats—out of which 3 were won by members of the Kurmi caste—to its tally as compared with the 2000 elections. In all it secured 17 out of the 81 Assembly seats. As a result, the party head Shibu Soren became the leader of the opposition in the state Assembly. On its side, the BJP-JD(U) alliance won 36 seats respectively with 30 going to the BJP, two seats less than in 2000, and six for the JD(U), three seats more than in 2000.

With regard to the ST MLAs, although they represented the largest group in the Jharkhand Legislative Assembly (37 per cent), they did not constitute a homogeneous group. There were at least four tribes represented—Santhal, Oraon, Munda and Ho—divided between several parties, mainly the BJP, the JMM and the INC (see Table 3.3). Moreover, it is interesting to note that the STs were not represented in the same way in the political parties. If the Santhals and the Oraons had a sizeable presence within the JMM and the INC, the Mundas constituted the largest ST group in the BJP-JD(U) alliance.

But, as 94 per cent of the ST MLAs won from the reserved constituencies, it might have been expected that the political identity

TABLE 3.2: CASTE AND COMMUNITY OF JHARKHAND MLAs IN 2000

(*in per cent*)

Castes and communities	Vidhan Sabha	BJP+*	INC	JMM	RJD
Upper Castes	17.3	20	18.2	–	11.1
Brahmin	1.2	–	9.1	–	–
Bhumihar	2.5	5	–	–	–
Bengali	1.2	–	–	–	–
Rajput	11.1	13	9.1	–	11.1
Kayastha	1.2	3	–	–	–
Backward Castes	23.5	25	9.1	8.3	33.3
Yadav	8.6	5	9.1	–	33.3
Kurmi	6.2	8	–	8.3	–
Koeri	4.9	5	–	–	–
Banya	3.7	–	–	–	–
Extremely Backward Castes	3.7	8	–	–	–
Scheduled Castes	9.9	5	–	16.7	55.6
Scheduled Tribes	35.8	38	54.5	58.3	–
Santhal	13.6	8	–	58.3	–
Munda	4.9	10	–	–	–
Oraon	8.6	13	18.2	–	–
Ho	3.7	–	27.3	–	–
Others	4.9	8	9.1	–	–
Religious Minorities	7.4	3	18	8.3	11.1
Muslims	6.2	–	18	8.3	11.1
Sikh	1.2	3	–	–	–
Unidentified	2.5	3	–	8.3	–
Total	100 N=81	100 N=40	100 N=11	100.0 N=12	100 N=9

Note: *BJP+: Bharatiya Janata Party, Janata Dal (United) and Samata Party.
Source: Survey by Cyril Robin.

TABLE 3.3: CASTE AND COMMUNITY OF THE MLAS IN JHARKHAND LEGISLATIVE ASSEMBLY IN 2005

(*in per cent*)

Castes and communities	Vidhan Sabha	BJP-JD(U) Alliance	INC-JMM	RJD
Upper Castes	11.1	11.1	–	42.9
Bengali	1.2	–	–	–
Bhumihar	4.9	5.6	–	14.3
Rajput	4.9	5.6	–	28.6
Backward Castes	27.2	36.1	19.2	14.3
Yadav	9.9	11.1	3.8	14.3
Kurmi	14.8	16.7	15.4	–
Koeri	1.2	2.8	–	–
Banya	2.5	5.6	–	–
Extremely Backward Castes	2.5	–	–	14.3
Scheduled Castes	11.1	16.7	7.7	14.3
Scheduled Tribes	37.0	27.8	53.8	14.3
Santhal	16.0	8.3	30.8	–
Munda	7.4	13.9	3.8	–
Oraon	9.9	5.6	15.4	–
Ho	1.2	–	3.8	–
Others	2.5	–	–	14.3
Religious Minorities	3.7	2.8	7.7	–
Muslims	2.6	–	7.7	–
Sikh	1.2	2.8	–	–
Unidentified	6.2	5.6	11.5	–
Total	100 N=81	100 N=36	100 N=26	100 N=7

Source: Survey by Cyril Robin.

of the new Jharkhand Legislative Assembly should have been characterized by a larger number of STs elected from general constituencies. Only two STs, one Congress and one JMM, were elected from a general constituency. Out of the 28 reserved seats for STs, the BJP and the JMM won 10 seats.

Regarding the OBC, their proportion in the Vidhan Sabha was significant with an increase, although not dramatic, from 19 seats in 2000 to 22 seats in 2005. This strong representation (29.7 per cent) was mainly due to the sociology of the BJP-JD(U) alliance in which the OBC representatives formed the largest group at 36.1 per cent and represented 50 per cent of all the upper crust of OBC MLAs. Moreover, this sizeable presence of the OBC in the Assembly was all the more noteworthy as they did not enjoy any reserved seats at this level in a so-called tribal state.

Within this category, the Kurmis,[19] whose number rose from five to eleven between 2000 and 2005, constituted 13.6 per cent of all the MLAs, i.e. the second largest group after the Santhals (16 per cent). Among them, four were BJP representatives (Kurmis are the largest caste represented with 16.7 per cent in the BJP-JD(U) alliance), four from the JMM, two for the JD(U) and one for the AJSU. This distribution of the Kurmis indicates that none of the political parties can avoid nominating the Kurmis for the Jharkhand elections and, as a legacy of the politics in Bihar, the upper crust of OBC represent an important electorate in Jharkhand. In addition, the gain of the Kurmis mainly happened in constituencies held by upper caste members till 2005.[20]

As a consequence, Jharkhand politics tends to be more and more polarized between tribals *versus* non-tribals—mainly the upper crust of OBC—and the 'tribal identity' of the state is clearly challenged. In addition, at the level of ministries, with three portfolios and the chief ministership for Arjun Munda (BJP), the STs only represent the second largest 'group' with 36 per cent of the ministers whereas the OBCs (Kurmis and Yadavs) account for 54.5 per cent.

CONCLUSION

Despite the sizeable presence of STs, both at the assembly and government level, the creation of the Jharkhand state seems to be more the victory of the BJP's Vananchal movement of countering the growing influence of missionaries in the tribal region than the outcome of the tribal Jharkhand movement for self-determination and self-rule. Indeed, the present state of Jharkhand corresponds more to the Dikus'[21] Vananchal concept with only the districts of Chhotanagpur and Santhal Pargana region of Bihar than to the Sarna[22] Jharkhand state 'conceived as a political unit carved out of the 21 adjoining tribal-dominated districts of Bihar, Orissa, West Bengal and Madhya Pradesh.[23]

One of the main reasons for the failure of the Jharkhandi parties to force their idea of a 'Greater Jharkhand' is the lack of a strong mass support movement. As we have noted earlier, these parties were confined to specific areas. As a result, if geographically the present Jharkhand state is a part of the Chhotanagpur Plateau, it is not the solution to the age-old autonomy movement and its political and tribal identity is much more vague.

Since November 2000, tribals are expecting the political parties to implement policies for the improvement of their well-being and development. But the tribal leaders are more focused on in-fighting than on mobilizing support for the cause of welfare of tribals and are accused of being influenced by electoral politics.[24] This has been the main reason for the Jharkhand parties losing their support base and the BJP building its political network throughout the state.[25]

With the development of the Vananchal movement, the leaders of the BJP in south Bihar succeeded in turning the tide of the Jharkhand movement in their favour. The ideology of the Vananchal movement has contributed to the weakening of the already fragmented Jharkhand movement, politically marginalized by the Congress party's several decades of divide-and-rule policy and overwhelmed by factionalism.

Besides, at the national level, the notion of a 'Greater Jharkhand' was less feasible, or less realistic than that of Vananchal. Indeed, as we mentioned before, the formation of a 'Greater Jharkhand' required to remove districts from three neighbouring states of Bihar whereas a Vananchal state was only carved out of Bihar.

Then, like what happened in the mid-1950s with the decision of the SRC to oppose the creation of a Jharkhand state, the way the state has been formed in 2000 went against the development of a strong regional identity.

NOTES

1. Census of India, 2001.
2. Alexius Ekka, 2000, 'Jharkhand Movement and Parliamentary Elections', *Economic and Political Weekly*, 29 January–4 February.
3. Agapit Tirkey, 2002, *Jharkhand Movement: A Study of its Dynamics*, Delhi: AICFAIP.
4. Simon Commission, constituted by seven members of the British parliament, nominated to study constitutional reform in India.
5. Tirkey, op. cit., p. 60.
6. Ibid., p. 61.
7. Ibid., p. 62.
8. Ibid., p. 63.
9. '*Sadaans*' means non-tribal people permanently settled in the Jharkhand region.
10. Ibid., p. 74.
11. Ibid., p. 86.
12. Interview with Theodore Kiro, Ranchi, 26 July 2005.
13. A.K. Roy did not merge his Marxist Coordination Committee with the JMM nor did Binod Bihari Mahato. Both were members of the CPI(M) District Committee and influenced the JMM ideologically. Tirkey, op. cit., p. 106.
14. Amit Roy, 2003, 'Second Phase of Jharkhand Movement', in R.D. Munda and S. Bosu Mullick (eds.), *The Jharkhand Movement: Indigenous Peoples' Struggle for Autonomy in India*, IWGIA and BIRSA, New Delhi.
15. In July 1993, four Jharkhand Mukti Morcha (JMM) Members of Parliament along with seven members of a breakaway faction of the Janata Dal (A) were allegedly paid at least Rs. 8.7 crore to ensure the survival of the P.V. Narasimha Rao government. Praveen Swami, 1998, 'The Givers and the Takers', *Frontline*, vol. 15, no. 9, 25 April–8 May.
16. AJSU was founded as the JMM youth wing on 22 June 1986, modelled after the All Assam Students Union. The founders of AJSU were disillusioned with the previous Jharkhandi political parties and wanted more militant agitations. AJSU organized general strikes and a campaign to boycott the Lok Sabha elections in 1989.
17. Vananchal is derived from *Vana* meaning 'forest' and *Anchal* meaning 'area'.
18. Kalyan Chaudhuri, 1998, 'Carving Out a Vananchal State', *Frontline*, vol. 15, no. 11, 23 May–5 June.
19. The Kurmis of Jharkhand are *Sadaans* and formed an economically

powerful class. R. Upadhyay, 'Jharkhand: March to Extreme Tribalism?', *South Asia Analysis Group*, 9 August 2002.

20. These constituencies are Gomia, Bermo, Jamshedpur West and Ichagarh; all located in the eastern region of Jharkhand.
21. *Dikus* refers to people who do not belong to Jharkhand (outsiders) and who are not tribal.
22. *Sarna* refers to the common spiritual beliefs of the tribals.
23. Indu Bharti, 'Behind BJP's Vananchal Demand', in R.D. Munda, S. Bosu Mullick (eds.), *The Jharkhand Movement: Indigenous People's Struggle for Autonomy in India*, IWGIA and BIRSA, Delhi, 2003, pp. 181–3.
24. Interview with Sanjay Bosu Mullick, Ranchi, 16 July 2005.
25. Kalyan Chaudhuri, 2000, 'The Day of Jharkhand', *Frontline*, vol. 17, issue 24, 25 November–8 December.

CHAPTER FOUR

Chhattisgarh: Redefining the Role of the State?

SAMUEL BERTHET

This paper argues that the creation of Chhattisgarh was a revealing episode in the history of Indian federalism. For, it resulted from national consensus endorsed by the Indian State (or 'Centre') and not from a regional movement achieving recognition. Post-Independence till the 1990s, regional movements were often perceived as separatism-in-action, or potentially confrontationist forces *vis-à-vis* the Indian State. In contrast, the emergence of Chhattisgarh, along with Jharkhand and Uttaranchal/Uttarakhand, was supported by national political parties and the administration. The economic changes of the last decade of the twentieth century and the consequent new paradigm of statehood contributed to this change in the Indian federal polity. We will analyse how the idea commonly accepted outside Chhattisgarh—that the new state is a tribal one —is unfounded. The policy of secluding/excluding tribals even while trying to integrate them into the mainstream at the cost of their loss of identity, is a continuing legacy in the new state. The initial perception of a tribal breach into the Hindi belt is not relevant as the main north Indian parties completely dominate the political scene. Chhattisgarh's predicament would be better perceived as issuing from more focused resource management of a mineral-rich hilly tableland, with possible conflicts arising from political decentralization through PRIs and integration of the region in question into a new energy race. Far from challenging the Centre,

Chhattisgarh's creation appears to be the result of assumed and evolving central prerogatives.

The years following the creation of Chhattisgarh are an interesting indicator of India's evolving federal system in phase with the overall economic development that has taken the country to the global economic forefront. States at the federal level have increasingly played a pivotal role in attracting private investment. Yet, only the cultural aspect is emphasized in official literature on the subject of the creation of Chhattisgarh.

Creation of a new state in India has traditionally been perceived as the outcome of regional assertion, articulated in terms of a particular cultural identity. The Government of Chhattisgarh has claimed that 'the creation of the new state of Chhattisgarh has been successful in imparting a sense of distinct identity to its people and an opportunity for the state to chart its own destiny'.[1] Popular identity is often cited in the official history of Chhattisgarh with reference to reformist movements such as Ramnamis and Satnamis or social ones like the Chhattisgarh Mukti Morcha.

Nevertheless, sociologists have demonstrated that popular culture can be made use of by an apparatus disconnected from its breeding ground, especially in the growing context of marketing identities and culture whether it is for commercial or political gain. This is particularly interesting in the case of Chhattisgarh, marked as it is by a 'folk' legacy, whether tribal or non tribal.[2] While the identity factor is often at the forefront of political discourse, it appears difficult to consider it as the most relevant approach to understanding the creation of Chhattisgarh. It might be more useful to revert to the basics of the analysis of the state as proposed by Marc Abélès in *Anthropologie de l'Etat*.[3]

The functionalist ideology depicted by him is well-represented in the philosophy of governance, which perceives political working as the combined process of various social components (state, private sector, civil society and NGOs) where conflict and balance of power are eluded. It dominated the discourse of ruling parties during the debate on the Madhya Pradesh Reorganization Bill and has been articulated in the discourse of the Chhattisgarh government (see *Vision Document*, Government of Chhattisgarh).

COMPONENTS OF CHHATTISGARHI IDENTITY AND POLITICAL SCENE

POLITICAL DIMENSION OF THE CREATION OF CHHATTISGARH AT THE LOCAL LEVEL

No sustained movement supported the creation of Chhattisgarh unlike, for instance, in the case of Vidarbha or Telengana region. This part of the former Central Province and Berar was a relatively late entrant under British rule as compared to many regions in peninsular India. Integration into the national political arena was similarly delayed, the political centres remaining on the coastal areas. The delay was due to princely rule over most of the area, and the specific regime designed for the administration of backward and excluded areas, where more powers would be conferred to the central administration.

The main factors highlighted by supporters of the Madhya Pradesh Reorganization Bill were governance and the economic potential of the region (one of the richest in terms of natural resources). These were introduced as part of the 'Agenda for a Proud, Prosperous India' put forward by the NDA government,[4] and supported by the Congress. Hence, Chhattisgarh can be considered a case study of a state's creation supported by the Centre courtesy the geo-economic perception of resource-rich regions in rural India as the veritable 'back office'.[5]

The political dimension of the birth of Chhattisgarh appears relatively minor in comparison to the economic one. The political scene was dominated by (i) internal rivalry in the Madhya Pradesh Congress leadership—with the Shuklas on the one hand, and Arjun Singh, Digvijay Singh and Ajit Jogi, on the other, (ii) the rise of the BJP, linked to a certain extent to OBC politics, and the alliance of the party with the regional industrial elite.

Baker's study of the elite in the Central Provinces, *Changing Political Leadership in an Indian Province*, serves as a milestone for any historical analysis of politics in Chhattisgarh. It depicts the rise of Ravi Shankar Shukla, a typical north Indian leader supported by the central apparatus, overshadowing more popular and down-to-earth local leaders such as Pyarelal Thakur. The Shukla hold over politics in Chhattisgarh ran through the 1960s, 1970s and 1980s with V.C. Shukla on the national scene, and S.C. Shukla in the state.[6] The exit of the Shuklas could provide a new chapter in Baker's study. It would argue in favour of the decline of the north Indian upper caste in central Indian politics. It might simultaneously signify the rise of an 'elite at the regional level' and not of an elite with a specific regional vision trying to implement a specific socio-cultural project, such as that of Pyarelal Thakur or Shankar Guha Niyogi, leader of the Chhattisgarh Mukti Morcha.

Key positions in the government after the first Vidhan Sabha election in the state were held by leaders who were not representative of the sociological pattern of the region, like Raman Singh and the Aggarwal family.[7] Their prominent role tends to conform to the association between the business community and the classic Hindu nationalist leadership. Representatives of the OBC and the ST community, the two main social groups, do not hold a prominent position.[8]

REGIONAL PROJECT OR CENTRAL MOVE?

Delimitation of the state's boundaries involves a process of identification for its inhabitants, either because the very creation of the state results from this feeling of a common identity, or because the delimitation of the state creates a new sentiment of belonging. Undoubtedly, it does not mean that the federal units created have a single identity, especially in the Indian context. According to the Indian Constitution, the creation of a state in India administratively singles out a region as a cultural unity, sustainable economically. According to the supporters of the Madhya Pradesh Reorganization Bill in both chambers, these two conditions were met in the case of Chhattisgarh.

The supporters of the Bill were representatives of the BJP and the Congress, as well as of some other national parties like the BSP and the CPI, the only 'regionalist' party unanimously and openly supporting the bill being the Shiv Sena, better described perhaps as a party with a strong regional base than a regionalist party.[9]

Most of the regional parties or those with a strong regional base [JD(S), TDP, AIADMK, SP] opposed the Madhya Pradesh Reorganization Bill. During parliamentary debates, none of the eight representatives supporting the Bill and originating from what was to become Chhattisgarh referred to the tribal component. Only S.C. Shukla made a reference to the STs, stating: 'There is no confrontation on the basis of caste line or on the basis of Adivasis and non-Adivasis.'[10] Among the four representatives who referred to the ST population, three strongly opposed the Bill: Baju Ban Riyan, CPI(M), elected from Tripura; Kunwar Akhilesh Singh, SP, elected form Maharajganj (UP); and Dr. Raghuvansh Prasad Singh, from Vaishali (Bihar).

The first requested the implementation of the Sixth Schedule in ST dominated districts, while the latter two made mention of a *dharna* staged by tribal people against the creation of Chhattisgarh and in favour of the Birth of a Gondwana state. The fourth, a sitting MP from the ST-reserved seat of Sidhi and elected on a BJP ticket, supported the Bill, asking for inclusion of other tribal dominated districts in Madhya Pradesh. The claim in favour of the inclusion of the districts of Shahdol, Sidhi, Mandla, Dhinkori and Umaria was also made by a number of other MPs. Again, some supporters of the bill asked for the inclusion of Shahdol, Sidhi, Mandla and Bhalaghat on linguistic grounds. None of these readjustments have been made. Neither the socio-cultural and linguistic factor nor the demand for a second States' Reorganization Commission has really been foreseen.

A first broad conclusion is that the creation of Chhattisgarh highlights a shift in the national parties (INC, BJP) which, for the first time, did not consider the creation of new states as a threat but actually encouraged and backed it. Of course, this is true only for those states which came into being in 2000, and not for other regions with statehood demands such as Vidarbha, Telengana or Coorg. Through Vananchal (Jharkhand),[11] Uttaranchal (Uttarakhand) and Chhattisgarh, the BJP linked the creation of three states to its organic Hindutva conception of India, with a common reference to a classical Hindu denomination. The perception of the Congress, in keeping with its traditional patronizing rhetoric of state welfare benefiting the poorest sections of the population and the minorities, also fits with the creation of 'backward' hilly and 'tribal' states.

CHHATTISGARH AND TRIBAL POLICY

The association of the tribal factor with the new state can be analysed more as an economic strategy in the global economy context making use of a popular cultural legacy, than as denoting specific political status. With regard to discourse related to identity claims, Jules-Rosette Benetta and Denis-Constant Martin analyse the use of popular culture as a label that does not automatically valorize the actors and the environment which lie behind its creation and expression:

> Discourses related to identity claims are often conjugate at the future tense (. . .). Those discourses once extracted from their social and cultural original context are distorted or can be used for commercial means (. . .). Commercial categories supplant those which spring from complex process of production of popular art and completely overshadow the complexities of this process and the reality of the places where it flourishes.[12]

This analysis is relevant to the case of tribal culture in Chhattisgarh. Tribal culture was, more than ever before, brought to the fore via the creation of Chhattisgarh, but rather as a tourist label than as an expression of the prominence of ST communities in the new state. It can be argued that the notion of tribal, and its various adjectival avatars such as ethnic, indigenous et al., is in itself a global category born with the rise of the modern concept of the state all over the world. In that sense also, the creation of Chhattisgarh and of tribal states—i.e. Jharkhand—can be perceived as the further integration of these regions in the modern state's prebends.

LEGACY OF ST COMMUNITIES

The idea that the emergence of Chhattisgarh was a pro-tribal political move is contradicted by the statements of representatives from the ST communities as well as by the administrative carve-up which has tended to further divide various communities along the states' boundaries. The tribal component in the state has increased, with the percentage of the ST population going from a total of 23.27 per cent in undivided Madhya Pradesh to 31.8 per cent in Chhattisgarh at present, almost one-third of the state's population.[13] It should, however, be kept in mind that the new state has an even more important OBC component, estimated at between 39 to 50 per cent, and an estimated Scheduled Caste (SC) population of about 12 per cent.[14]

The political centres of Chhattisgarh are located in the plains numerically dominated by the OBC communities in terms of population with a notable concentration of SC communities and dominated economically and politically by the business community, a very marginal population demographically. The plains areas of the Mahanadi and Seonath rivers, originally influenced by the tribal sociological pattern, evolved into a type of social pattern resembling that of a sub-region at the margin of the Hindi belt. Recast partially by Hindi and Hindu culture, the tribal pattern has remained, as Ajit Dhanda observed in *Area Study: Chhattisgarh*, a project conducted under the Anthropological Survey of India. In his conclusion, he underlines two points: the heterogeneity of the state and its tribal pattern, assessing that 'through patronization and chieftaincies, no matter how much elaborate the material superstructure of the area seems to have been, it did not take long to appreciate that Chhattisgarh had a powerful tribal base'. The sociologist and social activist Ilina Sen has also underlined the tribal pattern of Chhattisgarhi society still traceable through the numerous old Gond forts disseminated in the plains areas.

Bastar provided the example of negotiation between socio-ethnic diversities. Political changes through the centuries, observable in the Dusshera ritual, demonstrate that Hindu and tribal influences intermingled within the centre of political power. Similar rituals are likely to have been conducted in other parts of the hilly tableland. The tribal pattern of the northern, eastern and westernmost areas of Chhattisgarh is also evident from the sociological composition of its population.

Nevertheless, if Chhattisgarh is nowadays commonly introduced as a 'tribal state', it is very difficult to detect signs of tribal presence in Raipur, the very heart of this so-called tribal state, except in the state museum. The census would also indicate only a marginal presence of ST communities in Raipur urban district (4.14 per cent), suggesting that the tribal population has stopped at the very border of the political centre, and is left with few possibilities of interaction with it.

The tribal regions of Chhattisgarh can be distinguished as follows: (a) an area including parts of Jharkhand, north Chhattisgarh, north Orissa and West Bengal, (b) one encapsulating south Chhattisgarh, north-eastern Maharashtra, south Andhra Pradesh and the south-west Orissa and, finally, (c) the central-western Chhattisgarh and east Madhya Pradesh basin. These basins of tribal population in central and eastern India are spread along the borders of nine states.

The 34 reserved seats are split into different geographical and ethnic entities, and there is hardly any relation between the southern tribal-dominated part of the state, in Bastar, and the northern one, or the other small pockets scattered in other districts in the margins of the Mahanadi-Seonath basin.[15]

The sociological pattern of ST communities in Chhattisgarh could be divided into three main categories:

- STs living in the plains where they might previously have been dominant or prominent and where they were integrated into the caste system. Tribal culture has also for long been deeply influenced by the Hindu pattern in these regions, where nevertheless, they have nowadays by and large lost or abandoned their specific language or mythology. It is of interest to note that, in these areas, attempts have been made to revive Gond culture, but without being translated, till date, into a specific political movement capable of lobbying tribal concerns at the state level.[16] This acculturation, or even 'deculturation', has extended to the foothills, like for instance in Kanker district, the northernmost district of Bastar region, where the tribal language has almost disappeared.
- The tribals living in the hills were converted to Christianity by missionaries from the nineteenth century and by their Hindu counterparts from the mid-twentieth century onwards. They

have undergone fast socio-cultural transformation. They are mainly inhabitants of the northern districts of the state, but these proselytizing movements for conversions are recently spreading to south Chhattisgarh along with the development of a communalist agenda prone to conflicts.

- The tribals of the hilly tracts retain some basic elements of their socio-cultural specificities like language and mythology. They have to face growing pressure from missionaries, Hindutva organizations, Naxalites and fast-developing market forces, all in a context of difficult relations with the administration, especially the Forest Department.

A NEW POLICY TOWARDS TRIBALS?

Whether or not Chhattisgarh is granted the status of a tribal state is not the primary issue. The relevant question regarding federalism and governance is: does the birth of the state constitute progress in implementation of a different policy on tribal issues in the Indian peninsula, and more largely on the rural peasantry in all its diversity, or could it be used as an opportunity to change the existing developmental approach? This question is justified by the emphasis on the need for good governance in a region qualified as 'among the richest and inhabited by people among the poorest'.

As far as the land issue is concerned, the Chhattisgarh government seemed initially to have opted for a different approach to that of the Madhya Pradesh government. The latter, in a dramatic u-turn, opted for the evacuation of 'forest dwellers' after the BJP came to power.[17] The opposition to the BJP-led government in this state is growing among tribals who had, in fact, contributed to its electoral victory.[18] An interesting theoretical question may be raised in the context of this crucial livelihood issue. There is a contradiction between the BJP's ideology that defines ST identity in terms of a geo-environmental determinism characterized by forest-dwelling, and its concrete action favouring evacuation from the same forests.

The Government of Chhattisgarh has adopted procedures to transform an important number—421—of forest villages into revenue villages. However, the matter is pending and land remains a problematic issue. Delay in transforming forest villages into revenue villages has, in turn, transformed a political agenda into an electioneering promise. This issue could prove to be crucial in the next polls in the tribal dominated areas, given that the BJP's majority in the Vidhan Sabha depends on the reserved seats for STs. But transformation of forest villages into revenue villages could also pave the way to opening new areas to mining companies, and to the very industrialization process that tends to marginalize the local population by expropriation, degradation of livelihoods and influx of outsiders, all of which lead to the destruction of pre-existing social links.

Likewise, economic activity related to the collection and commercialization of Minor Forest Products (MFP) and Non-Timber Forest Products (NTFP) is stated to be a strong pillar of the tribal development policy in Chhattisgarh. The resilience with which middlemen have kept an unlawful grip on this trade through the past decades is evidence that strong and coordinated steps are required from the administration at the state level. Previous experience has proved that these steps should aim not at bypassing a sociological group whose knowledge may be an asset.[19] Legal implementation of the demarcation between each side's field of action could benefit both collectors and intermediaries through the transition from a trade dominated by supply of raw material to more systematic supply of refined MFP. Several deputy collectors of Bastar have raised this issue. The coming years will show if any significant break from long-lasting practices takes place, but there is no sign of such a shift as yet. The civil war in Bastar has only worsened the situation of the ST communities, transforming the forest land of tribal villages into wastelands following the displacement of the threatened population into refugee camps. Effective decentralization via some adjustment of the modalities for the application of the Pesa—thereby giving local bodies at the level of the village-cluster a certain political and economic weight with safeguards for real community-based management—would be an essential condition for real improvement.

UNILATERALISM WORKING AGAINST POLITICAL MOBILITY

The new state presents a strong tribal component with 34 seats reserved for Scheduled Tribes (ST) in a total of 90 Assembly constituencies. According to the 2001 census, STs accounted for about 31.8 per cent of the state's population, SCs for about 12 per cent. The majority, therefore, lies in the hands of non-tribal candidates. The new state has the biggest percentage of reserved seats for STs in any Vidhan Sabha if we consider only the Indian peninsula, not the north-eastern states. Its 34 reserved seats for STs out of 90 indicates a percentage of 37.77 per cent. When elected MLAs of the Madhya Pradesh Vidhan Sabha formed the new state assembly, almost 48 per cent of the Congress MLAs were tribal (23 out of 48). One representative of the ST community was chosen against the representatives of the Congress upper caste aristocracy, namely S.C. Shukla, former Madhya Pradesh chief minister, his brother and former Union Minister V.C. Shukla, and Motilal Vora, another former chief minister. An ST coming to power, winning against three Brahmins, may have seemed like a symbol of tribal empowerment. Only three years later, the first elections for the state's Vidhan Sabha restored a more complex balance of power where STs do not really have a predominant share. STs first had an important share of power in the new BJP government, roughly equal to Ajit Jogi's (35.8 per cent in the Raman Singh government, 34 per cent in the Congress one) but represented only 20 per cent of the cabinet ministers and were still by and large excluded from the key ministries.[20] In the newly elected government, representatives of the Indian urban elite such as Baniyas and Brahmins dominate. Moreover, in the present ruling party of Chhattisgarh, none of the three major leaders, namely Raman Singh, Dilip Singh Judev and Ramesh Bais, are STs.

Significantly, after the first reshuffle, three ST ministers were dropped. Therefore, the first elected government of Chhattisgarh reduced the ST share in power, which was quite significant in the previous dispensation. STs' power stakes are far inferior to their population share in the state, in spite of the government owing its success to electoral results in the reserved seats of tribal constituencies, where 70 per cent of its MLAs were elected. In these conditions, it seems difficult to assess whether the creation of Chhattisgarh, a so-called *tribal state*, is the product of the empowerment of tribal communities or leads in this direction. In the case of Chhattisgarh, the use of reservation as a way to political integration has not proved very successful in promoting political empowerment. One can view the gradual exit of tribals as Independent MLAs—from five in seven reserved seats in the 1951 elections,[21] and 10 in 1962 to zero today—as a symptom of this integration into the fold of mainstream politics. We can, therefore, corroborate the assertion made by Virginius Xaxa, in his study of reservations,[22] that the main effect of this policy is integration into mainstream politics and that it subsequently indicates the division of the tribal leadership along party lines. The observation is relevant to the case of Chhattisgarh: Arvind Netam has joined the BJP and Mahendra Karma the Congress. Yet there is still no significant tribal political party or movement.

Development of Panchayati Raj Institutions through implementation of the 73rd and 74th Amendments and their extension to the Scheduled Areas in 1996 were meant to promote the empowerment of tribals. This third tier of Indian democracy could raise the hopes of rural India and, hence, of the tribal dominated-regions. Simultaneous efforts made for better control of MFP and NTFP gatherers (mainly women members of the ST) represented an additional step for tribal communities, making inroads in the political arena through development of both local democracy and local economy. PRIs are still in their early years and are, therefore, difficult to properly evaluate, not to mention the necessary re-adjustment (need for an expanded scope of activities, especially at a financial level, and for building safeguards). The Panchayat Extension to the Scheduled Areas (PESA) has just started being implemented in Chhattisgarh while it has faced resistance from the state in Jharkhand.

The controversial setting up of industrial projects proves that a legal framework alone is not sufficient to force a departure from the coercive line of action against tribal livelihoods. The most cited case, during the Jogi government, involved the controversial consultation in 2001 of the Gram Sabha of Nagarnaar, Amaguda, Kasturi and Maganpur (Bastar) regarding a steel plant project under the National Mineral Development Corporation (NMDC), followed by demonstrations in 2002. The larger issue can hardly be addressed without a holistic approach adopted by decision makers as well as other institutional actors, such as NMDC or the forest department. Analysis of the political identity of tribals in Indian history and society initiated by Indian scholars, such as Surajit Sinha or Ajit K. Danda, has yet to be assimilated into the political discourse. Their comprehensive approach, and Danda's *Plea for Political Mobility (of the ST Population)*, are yet to find translation.[23]

To harbour the idea that tribals are not part of the modern world economy would be a serious error, historically as well as economically. Their continuing marginalization notwithstanding, their role in the world economy is evident at all levels—as migrant workers, wage earners (in the agricultural sector and others), MFP and NTFP collectors (whose annual turnover was evaluated at the end of the 1990s as being around Rs. 5 billion), craftsmen, healers, etc.

Integration of forest areas—where some tribals may have resided for centuries and where many others gradually moved through a combination of force and choice—into the global economy is well established. Without referring to the consequences on the Indian forests of the Napoleonic wars between England and France, the numerous World Bank and Asian Development Bank projects for joint forest management would serve as clear proof of such integration.

The notion of STs as a passive element of society is a common feature of the discourse of almost the entire political spectrum, including its extreme and most radical leftist element. It is used to justify radical intervention, whether from the legal authorities at the central or federal level, or from clandestine forces. The attempt to draw tribals into the mainstream means they are not yet considered an integrated part of society and have to move towards it, if necessary at the cost of their livelihood and lifestyle. Hence, radical change is demanded of the tribal population and not self-controlled evolution. Sustained by different views and ideologies, such is the common goal of all interventionist policies, whether political or religious.

The separatist factions within indigenous movements, supported by the World Council of Churches and Naxalite movements, also emphasize the distinctiveness and, to a certain extent, seclusion of STs from the rest of Indian society. The result of the latest ideology can be observed in the blasting of Panchayat buildings and, more generally, attacks on all government services. In areas under the control of Naxalites, the ban on trousers and roof tiles on houses and prohibition of *gothul* institutions are some instances of the endeavour to make tribal life conform to another model of life based on a set of values often antagonistic to their culture as practised through centuries. The foundation of the Naxalite movement's ideology is, of course, broader than the tribal issue. But, on the part of the Naxalites too, appropriation of the tribal cause is associated with a romanticized concept of tribal life. The action of Hindutva outfits, deeply rooted in Chhattisgarh, first in the northern districts and since the 1990s in the southern ones equally aim at imposing other set of values artificially: they demand change of names and Sanskritization. This trend began earlier with various ashrams, such as the Ramakrishna Mission. Their success is largely due to provision of social and health-related support to the local population in regions deprived of the most basic infrastructure. From all corners, STs find themselves unilaterally and sometimes forcefully under the influence of other socio-political groups.

Unilateralism affects STs at all levels of society, leaving them with few alternatives to trying to join the mainstream by hiding their identity. This seclusion is reflected in the primary stage of citizenship, i.e. during schooling, like R. Kumari and S. Radhakrishnan have observed in their study *Higher Education and Scheduled Tribe Youth*: 'The difference they visualize between themselves and the rest of the society is so wide that they get frustrated to the extent that they do not go home even for holidays.' This feeling of alienation, according to the authors of this study, is provoked both by the sense of superiority infused in those who have acquired a formal higher education and rejection by non-ST pupils and students. To remove obstacles to a two-way interaction between

STs and non-STs, what is required is the state's commitment to providing accessible and to valorizing primary education with regional languages as the medium so as to build a reciprocal relationship between the children of various communities.

INSULATION OF THE TRIBAL DISTRICTS

Demographic Dynamics

Data of the last census illustrate the unilateral relation of non-tribals towards tribals. In cities comprising districts where the ST population dominates, the ratio of the General Population (GP) category is overwhelmingly above the population under the ST category. In the cities comprising districts where the GP category dominates, the ratio of the ST category is still below its average in those districts as a whole. The movement of population from rural regions to cities, and from one district to another, is therefore one-way. The GP category dominates in the urban centre, and moves toward ST-dominated areas, without reciprocal movement. Though this assumption is based on a very general consideration, and though seasonal migration of labour may not appear in the data, it reveals a process of marginalization through the internal demographic dynamics within the state. This unbalanced process is also a fact in former tribal-dominated regions where the industrial plant has been implanted in order to integrate ST populations, such as in Durg-Bhilai. The industrial path to integrating tribal populations into the mainstream has rather led to further seclusion and marginalization. The only exception is Dalli Rajhara, the stronghold of the Chhattisgarh Mukti Morcha, which had a more holistic approach to social issues. A second element deepening the divide between tribals and non-tribals is the controversy over the conversion of the Kanker and Jagdalpur MLA seats from reserved for ST to general. It highlights the urban-rural divide inside tribal areas.

Data from the census confirm the marginalization of ST communities inside cities even within areas largely dominated by tribal communities. They reveal the current sociological dynamics that tends to further insulate ST communities from the centre of power.

TABLE 4.1: ST POPULATION IN MINORITIES IN CITIES IN THE ST AREAS

Name		Total population	ST population	% ST population
Surguja	Total	1,972,094	1,076,669	54.60
	Rural	1,834,913	1,053,644	57.42
	Urban	137,181	23,025	16.78
Bastar	Total	1,306,673	866,488	66.31
	Rural	1,176,652	842,516	71.60
	Urban	130,021	23,972	18.44
Raipur	Total	3,016,930	365,273	12.11
	Rural	2,099,312	327,238	15,59
	Urban	917,618	38,035	4.14
Bilaspur	Total	1,998,355	397,104	19.87
	Rural	1,511,661	366,097	24.22
	Urban	486,694	31,007	6.37
Raigarh	Total	1,265,529	447,703	35.38
	Rural	1,096,073	428,450	39.09
	Urban	169,456	19,253	11,36
Rajnandgaon	Total	1,283,224	341,688	26.63
	Rural	1,051,577	326,051	31.01
	Urban	231,647	15,637	6.75
Durg	Total	2,810,436	348,801	12.41
	Rural	1,738,127	284,766	16.38
	Urban	1,072,309	64,035	5.97

Source: Census of India, 2001.

It is particularly revealing in a region characterized by its numerous 'garh' or forts—a good number of which are ruled by tribal dynasties such as Rajgonds. This seclusion can also be seen as resulting from the administrative pattern that makes STs non-identifiable outside the states where they are not listed.

Another factor of seclusion and exclusion arises as a consequence of the action of the extreme left: anti-state organizations. In areas under their control, they have successfully attempted to prohibit the electoral process, even at the local level. They have also successfully hampered economic activities, even those based on the co-operative system, such as the collection of NTFP-MFP. The rise of Naxalite movements may lead in certain cases to greater lack of understanding of ST issues, ST demonstrations being systematically stigmatized as instigated by the Naxalites and, therefore, subversive, even when such movements are based on defense of basic rights legally guaranteed by the Constitution itself.

Administrative Regime of Exception

In the summer 2004, the Surguja-Jashpur-Koriya Development Authority and the Bastar Development Authority were set up in order to sharpen focus on the main under-administrated parts of Chhattisgarh. Less than four years after the creation of a state introduced as tribal, a need was again felt to perpetuate the distinctiveness of the two main tribal areas *vis-à-vis* the non-tribal ones. A new administrative framework has been provided to deal with the problem of the plains *versus* hill divide, which over 20 years of 'protective, regulatory, and developmental measures'—embedded in successive tribal sub-plans since the Fourth Plan—have failed to solve.[24] Can these administrative sub-entities in the tribal-dominated regions of Chhattisgarh, be considered a new step towards decentralization with the aim of hastening the development process? The decision is still recent and it is difficult to assess the accuracy and efficiency of its results. Nevertheless, the decision does not appear to favour local development through local empowerment, since the decision-making powers of these new entities are channellized through the chief minister and the district collector. It would therefore be used against the needed decentralization through local self-government institutions.

After the setting up of *Excluded Tracks, Scheduled Areas* and *Tribal Development Blocks*, the demarcation of these two new development authority areas underlines the fact that maintaining a special administrative and political order in regions identified as tribal is a continuing process. It also underlines the difficulties in devolving decision-making to the local tribal population through an authentic decentralized system and in refraining from a derogatory and interventionist mode of action. This would support the analysis of Savyasaachi that a process of de-centring, rather than of decentralizing, is under way.

MORE STATE, LESS SERVICES: GOVERNANCE AND NEW STATES

The opportunity offered by state formation must be seized upon to address the pressing developmental needs of the people of this 'rich land of poor people'. It is our fear that a failure to do so even after almost six decades of Independence will not be treated lightly by history.[25] (Planning Commission)

This remark of the Planning Commission is revelatory of the expectations raised by the creation of the state as well as the anxieties over the consequences to be faced in case they are not fulfilled. It clearly pinpoints the fact that despite the economic potential of these regions, the basic needs of the inhabitants of the new states has not been addressed. It supports the idea of repositioning the state apparatus in order to help it fulfil its responsibility of providing basic and vital amenities to the inhabitants of Chhattisgarh.

In its *Vision Document*, the Chhattisgarh government enunciated its objective: 'Build an ethos of public service and collective well-being'.[26] Provision of free and compulsory primary education for all is part of this plan.[27] But overall, the creation of Chhattisgarh is in consonance with the philosophy of governance whereby political and social issues are overshadowed by technical issues selling the prospect of a bright economic future. One outcome of the coming into being of the state is the region's increased ability to attract national and foreign investment. The attempt has been successful, with up to 11 per cent of the total investment in India directed towards the new state. Cottage industries are mushrooming side by side with mining plants that are being set up irrespective of environmental safeguards, as in the case of the sponge iron factories around Raipur. The ecological costs of such fast and unplanned industrialization are already visible around the capital city as well as in Raigarh. The experiences of the Bhilai Steel Plant, coal mining and thermal power plants, as well as the aluminium extraction plant in Korba have shown that large-scale industrial installations are not a sufficient condition for economic development. It can lead to displacement on the one hand, and influx of better qualified manpower from other regions, on the other, if the local market proves unable to provide the required conditions.[28]

While the Indian citizen relies increasingly on the federal state for delivery of public goods, Chhattisgarh tends to stand back and rely on private investment to fill infrastructural gaps, even for the most basic infrastructure.[29] This is clearly underlined in the new state government's *Vision Document:* 'Our focus is on two areas—good governance and good infrastructure. If we can provide these two, the rest will follow'.[30] The state is no longer a political power, or at least does not claim this role; it appears only 'an enabler and facilitator for the creative energies of its people'.[31] This attitude does not correspond to citizens' understanding of the working of the different tiers in India. Between 50 to 74 per cent of people expect basic issues such as electricity (74 per cent), crime (74 per cent), educational facilities (72 per cent), medical facilities (70 per cent), ration supply (67 per cent), roads (57 per cent), pollution (53 per cent) and drinking water (50 per cent) to be addressed by the state government as against 9 to 14 per cent expecting the same to be addressed by the central government; the rest (14 to 41 per cent) consider these as falling under the purview of local institutions.[32] It would appear logical that, from its inception, the state would have adopted the responsibility for reinforcing or building infrastructure for public goods distribution. Its political blueprint, introduced and implemented since 2000, appears in contradiction with general expectations and with the very reasons for the creation of the state, i.e. to redress the problem of poor infrastructure due to the neglect that the Bhopal regime was supposed to have shown towards the region. The government's choices for education in particular illustrate the fragility of its governance.

In a federal polity where the delimitation and creation of states are based on cultural cohesiveness, education could have been one of the top priorities for the new state: firstly to remedy the main lacuna of a region described as 'rich in natural resources and poor in human resources' and to prevent further unbalance, secondly, to give momentum to mass schooling by implementing the Eighth Schedule of the Constitution. After the creation of the state, the doors were opened wide for the inclusion of Chhattisgarhi in the list of official languages. While, in 2003, Dori, Santhali, Maithili and Bodo managed to obtain a place on the list, Chhattisgarhi—though considered the means of communication of a population estimated to stand at roughly 11.5 million and the seventeenth most spoken language in India—is yet to obtain this status. It is interesting to note that, unlike Chhattisgarhi, Oriya has received recognition as the language medium in some schools in the state. It appears that there is no lobby to promote Chhattisgarhi language within Chhattisgarh.

Before the birth of Chhattisgarh, an effort was made to organize and monitor tribal development with the creation of the Directorate, Tribal Area Development Planning, and the Tribal Research Institute. A scheme was initiated to implement the Eighth Schedule and, consequently, to back teaching in regional languages at the primary level. The new schoolbook from Bhopal were planned to be made available from summer 2005 onwards. But this effort-born of a long, and unachieved, programme of tribal development undertaken by the government of Madhya Pradesh—does not seem to find any enthusiastic response in a Chhattisgarh more preoccupied with the 'global village' ideology and with turning the state into an IIT and higher education hub. The question may be raised as to whether the creation of the new state will hasten or hamper the promotion of regional culture by the earlier governments of Madhya Pradesh, whose policies had evolved through precarious but steady effort.

Moreover, the programme initiated by the Madhya Pradesh Tribal Research Institute for the writing of school books in regional languages has not gained momentum after the creation of Chhattisgarh. Implementation of the programme began in August 2005, but without much advertisement. Again, in the context of the 'global village' concept, the authorities uphold the cause of English rather than of regional languages, going against Eighth Schedule requirements and studies which associate the success of schooling in the first years to the use of mother tongue.

The example of Dondi and Dondi Lohara in terms of schooling, with a net enrolment ratio of above 99 per cent for both blocks, shows how sustained and community-based efforts can drastically improve the situation.[33] These two blocks constitute the bastion of

Shankar Guha Niyogi's movement, Chhattisgarh Mukti Morcha, for social rights and access to health services and education.

Another reason for statehood was the high degree of illiteracy among ST communities and other sections of the population. Promotion of literacy, a condition for the development of the new state, implies state-supported action, which Madhya Pradesh initiated with some success as well as with a few failures in the 1990s. The government of Chhattisgarh under Ajit Jogi, former disciple of Digvijay Singh, took a radically opposite path to his mentor. In 2001, he chose to emphasize the partnership of private investors in education through the Chhattisgarh Private University Act, which led to the creation of 97 private universities in three years.[34] Finally, in 2005, the Supreme Court declared illegal the creation of universities without meeting the requirements of the University Grants Commission.

The overall picture of a disorganized higher education system is worsened by a still very weak primary education pattern.[35] Meanwhile, Chhattisgarh's successive governments seem to have altogether discarded the option of setting up a new education system as per the requirements of the state. The significance of the use of the mother tongue during schooling in a state where illiteracy is a major problem (57.09 per cent of the total population of Chhattisgarh, according to the 1991 census), remains a crucial issue still to be addressed. And there are not yet instances in India or outside India where the private sector endorses the responsibility of mass and democratic schooling. Therefore the development paradigm based on the private sector acting as an intermediary for basic infrastructure reveals to be misconceived, even in an IT advanced state with an already developed infrastructure base and a much higher literacy rate, such as the state of Karnataka for instance.

Delivery of yet another public good appears uncertain: transport. A glance at the map of the state would show that 13 out of 16 districts border one or the other of seven neighbouring states. The lengthy shape of the state is such that various districts inevitably develop closer links with the urban centres of neighbouring states than with Raipur, and maintain closer cultural affinities with neighbouring regions than with other parts of the state. Chhattisgarh's districts were, according to their location, within the sphere of urban centres such as Jabalpur in Madhya Pradesh, as also of those in other states, like Vishakhapatnam in Andhra Pradesh or Nagpur in Maharashtra, the former capital of the Berar. This is, indeed, part of the overarching impact of the railway network, especially in a region lacking in transport infrastructure. Previous administrative boundaries are other important factors.

The lack of connectivity of Jagdalpur for mining purposes, the main centre of Bastar region, with the state capital by railway, even while it is connected to Vishakhapatnam, may be a basic fact but it is also significant in many ways. Likewise, we may note the absence of direct connections between the northern region and the state capital, whereas it has direct links with the neighbouring states of Madhya Pradesh, Orissa and Jharkhand. Bilaspur being the most profitable railway station in India, accounting for 16 to 17 per cent of the total income of Indian Railways, this lacuna is not linked to pecuniary scarcity but to non-redistribution at the local level of locally generated resources, an issue that the creation of the state has not resolved.

The governments of Chhattisgarh chose to rely mainly on private investment to improve lacunae in terms of basic infrastructure, thus leading to the privatization of government road transports. As a result, communication between the three districts of Bastar and the rest of Chhattisgarh, as well as internal communication in those districts, rely exclusively on the private sector. In case of non-profitability or adverse natural circumstances, the population is not insured against lack of or inadequate connectivity. Moreover, the face-off between the private sector and the Naxalites can lead to obvious pitfalls, of which the majority of the population might be the first casualty and which could further weaken the state. That is what we are witnessing since 2005, with a radical situation unfolding that is being increasingly compared to the prevailing situation in the north-east and Kashmir. In a region that has by and large been deprived of infrastructure related to public goods delivery, the philosophy of governance implemented by the state might be questioned. The state of Chhattisgarh has eluded its role of basic public amenities provider to all. It relied on the concept of public/private partnership and decentralization as per ther theoretical concept of governance. Unless and until it plays the role of basic public amenities provider through massive state investment, it seems unlikely that the unbalanced structure of the state would change significantly and that the population of Chhattisgarh would gain any benefit from the new administrative situation. But in the process, politicians would have lost the recourse of putting the blame on a too distant capital.

CONCLUSION

Since 2000, pro-Chhattisgarhi communalist feelings have appeared, akin to the pro-Jharkhandi manifestations.[36] These 'pro-local' demonstrations arising from social frustration represent a new phenomenon in Chhattisgarh, described as opposed to the Chhattisgarhi *ethos* praised for valuing integration. Curiously enough, it has not been supported by a strong linguistic revivalism. In the long run, a cohesive regional sub-entity is certainly a less threatening element for the nation than fragmented communities subject to social frustrations. In Chhattisgarh, the latter are the direct outcome of a philosophy of governance that does not include in its agenda the issues of state-funded and state-implemented delivery of basic infrastructure and public goods in a manner ensuring that the local population takes advantage of the economic and social opportunities offered by industrial development. True, the governance paradigm has the advantage of offering flexibility. But this flexibility is relevant only if basic infrastructure is built along with a political framework that defines the role of the citizen. The functionalist vision of political working should incorporate some aspects of the relations between different social classes and cultural groups, so that the citizen can reinvent the role he plays to suit the new functioning of society. The creation of a new state should be accompanied by new reflections on a transformed citizenry integrating the three tiers of Indian democracy.[37]

The creation of Chhattisgarh cannot be perceived as symptomatic of the rise of regional forces in the Indian political arena. The role of the Centre and the federal states may require reassessment in the wake of the 1990s' federal governance philosophy. The perpetuation and reinforcement of separate administrative processes and geographical delimitation underline lack of share that the ST have in the decision-making as well as in the political and economic activities, the very instruments that would ensure on a day-to-day basis their normal representation without the need for extraordinary or derogatory functioning. Increased and effective empowerment of members of the ST communities in particular, and of the citizens in general, and implementation of their rights would be the best way to ensure such representation. Along with the implementation of these rights, as defined in the Constitution, another prerequisite is the integration of socio-economic patterns as well as specific environmental practices in policymaking. All these moves are supposed to be part of the agenda of decentralization, of which the creation of Chhattisgarh was itself supposed to represent a significant step.

India gaining the position of a world power raises a crucial question at the internal level: will the country create a new pattern of development, taking into consideration the various components of the population as well as environmental requirements? There are no easy answers. But the evolution of Chhattisgarh, a state created in the name of a *new India*, is certainly an indicator of the issues that linger and the possible conflicts that will arise from questions left unaddressed in the name of liberal efficiency whereby international economic parameters matter more than local social and environmental realities. Chhattisgarh throws light on a philosophy of governance that seems to no longer consider the citizen as a stakeholder.

APPENDIX 1

Tribal Communities Scheduled by the Government of Chhattisgarh[38]

1. Agariya
2. Andh
3. Baiga
4. Bhaina
5. Bharia Bhumia, Bhuinhar Bhumia, Bhumiya, Bharia, Paliha, Pando
6. Bhattra
7. Bhil, Bhilala, Barela, Patelia
8. Bhil Mina
9. Bhunjia
10. Biar, Biyar
11. Binjhwar
12. Birhul, Birhor
13. Damor, Damaria
14. Dhanwar
15. Gadaba, Gadba
16. Gond, Arakh, Arrakh, Agaria, Asur, Badi Maria, Bada Maria, Bhatola, Bhimma, Bhuta, Koilabhuta, Kolibhuti, Bhar, Bisonhorn Maria, Chota Maria, Dandami Maria, Dhuru, Dhurwa, Dhoba, Dhulia, Dorla, Gaiki, Gatta, Gatti, Gaita, Gond, Gowari, Hill Maria, Kandra, Kalanga, Khatola, Koitar, Koya, Khirwar, Khirwara, Kucha Maria, Kuchaki Maria, Madia, Maria, Mana, Mannewar, Moghya, Mogia, Monghya, Mudia, Muria, Nagarchi, Nagwanshi, Ojha, Raj Gond, Sonjhari, Jhareka, Thatia, Thotya, Wade Maria, Vade Maria, Darol
17. Halba, Halbi
18. Kamar
19. Karku
20. Kawar, Kanwar, Kaur, Cherwa, Rathia, Tanwar, Chattri
21. Khairwar, Kondar
22. Kharia
23. Kondh, Khond, Kandh
24. Kol
25. Kolam
26. Korku, Bopchi, Mouasi, Nihal, Nahul, Bondhi, Bondeya
27. Korwa, Kadaku

28. Majhi
29. Majhwar
30. Mawasi
31. Munda
32. Nagesia, Nagasia
33. Oraon, Dhanka, Dhangad
34. Pao
35. Pardhan, Pathari, Saroti
36. Pardhi, Bahelia, Bahellia, Chita Pardhi, Langoli Pardhi, Phans Pardhi, Shikari, Takankar, Takia [in (i) Bastar, Dantewara, Kanker, Raigarh, Jashpurnagar, Surguja and Koria district, (ii) Katghora, Pali, Kartala and Korba tahsils of Korba district, (iii) Bilaspur, Pendra, Kota and Takhatpur tahsils of Bilaspur district, (iv) Durg, Patan, Gunderdehi, Dhamdha, Balod, Gurur and Dondilohara tahsils of Durg district, (v) Chowki, Manpur and Mohala Revenue Inspector Circles of Rajnandgaon district, (vi) Mahasamund, Saraipali and Basna tahsils of Mahasamund district, (vii) Bindra Navagarh Rajim and Deobhog tahsils of Raipur district, and (viii) Dhamtari, Kurud and Sihava tahsils of Dhamtari district]
37. Parja
38. Sahariya, Saharia, Seharia, Sehria, Sosia, Sor
39. Saonta, Saunta
40. Saur
41. Sawar, Sawara
42. Sonr

NOTES

1. *Vision Document*, Government of Chhattisgarh, 2001.
2. Denis-Constant Martin, 2000, 'Cherchez le Peuple, Culture, Populaire et démocratie' dans la Critique internationale no. 7, pp. 169–83.
3. March Abeles, 1990, *Anthropologie de l'Etat*, Paris: Armand Colin.
4. Ministry of Home Affairs, Annual Report, Chapter VII, 'Creation of New States', 7.5.
5. See Savyasaachi in the present volume.
6. Ravi Shankar Shukla was the chief minister from 1947 till his death on 31 December 1956, Shyama Charan Shukla from 1969 to 1972, 1975 to 1977 and 1989 to 1990. V.C. Shukla held the information and the foreign affairs portfolios in the Union cabinet under Indira Gandhi.
7. Lakhi Ram Aggarwal, former Rajya Sabha member, considered to be the

party's godfather; his sons Finance and Industry minister Amar Aggarwal, and Brij Mohan Aggarwal.

8. Samuel Berthet, 'Chhattisgarh: Tribal, OBC, Reformists Movements and Mainstream Politics', in Christophe Jaffrelot (forthcoming), CSH-CERI-CSDS, Delhi.
9. Among national parties, the CPI(M) opposed the bill.
10. Bhagatram Manhar, S.C. Shukla, Punnu Lal Mohale, Charan Das Mahant, Lakhi Ram Aggarwal, Surendra Kumar Singh, Dilip Singh Judev, Tarachand Sahu.
11. See the article Cyril Robin in this volume.
12. Jules-Rosette Benetta, Denis-Constant Martin, 1997, op. cit., pp. 32–3,
13. Census of India 2001. Another central government-supported agency, Medind (Bibliographic Informatics Division—National Informatics Centre—Department of Information Technology), proposes a figure of 37 per cent without quoting its sources. See medind.nic.in/haa/t04/i1/haat 04i1p25.pdf
14. Medind proposes a figure of 15 per cent. See above.
15. Out of 16 districts there are 13 districts partly or wholly classified under the Scheduled Areas legislation in Chhattisgarh, Ministry of Law and Justice (Legislative Department), Notification, The Scheduled Areas (States of Chhatisgarh, Jharkhand and Madhya Pradesh), order, 2003 in the Gazette of India, Extra, Delhi, 2003.
16. It is the case for instance in north-east Maharashtra or in Bilaspur. B.M. Mukherjee and F. Mollick, 'Gond Revivalism and Reintegration', in D.K. Behera and G. Pfeffer, 1999, *Contemporary Society, Tribal Studies*, pp. 173–9, Delhi: Concept Publishing Company.
17. 'Uma in Forest Land Sop Rush', *Telegraph*, 26 January 2004, and 'Uma Seeks Support to Clear Forest Encroachments', *The Hitvada*, 1 August 2004.
18. 'Stop Exploitation of Tribals: Jamuna', *The Telegraph*, Saturday 7 May 2005.
19. Pravir Krishn, 2004, 'Chhattisgarh, MFP and Politics of Development in Tribal Areas', Delhi (unpublished), presentation given to the seminar, Jharkhand, Chhattisgarh and Andhra Pradesh: Decentralisation and Federalism in the Union of India', October 2004, Centre de Sciences Humaines, India International Centre, Delhi.
20. Ram Vichar Netam, 'SC, ST, Backward and Minority Development, Revenue and Nankim Ram Kanwar, Rehabilitation and Agriculture, Animal Husbandary, Fishries, Co-Operative, Law and Legal Affairs'.
21. See Election Commission of India, Statistical Report on General Election,

1951, to the Legislative Assembly of Madhya Pradesh, Delhi, pp. 4–10 and 231.

22. Virginius Xaxa, 2005, 'Electoral Reservations for the Scheduled Tribes: The Legitimation of Domination', in Stephanie Tawa-Lama Rewal, *Political Representation and Social Change: The Working of Electoral Reservations in the Indian Democracy*, Delhi: Manohar.
23. A.K. Danda, 'A Plea for Political Mobility', pp. 474–95, in Mrinal Miri *Continuity and Change in Indian Society*, Simla: Indian Institute of Advanced Study.
24. Divya Shrivastava, 2000, *The Development of Scheduled Tribes in Madhya Pradesh*, pp. 182–3, Delhi: Gyan.
25. Planning Commission, 'Concluding Remarks', *Water Policy for Drought Proofing—Chhattisgarh*, Delhi, p. 306.
26. Chapter VIII, 'Providing Good Governance', p. 1.
27. 'Compulsory and free primary education would be provided through active involvement of local bodies at the panchayat and municipal levels', '*Developing Human Capital*, Chapter VII , p. 5.
28. V. Dhagamwar, S. De and N. Verma, 2003, *Industrial Development and Displacement: The People of Korba*, Delhi: Sage.
29. Pradeep Chhibber, Sandeep Shastri and Richard Sisson, 2004, 'Federal Arrangements and the Provision of Public Goods in India', in *Asian Survey*, vol. XLIV, no. 3, May–June, pp. 339–52.
30. Quoted from http://chhattisgarh.nic.in/profilenew/profile1.htm., Director of Public Relations, Government of Chhattisgarh, echoing this quotation is the following expression: 'Unburdened by Governance Legacies' in Governance http://chhattisgarh.nic.in/governance/govern.htm, ibid.
31. Ibid.
32. 'Federal Arrangements and the Provision of Public Goods in India', op. cit., p. 350.
33. Zacharia, 2003; quoted in *Education of Tribal Children in India*, p. 14, www.education.nic.in/htmlweb/ssa/education_tribal_children.pdf
34. Some 125 applications have been sent for registration after the provisions of Chhattisgarh Private University Act, 2001were passed. On a first move 97 were registered. Among those 57 were denotified in 2004 by the state government for having failed to conform to the norms. 'Pvt. Varsities up for Sale in Chhattisgarh', *The Hitvada* (Raipur edition), 4 August 2004.
35. The number of government schools in the state capital itself is very low and in the rural areas private universities are dominating the scene. See for instance: 'Education System in a Mess, Courtsey Apathetic Govt', in *The Hitvada* (Raipur edition), 3 August 2004.

36. '21 Hurt as CISF Opens Fire at Sipat', in *The Hitvada* (Bilaspur edition), 22 August.
37. These debates find very instructive reflections in the Chhattisgarh-net web forum, under the mediation of Shubhranshu Choudhury.
38. The *Madhya Pradesh Reorganization Act 2000* received the assent of the President on 25 August 2000, assent published in M.P. Gazette (Extra-ordinary), dated 18 September 2000 at pages 1115–16(41).

REFERENCES

Baker, D.E.U., *Changing Political Leadership in an India Province: The Central Provinces and Berar (1919–39)*, Delhi: Oxford University Press.

Chandra, N.D.R., 2003, *Chattisagarha Vikasa Patha Ki Ora (Chhattisgarh Towards the Path of Development: Madhyapradesa Punargathana Vidheyaka)*, Bhopal: Author's Press.

Danda, A.K. (ed.), 1977, *Chhattisgarh: An Area Study*, Calcutta: ASI.

Government of Chhattisgarh, 2005, Human Development Report, Delhi.

R. Kumari, S. Radhakrishnan, 1989, *Higher Education and Scheduled Tribe Youth*, Delhi: Radiant Publishers.

Lalit Surjan (chief ed.) and Vinod Verma (ed.), 1997, *Madhya Pradesh*, Raipur: Patrakar Prakashan.

Mceldowney, Philip, 1980, 'Colonial Administration and Social Developments in Middle India: The Central Provinces, 1886–1921', Ph. D. thesis, University of Virginia.

Miri, Mrinal (ed.), 1993, *Continuity and Change in Indian Society*, Shimla: Indian Institute of Advanced Study.

Sen, Ilina, 1992, 'Women Workers in the Mines of Chhattisgarh', in Heuze (ed.), *Travailler en Inde, Purusartha*, no. 14, Ehess, Paris, pp. 271–89.

Sundar, Nandini, 1996, *Sovereigns and Subalterns: Anthropological History of Bastar*, Delhi: Oxford University Press.

Map 4.1: Chhattisgarh: An Area Survey—A.K. Danda (1977), Anthropological Survey of India, Calcutta

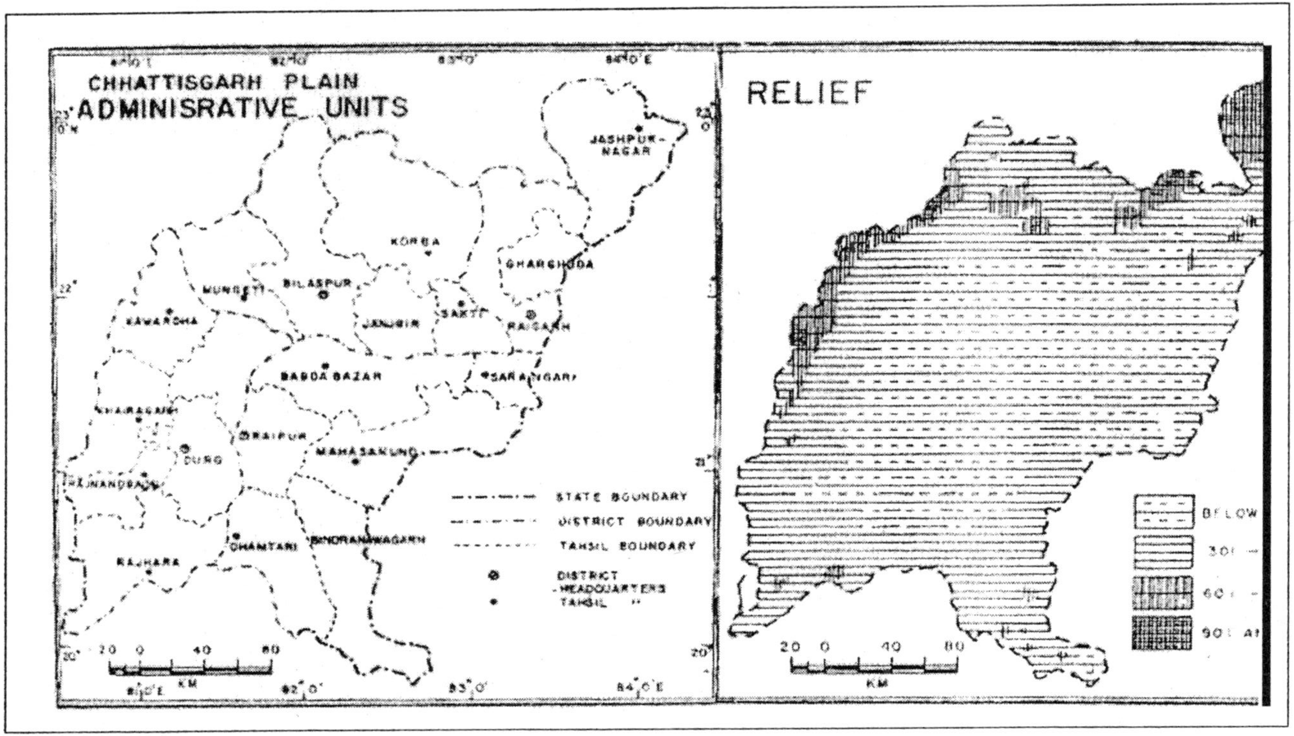

Map 4.2: India, A Regional Geography, R.L. Singh (1995), National Geographical Society of India, Varanasi

CHAPTER FIVE

Decentralization, Local Knowledge and Labour Absorption: The Case of Chhattisgarh

DIPANKAR SENGUPTA

INTRODUCTION

While the initial reasons for the strong bias in India's Constitution in favour of the union government *vis-à-vis* the states in the division of powers were political, they were accentuated by the model of economic development that the union government followed. The Nehru-Mahalanobis model of industrialization coupled with the Congress's model of socialism and implemented with licences and permits (instead of a tax-cum-subsidy policy) to guide investment ensured that not only was administrative powers concentrated in the hand of the centre, but over time states also became financially weaker. A model of industrialization with a heavy accent on heavy industries required resources. Socialism dictated that the state should own such industries. Inter-sectoral consistency meant that autonomous action by private agents as well as non-central government agencies should be eliminated which was achieved with the central government reserving for itself all powers regarding investment. Additionally given the model's investment requirements it was the centre that ensured that resources were concentrated in its hands.

Decentralization of sorts took place after the economic reforms that commenced after mid-1991. As the central government did away with the system of licences and permits to control and guide investment, the states were empowered by default. The states too in theory have some leeway in planning their own economic growth/development. However, by 1991, the states were in such financial condition that this empowerment by default was in reality not particularly relevant. When the ability of state governments to frame appropriate policies in a liberalized economy thrown open to international trade was severely circumscribed (in large part due to inherited financial conditions) could one envisage a role for panchayats in such a milieu?

This paper argues that in a large economy like India and given the wide diversity in conditions in the various parts of the country a centralized polity is singularly unsuited to meet the requirements of the global market economy. The reason is that such a system robs the economy of much needed flexibility and puts India at a disadvantage *vis-à-vis* its competitors by making the country a high cost economy, particularly in the case of agriculture. It is a decentralized economy with empowered panchayats that is best suited to utilize India's most abundant resource, labour, and turn it into physical capital especially in the field of irrigation. Related to this is the argument that sustainable development too requires different sets of policies based on the peculiarities of the relevant locality. In this context the failure of Andhra Pradesh to implement rainwater harvesting schemes to Gujarat's more successful effort is contrasted and lessons drawn for Chhattisgarh. We argue that Chhattisgarh is not yet ready in terms of empowering its local bodies to take advantages offered by a global economy as it has not learnt the right lessons from case studies that document successes and failures both inside and outside Chhattisgarh.

The organization of this paper is as follows: in the first section we set out an economic argument for a measure of political decentralization. This is followed by a survey of literature that compares the effect of decentralization on relevant economic variables. We then discuss very briefly the nature of a water-harvesting project and the costs and benefits involved as well as how to implement such projects. We then compare the two great state-wide rainwater harvesting projects taken up in 2000 by Andhra Pradesh (where the state government implemented the scheme itself) and Gujarat (which implemented the project through the Panchayats). This is followed by a discussion on a success story as well as a failure in Chhattisgarh itself. We draw some lessons from this comparison and based on Chhattisgarh's plans for water management evaluate how far these plans empower local bodies in this exercise.

When evaluating the performance of local self-governments, we focus on a single issue—its ability to supply water, an essential input for agriculture. The narrowness of this approach can be justified by the fact that over 60 per cent of India's population is still dependent on agriculture. As the potential of the Panchayati Raj Institutions (PRI) to affect material conditions of production is considerably higher than their urban counterparts, we stick to these institutions.

TOWARDS A THEORY OF DECENTRALIZATION

What is the economic argument for decentralization? A case for decentralization may be made on the same grounds on which von Hayek[1] defended the market economy *vis-à-vis* the planned economy. In so far as one of the roles of the state is to provide public goods like infrastructure where externalities are involved, a theory may be advanced. It must be recognized that most economies are not homogeneous entities. There is a wide variation among various regions and localities within regions. Consequently, economic infrastructure that has to be created is not always standardized or uniform. Planning for infrastructure in a non-uniform environment, especially when local economic activity is affected by local factors requires the collection of relevant data—available locally—and then processing this data into information. Ideally, it should be this information that is the basis of planning for certain kinds of infrastructure. This is especially true for agriculture and a host of agro-industries. To that extent infrastructure required to support that industry/economic activity will be peculiar to the locality as its nature and quantum will depend on local conditions. Thus that portion of infrastructure will be best planned, executed and managed by the members of the locality itself. The reasons are simple. The members of the locality or their representatives being first hand observers of local conditions should know the best way to create an appropriate supporting local infrastructure and should be able to do so in the most economical manner. Indeed, for projects relating to watershed management, local self-governing bodies can mobilize free labour (by suitable innovation as regards distribution of benefits) from its citizens, which in the context of South Asia usually means unutilized labour.

If, on the other hand, the central government is entrusted with the responsibility of providing all infrastructural requirements, then it has to collect information from all the localities, aggregate this information and process it to arrive at a plan to provide infrastructural support. This is obviously a monumental task and one that is not easily accomplished. Additionally, in the process of aggregating information, it is likely that some information of value will be lost. To that extent the plan created will be *faulty/sub-optimal*. Furthermore, given the magnitude of this exercise it is also likely that the *lag* between the perception of the problem and action will be larger. Fourthly the possibility is that the link between local public good requirement and a local solution will be broken. While local demands will be aggregated, the solution that is proposed will be a centralized and uniform one (as we will see in the case of Surguja district discussed later in the paper). Take the case of the construction of a multi-purpose irrigation dam to cater to the needs of a large number of people spread over a large area distributed into various localities. This solution, while at times the only and perhaps the best solution, may not always be so. For one, the capital costs of such projects are very high. Secondly, they can take a long time to complete. Thirdly, it has a tendency to submerge the most fertile areas and thus the most populated areas and displace a section of people 'for the greater common good'. However in the absence of effective decentralization, the solution like the one above will be the only way out. Before discussing the effect of the redistribution of powers, a look at the public good requirements of the Indian economy integrating with the global economy is useful.

What are the public goods that the Indian economy requires now that it has decided to integrate with the world economy? Obviously the public goods that must now be provided must supplement the strengths of the Indian economy. Given the fact that India is a labour surplus economy, this means that public goods provided must be those that amplify the strengths of those sectors of the economy that are labour-intensive. This covers agriculture and labour-intensive manufactures like apparel/garment manufacture. In the future it could also include assembly of electronic goods that is the labour-intensive component of manufacture of electronic goods. The latter sector generally comprises small firms[2] that have a tendency to agglomerate/localize in a particular region. For an economy the size of India, these regions will possibly spread all over the country, with different regions supporting different clusters of industries.

However, whether agriculture or industry, both these sectors have a set of common public good requirements. But the prime requirement for agriculture is water. Apart from civic requirements, water is needed for irrigation and industrial uses and water supply must be predictable and regular. Now provision of water is, by and large, in the domain of the state and central governments, and logically so, as the usual mode of meeting requirements on a mass scale is met by the construction of large dams which is beyond the capacity of local civic authorities, be it urban or rural. However, such projects are highly capital-intensive and not without their share of controversies, not the least because of doubts over their long-run cost-effectiveness. The alternative is to go in for decentralized solutions but one that depends on local participation, like roof top/rainwater harvesting. Given their nature they are best administered by the local civic authorities like the PRIs. If these schemes are successful, then not only are significant savings effected, the conflict between agriculture and industry over electricity can also be lessened. This is because if the experience of the Tarun Bharat Sangh (see below) is anything to go by, the rise in the water table reduces power consumed in pumping water to the fields. Lower power requirements from agriculture can only mean more and cheaper power for industry as State Electricity Boards with a lower financial burden will be able to invest more in power generation as well as maintenance of existing infrastructure. This will lead to a lowering of costs as well as removal of infrastructural bottleneck. Additionally money saved by the state due to the substitution of the capital-intensive water supply project can be spent on transport and ports to lower costs and add to competitiveness.

The effects of centralized solutions on national competitiveness will be easy to measure. In so far as the costs have to be financed by taxes, a rise in indirect taxes will ensure that costs across the board increase, affecting competitiveness. It is also possible that the project, usually a mammoth multipurpose dam, may have other benefits like the generation of hydel power,[3] the vast enhancement of agricultural productivity which may more than compensate for the costs incurred. However, even if cost benefit exercises conclusively prove that cheaper decentralized alternatives exist, in the absence of effective decentralization, the centralized capital-intensive scheme will be the only feasible option irrespective of the cost-benefit calculations. Indeed, there are now cases that demonstrate what happens when infrastructural projects best suited for local planning and implementation are actually executed centrally.

SURVEY OF LITERATURE

Do empirical findings confirm the above thesis? It must be conceded that studies that have examined the connection between the spread of local democracy and economic growth/investment have shown mixed results.

Rosensweig and Foster[4] report (based on a study of 250 villages in India) that the replacement of local/traditional methods of village administration with democratization has the effect of changing the nature of expenditure from irrigation projects (preferred by the rich peasants who had hitherto been *de facto* rulers through the village headman) in favour of road building (favoured by the poor as it increases employment). Expenditure on education also receives a boost. They also report that fiscal decentralization not only boosts local governments' incomes but also lowers the cost of public investments. But the consequence for overall economic growth seem to be limited.

Ratna Reddy et al.[5] analysing the impact of participatory watershed development in certain districts of Andhra Pradesh conclude that participation is a necessary condition but by no means a sufficient one for overall improvement in livelihood. For that other complementary programmes like horticulture and dairy development programmes are required. They also conclude that the benefits from such programmes are not spread equally; the rich benefit more than the poor do.

Hari Prasad and Sengupta[6] report that when it comes to sustainable development, measured by them as the rate of extraction of ground water, the existence of vibrant PRIs have a negative and significant impact on ground water depletion.

An illuminating view of decentralization may be acquired if we briefly look at what has been reported for the OECD countries. Garello[7] warns against drawing simplistic relations between decentralization and growth, emphasizing that fiscal coherence (i.e. the match between a tier of government's power to spend with its ability to raise resources) be given as much importance. Tentative results suggest that fiscally coherent states (whether centralized or decentralized) have done well while fiscally decentralized states lagged behind.

The results reported above are a small sample of a large number of studies carried out, much of which are not dissimilar in their conclusions: while failure is not reported, the link between decentralization and growth is not established beyond doubt either. Yet, we persist in our arguments that decentralzation in India is itself a recent development (discounting the states of Maharashtra, Gujarat, West Bengal and Kerala) and it is possible that so far as these institutions are still in the process of learning. Before we argue our case further, we analyse the success of the Tarun Bharat Sangh in the field of water management. It cannot be disputed that if India is to do well in agriculture then this vital input must be secured and the case outlined below is a good success story that may be analysed.

THE CASE OF THE TARUN BHARAT SANGH

The successes of the Tarun Bharat Sangh (TBS)[8] in watershed development projects in Rajasthan have opened the eyes of policy makers to the possibility of rainwater harvesting as a tool for ensuring water supply even in areas with scanty rainfall. It is best exemplified by the experience of Alwar district that had been declared a 'dark zone' (no ground water) in the 1980s by the authorities and activities like agriculture had almost ceased to exist. It is here that the Magsaysay Award winner Rajendra Singh, the founder of the TBS, with the help of the villagers of Kaonta Bhaontala constructed the first check dam in 1985. In 1986, they constructed a *johad* (a traditional crescent-shaped pond) at the source of the river Arvari which had become a seasonal rivulet. Other villages too followed suit constructing *johads* in the other catchment areas of the Arvari. When the number of ponds touched 375, the Arvari that had almost ceased to exist, revived and from 1994 became a perennially flowing river. What TBS has accomplished is a vindication of the Nurkse-Vakil-Brahmanand[9] thesis, that in a labour-abundant economy like India, labour combined with very little capital can bring about a remarkable economic transformation. The economic impact can be gauged from the effect of the investment made by the villagers of Neembi. On an investment of Rs. 50,000 to build two checkdams, Neembi produces vegetables and milk worth Rs. 3 crore. This is not the kind of capital-output ratio that can be easily ignored, especially by states which are financially constrained.

However it was ignored till 2000 when large areas in India were struck by drought. It was suddenly discovered that the villages under the TBS's area of operations did not suffer from want of water, even though Rajasthan was suffering from drought for three consecutive years. Indeed in some areas the ground water lay only three feet from the surface.

TBS's success must be studied carefully if it is to be implemented widely. For the implementation of such exercises, the amount of labour required, the know-how required as well as the information of local geographical and hydro-geological conditions is crucial.

Briefly summed, the following seem to be the characteristics of the projects undertaken by the TBS. By and large information about the latter is extremely localized. This would preclude the possibility of a state-wide exercise/effort to undertake rainwater harvesting schemes planned and implemented from a state capital. Indeed, participation and planning (and in this case even finances) were locally procured.

However not all state governments heeded this lesson. Indeed the Government of Rajasthan attempted on a number of occasions to demolish the structures that the TBS had set up, failing each time in the face of determined opposition from the villagers who have benefited from this scheme. The grounds ran from legal (the state claimed that the TBS had no right to construct the check-dams) to technical (the structure of the check-dam was deemed to be unsafe). However, a group of eminent persons which included engineers disputed the state government's claim. In this din, the enormous benefits of the TBS's activities relative to the modest investments made were ignored till drought struck India in 2000. Prime ministerial pronouncements that rainwater harvesting should be looked into were heard and two states decided to undertake this on a wide scale. These were Andhra Pradesh and Gujarat.

THE POWER OF PANCHAYATS: TWO APPROACHES[10]

The Government of Gujarat launched the Sardar Patel Participatory Water Conservation Programme (SPPWCP), choosing to act through the PRIs. The state government invited proposals from the panchayats and faced an overwhelming response. Initially, the state government had budgeted for approximately 2,500 check-dams at the cost of Rs. 100 crore. However, the response and innovation of the PRIs in the state ensured that while the number of sanctioned dams quadrupled to 10,500 the budget only doubled to Rs. 200 crore. Impressively enough, the state government asked the villagers to bear 40 per cent of the cost. Planning and execution of the project were done by the PRIs themselves. The results of the SPPWCP have been described as 'good' although there are problems with overly stressing check-dam construction as we will argue later. While there have been cases of corruption, these have been limited. The best results have taken place in those villages where civil society was involved.

The case of Andhra Pradesh is another matter altogether.

The *Neeru Meeru* Scheme in Andhra Pradesh, unlike the one in Gujarat, did not rely on local participation. Here the state relied on contractors and bureaucrats and the results have been poor. Being centralized, they have fallen prey to certain members of the ruling party who utilized the scheme to set a system of patronage. This is easy, as those managing and executing the scheme do not live amongst those who are its beneficiaries. The scheme as it was implemented chose to use mechanised techniques like earth excavating machines as opposed to labour-absorbing methods which is more suited to a state where labour is cheap. There is not much that the PRIs can do about it, as to be beneficiaries of this scheme the panchayats have to sign a Memorandum of Understanding with the district authorities that gives the bureaucracy effective control of the execution of the scheme. Effective local participation has been reduced to self-restraint over crops that can be cultivated, i.e. the villagers must not cultivate water-intensive crops. Indeed in the event of failing to keep to guidelines the district authorities may initiate action to recover disbursed monies and suspend the programme.

However, while the PRIs have responsibilities, they have *de facto* few powers. For example, de-silting of ponds and tanks are vital to the recharge of underground acquifers. However given the Andhra government's proclivity to favour larger schemes, the smaller tanks did not get the necessary attention.[11] Indeed the minor irrigation department that got more funds to implement the *Neeru Meeru* spent 80 per cent of its outlay on salaries. Consequently in many villages de-silting could not be taken up.

The defining characteristic of the *Neeru Meeru* programme has been the manner in which planning and implementation has been in the hands of the concerned government departments and contractors. The communities have been largely bypassed. This was compounded by the fact that diversions of funds were reported even from the plan of action that the department-contractor combine had drawn up. Clearly this was enabled by lack of popular participation in the planning and implementation process. The greatest damage may have been the opportunity lost in institutionalizing a process/mechanism that would have laid the foundations for grassroots planning for sustainable development. The importance of the last point cannot be overstressed. While tank desiltation is rightly stressed from time, to time, administrations with urban biases do not have an integrated view of the project that they plan.

Thus other important components like '. . . bunds, sluice, feeder channels, spillways, catchment area treatment, encroachments of tank beds, chain of tanks etc., are not given due importance'.[12] One reason is technological—having opted for a mechanized approach through earth-moving machines, it becomes more difficult to accomplish the other tasks as they do not lend themselves easily to applications of heavy machinery. More importantly, the treatment of the other components clearly demand the possession of local knowledge of conditions which a centralized authority cannot have. A comparison of costs of desiltation between the mode that uses labour-intensive techniques and the one that uses earth-moving machines in the context of the *Neeru Meeru* programme, carried out by Watershed Support Services and Activities Network (WASSAN) reveals that the latter is only marginally cheaper than the former. However, as WASSAN points out that its study does not adjust for the subsidy on diesel.[13]

The results of not involving the panchayats are clear. The then chief minister of the state Chandrababu Naidu had to admit that even after having 'spent around Rs. 1,700 crore under *Neeru Meeru* to augment the groundwater table and conserve water in the state during the last four years. . . . All this has come to naught.'[14]

Thus it can be reasonably argued that states who have long nurtured PRIs are also states where participatory schemes will be successful.

But that is not all. The planning for such projects which require, as we have previously argued, specialized and local knowledge acquired by local people over a long period of time cannot be transferred to external agents like contractors in a small period of time. Additionally what must have contributed undoubtedly to Gujarat's success must have been the fact that 40 per cent of the investment required had to be raised locally as per the state government's guidelines. Thus the villagers had added incentive to see that their investment was productive. The villagers in Andhra Pradesh having invested nothing themselves had less incentive. Here Garello's point about fiscal coherence becomes particularly relevant. A local government which does not have to fully or partially finance a scheme that it has to implement is likely to be less concerned about the productivity of such investment than one where it is asked to share the cost. Similarly its inputs regarding information are likely to be more relevant when the project in question is a thoroughly local one. Taken further we can argue that the greater is the responsibility of the local government in financing its own activities, greater is the concern it is likely to have regarding the productivity of the project.

Indeed, as in the case set out below a village may even take it upon itself to finance the entire project itself.

FINANCING ONE'S OWN PLAN: THE CASE OF GANDHIGRAM[15]

Gandhigram in Kutch, in the face of state government inaction, decided to mobilize the resources it requires to build a check-dam in the year 1999. It organized a Rs. 15 lakh loan from an NRI, a Rs. 5 lakh loan (at 16 per cent intrest) from the Kutch Gramin Bank and voluntary labour from the residents would contribute an additional Rs. 7 lakh. The loans were to be paid back in five years. Each resident agreed not to irrigate more than 5 acres of land and share in the maintenance costs. As this dam would help them grow an additional crop, the profits from this enhanced income were expected to pay for the dam. Again the ability of the local government to encourage/enforce cooperative behaviour enabled it to execute this project. State governments, which are far more remote from the villagers than the PRI representatives, would find it impossible to elicit cooperation of this magnitude and certainly not from all villages of the state. Thus, the link between decentralizing power and increasing effectiveness of expenditures on infrastructure cannot be ignored. As the capital-output ratio declines with decentralization, the foundations of an efficient economy are laid.

DECENTRALIZATION FOR ECONOMIC EFFICIENCY: IS CHHATTISGARH READY?

Before an analysis of whether Chhattisgarh is decentralized enough for economic efficiency, an appraisal of Chhattisgarh's resources may be revealing.

It must be noted that Chhattisgarh was Madhya Pradesh's rice bowl, producing over 24 per cent of the state's agriculture production (over 6 million tonnes valued at Rs. 6,800 crore. Seventy per cent of MP's paddy production (a water-intensive crop) came from this region. This again is not surprising as Chhattisgarh's water resources are considerable being served by four river basins of which the Mahanadi and Godavari basins dominate followed by the Ganga and the Narmada basins.

TABLE 5.1: WATER RESOURCES OF CHHATTISGARH

Surface Water in Million Cubic Metres	
Estimated utilizable potential	41,720 mcm
Potential area that can be irrigated	4.3 million ha
Actual area irrigated	1.34 million ha
Ground Water	
Net utilizable potential	11,960 mcm
Actual potential utilized	n.a.

Source: Water Resources Department, Government of Chhattisgarh.

However, this water is regionally concentrated as well as seasonally distributed. (Table 5.2). The distribution from year to year is also highly uneven.

This variation makes paddy cultivation truly a 'gamble on the monsoons'. This is shown in Table 5.3 where the drought of 2002 had a dramatic impact on paddy production in the monsoon-dependent *kharif* season, even though acreage was not affected.

Consequently irrigation is of utmost importance, especially if Chhattisgarh is to create a position for itself in the rice market. Here utilization of the irrigation potential is considerably below the national average, especially when it comes to minor irrigation schemes.

It is little wonder that crop yields in the state are considerably below national and international standards.

TABLE 5.2: YEARLY RAINFALL: DISTRICT-WISE AND YEARLY VARIATIONS

	1994	1995	1996	1997	1998	1999	2000	2001	2002	2003	mean	SD	CoV
Raipur	1,237	990	748	1,287	893	758	514	1,321	726	1,356	983	285	0.29
Mahasamund	1,605	882	686	1,125	812	921	613	1,113	978	2,054	1,079	418	0.39
Dhamtari	184	1,328	1,323	1,317	1,040	1,259	881	1,475	770	1,555	1,113	390	0.35
Durg	1,404	1,057	1,009	1,220	1,448	1,205	767	970	771	1,433	1,128	242	0.21
Rajnandgaon	1,819	1,070	614	1,087	989	1,089	880	1,249	907	1,316	1,102	304	0.28
Kabirdham	1,263	1,172	1,141	1,357	1,398	1,327	814	1,165	708	1,006	1,135	218	0.19
Bilaspur	1,795	1,100	1,058	1,234	1,375	917	675	1,028	858	1,242	1,128	295	0.26
Janjgir	1,660	936	892	1,086	1,268	1,014	933	1,273	931	1,561	1,155	262	0.23
Korba	2,224	1,104	1,331	1,361	1,425	2,106	1,309	1,411	1,020	1,779	1,507	381	0.25
Raigarh	1,145	1,860	1,083	1,189	1,256	1,177	1,190	815	1,262	1,555	1,253	266	0.21
Jashpur	805	1,359	1,721	1,582	1,662	1,613	1,152	1,591	1,212	1,647	1,434	281	0.20
Surguja	2,025	1,068	1,315	1,505	1,276	1,344	1,205	1,652	1,165	1,606	1,416	271	0.19
Koriya	1,655	1,349	1,162	1,433	1,386	1,381	1,181	1,463	926	1,786	1,372	233	0.17
Jagadalpur	1,787	1,310	1,262	1,190	1,067	1,407	967	1,738	902	1,568	1,320	291	0.22
U.B. Kanker	1,411	1,941	1,272	1,025	1,261	1,375	1,040	2,157	991	1,918	1,439	399	0.28
State Average	1,468	1,235	1,108	1,267	1,245	1,273	973	1,367	954	1,575	1,246	188	0.15

TABLE 5.3: RICE PRODUCTION: DISTRICT-WISE VARIATION

District	Area				Production				Productivity			
	2001–2 Achiev.	2002–3 Achiev.	2003–4 Achiev.	2004–5 Programme	2001–2 Achiev.	2002–3 Achiev.	2003–4 Achiev.	2004–5 Achiev.	2001–2 Achiev.	2002–3 Achiev.	2003–4 Achiev.	2004–5
Raipur	483.95	478.8	482.34	470	718.7	373.94	871.58	861	1485	781	1,806	1,832
Mahasamund	225.13	222	223.47	207	443	132.31	440.23	424	1968	596	1,970	2,048
Dhamtari	128	127.2	126.96	122	256.1	132.54	219.51	223.5	2001	1042	1,729	1,832
Durg	390.1	378.4	370.8	362	739.6	276.23	598.1	700	1896	730	1,612	1,934
Rajnandgaon	236	229.2	221.9	217	342.9	158.6	327.52	335.5	1453	692	1,476	1,546
Kabirdham	82	79.3	78.5	73	109	48.93	114.45	119.78	1330	617	1,458	1,641
Bilaspur	296.5	276	282.64	277	533.4	216.1	476.81	530	1799	783	1,687	1,913
Janjgir	235.2	236.7	239.11	227	461.2	300.84	482.28	459.67	1961	1271	2,017	2,025
Korba	104.1	96.4	101.29	95	181	69.31	147.98	180.98	1739	712	1,461	1,905
Raigarh	225.5	219.1	219.08	212	379.5	210.77	363.27	370.7	1683	962	1,518	1,749
Jashpur	169.7	162.4	154.07	152	208.6	133.33	254.22	260	1229	821	978	1,711
Sarguja	296.1	295.4	292.54	287	460.4	314.77	360.7	359.75	1555	1256	1,233	1,253
Koriya	71.7	64.8	66.25	63	92	46.91	95.33	100.35	1283	724	1,439	1,593
Jagdalpur	258	251.1	253.33	247	360.7	241.55	414.44	407.55	1398	962	1,636	1,650
D.B. Dantewada	221	200.5	218.25	205	330.1	97.04	326.93	312	1494	484	1,498	1,525
U.B. Kanker	162.07	151.8	146.99	140	285.7	133.12	257.37	228.2	1763	827	1,751	1,630
Total	3,585.1	3,469.1	3,477.5	3,356	5,901.9	2,886.29	5,750.72	5,872.98	1,646	832	1,654	1,750

TABLE 5.4: WATER RESOURCES

Type of Scheme	Chhattisgarh			India
	Potential created (lakh ha)	Potential used (lakh ha)	% utilization	% utilization
Major	5.94	4.53	76	–
Medium	2.68	2.44	91	87
Minor	4.97	2.35	47	89
	13.59	9.32	69	87

Source: Water Resources Department, Government of Chhattisgarh.

TABLE 5.5: AVERAGE YIELD COMPARISON

	Average Yield (kg/ha)				
		India			
	Chhattisgarh	Unirrigated	Irrigated	China	Egypt
Paddy	1,005	1,050	2,090	5,807	7,659
Jowar	1,138	1,080	1,320	N.A.	N.A.
Maize	1,485	1,560	1,980	N.A.	N.A.
Wheat	924	1,830	3,180	3,295	5,255

Source: Commissioner of Land Records. Gwalior, GOI (1993) and CMIE (1996).

Given these resources and shortcomings, what are the strategies that Chhattisgarh can adopt to maximize economic benefits? The experiences of the TBS as well as the experiences of Gujarat and Andhra Pradesh do point in certain directions. This is strengthened by some case studies in Chhattisgarh itself.

CHHATTISGARH'S SUCCESSES AND FAILURES: THE RAJKHETA STORY AND THE SURGUJA FAILURE

The story of Rajkheta village in Surguja district of Chhattisgarh, like that of the TBS, highlights the importance of 'catching water where it falls' (Arjjumend).[16] While Surguja district has received an average of slightly over 1,400 mm of rainfall over the last ten years the year-to-year fluctuation is not low (Table 5.2). Moreover the sloped terrain lends itself to soil erosion accentuated by demands of livestock, which in the face of degraded grasslands will feed on remaining vegetation.

Tribal-dominated Rajkheta has witnessed pristine forests being degraded with predictable ecological consequences. Thus declining land productivity led to seasonal migration of labour.

The Surguja Gram Vikas Sansthan (SGVS) started its activities in 1994–5 with a view to conserving water given the seasonal variations of water availability. The SGVS chose as its goals water management, soil conservation, agricultural development and people's empowerment.

Participatory involvement was sought by public discussions involving the community whereby relevant information was disseminated and obtained. Equally important, tribal families by participating in these discussions realized that they could voice their concerns as well as help to make decisions. Thus for the first time it was recognized publicly that not only was water a scarce resource (as opposed to a free good), but that it was mismanaged.

It may be noted that activities like soil conservation are necessarily labour-intensive which was well in keeping with the village's factor endowments at least for some seasons. So are water conservation exercises. But these are also heavily dependent on local information like details of the village drainage system. Indeed, it was on the close examination of this drainage system that the sites of the check-dams were decided.

While the locals were sceptical about the effectiveness of the check-dams they nevertheless participated in the project contributing to it with labour. It can be reasonably argued that community involvement in planning and implementation was at least in part responsible for people's participation even when they remained unsure of success. The impact of this project has been impressive. Soil erosion has been checked. The water table has risen considerably and some ponds even support pisciculture. The irrigated area has risen from 13 acres in 1995 to 300 acres in 2001. As a result of water availability, productivity has also risen. Productivity of paddy cultivation has risen from 0.98 metric tonnes per hectare to 1.97 metric tonnes per hectare which is only slightly below the national average and almost twice the state average. Wheat cultivation productivity has also doubled from 1.23 metric tonnes per hectare in 1995 to 2.47 metric tonnes per hectare in 2001 which is much higher than the state average. All this has occurred by the mere increase of water availability. An indication of this can be gauged by the fact that land available in the *rabi* season increased from 5 per cent to 50 per cent of the total cultivable area. The figures for the *kharif* season are 70 and 98 per cent respectively. All in all, Rajkheta has experienced enhanced agricultural production and the commencement of vegetable cultivation has enhanced incomes.

Water distribution is managed by water user groups called *pani panchayats* consisting of user farmers with an elected president, secretary and treasurer. The distribution of water is rule-based; usually each farmer is given water for one acre and this exercise repeated in subsequent rounds. The collection of fees and management of the water pumps and other tasks are managed by water user groups formed for these purposes. The revenues generated are deposited by the apex body, the Watershed Committee, which uses it for tube well and channel maintenance. The man-days of employment generated by this project is also considerable.

The total monetary investment in the Rajkheta project is admittedly on the higher side amounting to Rs. 31 lakh. Finance for the project came from Christian Aid and the Lutheran World Relief Services (USA) with Action for Food Production of Delhi providing technical assistance. The local community's labour was evaluated at Rs. 6 lakh (Sharma)[17] which goes to reveal the extent to which surplus labour can be converted to capital. The per hectare cost (defined as total cost divided by increase in area irrigated) is approximately Rs. 32,000. However, if Rajkheta should be treated as a pilot project, costs are expected to halve as it is duplicated (Sharma).[18]

THE IMPLICATIONS FROM RAJKHETA

What makes Rajkheta a success? A simplistic answer that talks about participatory approaches to such projects may not be satisfactory. There is evidence from the Drought Prone Area Programme

(DPAP) in Chitradurga, Karnataka, that intended beneficiaries may choose *not to participate* in such programmes even when such programmes are open to participatory involvement (Vaidvelu).[19] The constraints as pointed out are twofold: the problem of the farmer participating in somebody else's programme (i.e. the government's) and the lower level government functionary fulfilling policy objectives decided at the national level. The shortcomings lay in the following areas:

1. Farmers were not sufficiently informed of the objective of the programme and as to why their cooperation was needed.
2. The Self-Help-Group formation was not preceded by training and seemed to be without purpose.
3. The plans were drawn without inputs from the villages—for the villagers this was the responsibility of the state.
4. Farmers did not have to contribute to the scheme.

It can be easily seen that Rajkheta suffered from none of these shortcomings. Even financially it may be pointed out that residents of Rajkheta contributed over 16 per cent of an expensive pilot scheme's total investment when central government norms suggest a contribution of 10 per cent.[20] In the case of duplication when costs may be cut to half, this contribution would rise to over 32 per cent.

While Chhattisgarh has a success in the form of Rajkheta it also has a failure in the form of the watershed project at Surguja which highlights the problems of a uniform, guideline-operated time-bound scheme implemented by a centralized agency of the state. A study of this project[21] revealed how informationally incapable the implementing agency was which led to it prescribing uniform actions for diverse situations as exemplified by equal subsidies for unequal households. Another way in which this artificial uniformity skewed benefits was by biasing benefits in favour of the size of landholdings instead of providing for inter-household negotiations and bargaining. It is not difficult to see why poorer farmers would be less interested in the sustainability of this scheme.

Centralized approaches to watershed development have certain uniform practices. One of them is check-dam construction which benefits only 15–16 per cent of the households directly (Shah).[22] The smaller less obvious but necessary 'add-ons' like *nala* plugs (small checks on the drainage lines which cause water to seep under ground) or contour *bunds* (to reduce soil erosion) generally get left out as their benefit is not immediate. As has been pointed out

> Building watershed harvesting structures as part of the watershed development projects is a very easy task—any contractor endowed with a bit of money can do so. But building an effective structure, which starts off a process of self-management and self-regeneration in a village community, is a much more difficult task (Sharma).[23]

LESSONS LEARNT

What lessons then has the state learnt from all these case studies? Firstly, it is worth recalling that Chhattisgarh, being part of Madhya Pradesh before 2000, also inherited Madhya Pradesh's system of PRIs which was put in place due to the efforts of the former chief minister of MP Digvijay Singh.

The question we must ask ourselves is whether Chhattisgarh is empowering what is already in place in order to let the PRIs play their role in transforming the state's agriculture into a competitive sector and take advantage of the regional redistribution that is certain to follow as India's economy including her agriculture is being thrown open to foreign competition?

In so far as planning for securing water supplies are concerned the picture appears to be negative. A perusal of the documents detailing the infrastructure plans[24] adopted by the state indicate that the leeway given to the PRIs is certainly not as much as that witnessed in Gujarat in the case of the implementation of the SPPWCP.

The state government has decided to continue with the Madhya Pradesh Farmers' Participation in Management of Irrigation Systems (MPFMIS) Act. The Act provides the framework for the participation of farmers in the *operation and maintenance* (O&M) activities of *existing* activities through a three-tier structure:

1. At the primary level there are Water Users Associations (WUA) for minor canals of a major project or an entire minor project.

2. A distributory committee at a secondary level for distributaries of large projects or an entire medium-sized project.
3. Project committees at a tertiary level for large projects.

The critical functions that these farmers organizations are supposed to do are to ensure equitable distribution of water, resolve disputes, plan and execute maintenance operations within their jurisdiction, raise resources via user fees and maintain accounts. There are of course some problems with the functioning of this Act. For one O&M funds are inadequate (with the state spending the bulk of funds on investment). This leads to poor performance in the form of unreliable supply. Dissatisfied farmers do not pay up leading to a worsening of the situation. It may still be argued that this is a financial problem and that for maintaining existing schemes this Act may be unobjectionable; but for enhancing irrigation potential clearly this is not enough, which is precisely what Chhattisgarh needs.

And given the fact that it is in the irrigation potential under small schemes that is grossly underutilized, it becomes clear that it is rainwater harvesting that Chhattisgarh requires. For this, however, merely involving WUAs in O&M operations is not enough. They have to be involved in planning and implementation and should ideally come up with a part of the finance (however small).

However, the state does not plan to entrust this responsibility to the panchayats. The Chhattisgarh State of the Environment Report 2004 talks about the shortcomings of the Water Resources Department (WRD) and the fact that with the break up of the state the skill/human capital has 'continued to reside primarily in Bhopal' and the WRD would have to be developed locally at Chhattisgarh. This is not the attitude of a state that aims to decentralize powers and planning of irrigation to the PRIs. On the other hand, the plan document advises Chhattisgarh to legislate to regulate ground water resources so as prevent over-exploitation. It also points to the limited capacity of the state to fund development in this area and yet does not talk about involving the PRIs in this sector. There is of course a discussion about reactivating and further developing WUAs but only as better managers in the O&M process, not as planners and initiators of irrigation projects.

Clearly, if the experience of Andhra Pradesh is anything to go by, this is not the optimal approach. Chhattisgarh's shortcomings are in the area of minor irrigation schemes. This can be remedied by rainwater harvesting projects that are best designed and implemented by the beneficiaries themselves as Gandhigram and Rajkheta so well demonstrate. To expect the relevant government department employees to acquire this expertise and then design and implement the projects with the WUAs in the subsidiary role of O&M managers is to neglect the lessons of the TBS's successes in Rajasthan. Indeed, the proposal to regulate groundwater is also fraught with danger; at one stroke the state empowers itself with the power to decide who will exploit this ground water but without the responsibility to augment groundwater resources. A better way would be to bring PRIs into this process and share the power and responsibilities of managing groundwater with them.

A non-participatory approach in a situation of unutilized irrigation potential does not augur well for agriculture in this state, especially given the fact that rice grown in this area is a particularly voracious consumer of water.

It may be argued therefore that Chhattisgarh has not learnt from success stories and failures located in the state itself. As in Chitradurga (and unlike Rajkheta) there seems to be no attempt in the state's water policies to involve intended beneficiaries in the design of the project. These policies become yet another instance of intended beneficiaries participating in 'someone else's' project. Unlike in Rajkheta and like in Chitradurga the fact that beneficiaries have to share some of the costs is not made explicit. Nor is the mode of benefit sharing spelt out.

It must be admitted though that *Gaon Ganga*,[25] launched on the 19 November 2000, does emphasize community participation and the creation of community user groups. But this is more in nature of a response to the crisis of recurring droughts rather than a well-thought out attempt to incorporate the PRIs into the planning mechanism.

The scheme that mirrors the attitude of the government is the *Khet Ganga* project for irrigation in the rain shadow regions of the state. Launched in February 2002, it focuses on enabling the farmer to *tap* groundwater potential and financing of drilling wells rather than constructing structures that conserve water and enhance ground water reserves.[26]

This is not to say that the *Khet Ganga* project does not have its merits. But its sustainability lies in the successful implementation of the *Gaon Ganga* that follows the Rajkheta model, where not only does the local community participate in planning and part-finance the projects that go on to augment water supply but also exercises control over water extraction in a manner that is rules-based, the rules being generated from negotiations between stake-holders.

In so far as the statutory body that can raise finances at the village level is the panchayat, there is really no alternative to involve the PRIs at every stage of the *Gaon Ganga* giving it responsibilities and powers as well as providing it with scientific inputs such that the chances of Rajkheta being duplicated is maximized. Secondly, as panchayats are also involved in other state-sponsored schemes that promote agricultural productivity and marketing they are in perfect position to provide synergy between the various schemes and amplify the effectiveness of watershed development projects. This takes care of the problems reported by Reddy et al.[27] The problem reported by Rosensweig and Foster[28] can be remedied by tying grants to watershed developing programmes and insisting on matching contributions from the panchayat which may either raise them through its general funds or from contributions through water users.

From the point of view of labour absorption, a decentralized approach makes it more likely that labour-intensive methods will be used to create the necessary structures like check dams, *nulla* plugs and contour *bunds*. Given India's and Chhattisgarh's factor endowments of a vast pool of surplus labour that is available, at least seasonally, this ensures capital accumulation at relatively low costs.

A centrally administered scheme that evokes no sense of ownership among the beneficiaries either by way of planning in its participation or financial contribution can actually witness the use of capital-intensive techniques even though labour is available.

Vaidvelu[29] points out how the DPAP in Chitradurga resorted to using earth-moving equipment instead of using labour as deadlines had to be met.

CONCLUSION

It is not being argued that bringing in the PRIs will necessarily enhance the state's irrigation assets. It is quite likely that PRIs, being new institutions in this state, will not be as dynamic as Gujarati's PRIs have been or construct a Gandhigram which was planned, implemented and financed from start to finish locally. (However, as we have seen even a poor village like Rajkheta has accomplished something similar albeit with external finance.) But to put a bar on their (PRIs) freedom is a sub-optimal action because it precludes the possibility of a TBS- or SGVS-like organization from taking root in the state and making rainwater harvesting a way of life. Even if such an organization arose, such an entity as TBS in Rajasthan and SGVS in Chhattisgarh would be in the unenviable position of trying to enhance the productive capacity of the state in violation of state laws! The possibility of one enterprising panchayat leading the way and the others following is also discounted. In states like West Bengal observers have noted the success of enterprising panchayats and have asked their local panchayat officials why that success cannot be emulated (Ghatak and Ghatak).[30]

Thus we cannot conclude on the basis of the Government of Chhattisgarh's actions or on the basis of its plan documents that PRIs have a meaningful role to play when it comes to planning for the supply of certain public goods like water. In so doing the state is unwisely sidelining a key player, thus making its own job cumbersome and expensive. In such a situation it is unlikely that Chhattisgarh will be able to utilize the opportunities that geographical redistribution of agricultural production will bring about as India gets more and more integrated with the global economy. It is clear that in this respect Chhattisgarh has inherited the Andhra Pradesh mindset and has chosen not to follow Gujarat.

While admitting that the economic case for decentralization is not iron-clad, anecdotal and empirical evidence suggest that there are some benefits to be had if democratic decentralization does come through. While evidence linking growth with democratic decentralization is not strong, what is visible is the lowering of costs when certain projects are transferred to local self-governments. This is even more so when the body in question is asked to bear a part of the cost of the project. The linkage between power and responsibility is observed both in empirical studies and the anecdotal evidence surveyed. But this is not the evidence that apparently informs the decisions of the Government of Chhattisgarh when it plans for its agriculturists.

As with the case of Andhra Pradesh, Chhattisgarh's centralized efforts to enhance its irrigation facilities may well face difficulties and the Chhattisgarhi farmer may have to deal with increasing costs and lose out to his competitors.

NOTES

1. F. von Hayek (ed.), 1935: *Collectivist Socialist Planning*, London: Routledge, Kegan and Paul.
2. Small as is being defined here may not tally with the Government of India's definition of what comprises the small sector.
3. For instance the Bhakra-Nangal Project or even the Sardar Sarovar project.
4. A.D. Foster and M.R. Rosensweig, 2001: 'Democratization, Decentralization and the Distribution of Local Public Goods in a Poor Rural Economy'. http:// econ.bu.edu/dilipm/ec722/papers/25fosterrosenzweig.pdf
5. V. Ratna Reddy, M. Gopinath Reddy, S. Galab, John Soussan and Oliver Springate-Baginski, 2004: 'Participatory Watershed Development in India: Can it Sustain Rural Livelihoods?', *Development and Change,* vol. 35, no. 2.
6. C.G. Hari Prasad and Dipankar Sengupta, 2005: 'Democratic Decentralisation in India and the Management of Groundwater—An Interstate Analysis: 1980–2000', presented at the conference 'Water Poverty and Social Crisis: Perspectives for Research and Action' at Agadir, Morocco, organized by IRD, Agadir University, IDRC, and the Ford Foundation, 12–15 December 2005.
7. Pierre Garello, 2004: 'An Index of Fiscal Decentralization for OECD Countries' presented at the conference 'The Role of Government in Asian Economies', Hong Kong, 16–18 September.

8. 'The Arvari, Coming Back to Life', *Down to Earth*, 15 March 1999.
9. R. Nurkse, 1967: *Problems of Capital Formation in Underdeveloped Countries*, New York: Oxford University Press, See also C.N. Vakil and P.R. Brahmanand, 1956: *Planning for an Expanding Economy*, Delhi: Vora & Co.
10. This section borrows heavily from the article 'Tryst with Rain', *Down to Earth*, vol. 9, no. 11, 31 October 2000.
11. 'Saga of Tanks', *Catchwater*, vol. 4, no. 6, December 2002, January 2003 downloadable from http://rainwaterharvesting.org/catchwater/dec2002/in_focus1.htm
12. *Voices from the Ground: Issues in Tank Desiltation under 'Neeru-Meeru'* prepared by Watershed Support Services and Activities Network (WASSAN) in collaboration with NGOs and printed with financial support from SDC/IC–NGO Programme, Andhra Pradesh.
13. Ibid.
14. 'Naidu Red-faced over Heatwave Deaths', *The Telegraph*, 6 June 2003.
15. 'Bank Loans to Harvest Water: A Community in Kutch Mobilises Resources to Meet its Water Needs', *Jalvani*, vol. 3, no. 2, 2000.
16. See Hasrat Arjjumend, 2003: 'Innovations in Rainwater Harvesting: Case of Rajkheta in Chhattisgarh', *LEISA India*, June, for a detailed and structured analysis of the Rajkheta story.
17. See Sudhirendar Sharma, 2001: 'Return of the Native: Catching Water Where it Falls', *Humanscape*, January, http://www.humanscape.org/Humanscape/new/jan01/hs010107.htm
18. Sharma, ibid.
19. See G. Anand Vaidvelu, 2005: 'Choosing "not" to Participate: Evidence from the Drought Prone Area Programme (DPAP) in Chitradurga, Karnataka', IWMI-Tata Water Policy Programme, Water Policy Research Highlight.
20. *Guidelines for Watershed Development*, Ministry of Rural Areas and Employment, Government of India, New Delhi, 1994.
21. S. Sharma, 2001: *Where Every Drop of Rain Counts: Case Study on Natural Resources Regeneration and Management in Surguja District of Chhattisgarh*, Delhi: The Ecological Foundation.
22. See Amita Shah, 2001: 'Who Benefits from Participatory Watershed Development? Lessons from Gujarat', IIED Gatekeeper Series 97, IIED, London, 2001, downloadable from http://www.iied.org/NR/agbioliv/gatekeepers/documents/GK97.pdf
23. Sudhirendar Sharma, 'Rainwater Harvesting Yet to Drought Proof India',

downloadable from www.water-2001.de/datenbank/162478313.49196.84/watershed1.doc

24. This section borrows heavily from the 'Infrastructure Development Action Plan for Chhattisgarh' prepared by PriceWaterhouse Coopers on behalf of the Government of Chhattisgarh.
25. *Gaon Ganga*, http://chhattisgarh.nic.in/schemes/gaon_ganga.htm
26. *Khet Ganga*, http://chattisgarh.nic.in/schemes/khet_ganga.htm
27. Reddy et al., op. cit.
28. Rosensweig and Foster, op. cit.
29. Vaidvelu, op. cit.
30. M. Ghatak and M. Ghatak, 2000: 'Grassroots Democracy: A Study of the Panchayat System in West Bengal', prepared for the Conference on Experiments in Empowered Deliberative Democracy, Wisconsin–Madison, January.

CHAPTER SIX

Distorted Development and Possibilities of Alternatives in Chhattisgarh

ILINA SEN

We try in the pages that follow to examine contrasting visions of development in the new Indian state of Chhattisgarh. Although the discussion is anchored in Chhattisgarh, the backdrop is provided by the creation of the new states of Jharkhand, Chhattisgarh and Uttaranchal at the turn of the century that gave a new dimension to the decentralization discourse in Indian polity.

The state of Chhattisgarh came into being on 1 November 2000. Carved out of the 16 easternmost districts of Madhya Pradesh, the present Chhattisgarh comprises parts of pre-Independence Central Provinces and Berar, as well as areas formerly incorporated in the adjoining *riyasats* (princely states). This history, of the partial experience of colonial British Indian administration and the partial domination of feudal *riyasats*, continues to affect the new state even today. In a similar way, geographical factors, the central plains of the Mahanadi surrounded by relatively inaccessible hills and plateau (broadly coexisting with the British and the princely domains respectively) are important in understanding the present character of the state. It is a state over large parts of which the forest intrudes into many aspects of rural life. Perhaps it is possible to extend the arguments to other areas with a similar developmental history.

ENVIRONMENT AND ECONOMIC SETTING

The Chhattisgarh region is an area that is an ecologically, linguistically, and culturally distinctive region. Administratively it comprises 16 districts, carved out of the original seven districts, viz., Raipur, Durg, Rajnandgaon, Bilaspur, Surguja, Raigarh and Bastar. The last three districts lie on the fringes of the region and are considerably influenced by the culture and ecology of the areas they border—Mirzapur, Ranchi, Gumla, Gadchiroli, the KBK districts of Orissa, and the Telengana districts of Andhra Pradesh. The Chhattisgarh region has a large area under forest cover, rich mineral reserves (tin, limestone, quartzite, iron ore, bauxite, alexandrite), and a large tribal population. The river Mahanadi flows through the central part of the region, and the plain areas in the river valleys are famous for rice cultivation, with input-intensive HYVs having replaced traditional seeds in much of the region. Along the railway, that passes through the valley centre, there has sprung up over the last twenty years, an industrial belt with the public sector giant Bhilai Steel Plant, three large cement plants, steel rolling and re-rolling mills, and a large mixed industrial estate. This massive industrial endeavour is backed up by a series of dams on the upper Mahanadi and electric power from the National Thermal Power Corporation (NTPC) units at Korba.

The population is mixed around this industrial and urban belt. In the rural areas of the Mahanadi Valley, Other Backward Classes (OBC) like the Sahus and the Kurmis dominate agriculture, and the Satnamis constitute a major Scheduled Caste (SC) component. Chhattisgarh has approximately 34 per cent Scheduled Tribe (ST) population, 12 per cent SC population, and more than 50 per cent OBCs. While the process of modernization seems to be apparent in the valley areas, the situation in the forest and hill areas on the periphery of the district is quite different. Although being affected more and more by invasive forest and mineral exploitation, traditional lifestyles and population compositions have survived to a far-greater extent here. Some of these areas, dominated by the Gond, Halba and Kamar/Bhujia and Oraon tribes, have recently been covered under the provisions of Panchayati Raj Extension to Scheduled Areas (PESA).

Like the neighbouring state of Jharkhand, Chhattisgarh is also a resource-rich state. It is rich in minerals, forest produce as well as fertile alluvial plains. It has huge reserves of iron ore, bauxite, coal as well as, it is whispered, uranium. These minerals have gone on to fuel the industrial zone cutting through the belly of the state, and have also given rich royalties to the old and new government through export deals. The most well-known export agreement is between the Japanese government and the National Mineral Development Corporation (NMDC) in which, for the last three decades, iron ore from the Bailadila mines in the state of Bastar have been exported to Japan through the Vishakhapatnam port, to which a special access railway has been built with financial support from the Japanese.

Geographically, Chhattisgarh consists of three natural formations. The first is a continuation of the plateau of Baghelkhand that joins up with the Jharkhand plateau along the northern borders of the state. Since the area is next to the Maikal ranges from where the Narmada and the Son originate, the plateau is drained primarily by the Son that divides Chhattisgarh from the rest of Madhya Pradesh. The area is rich in Kosa silk propagation (Champa in Bilaspur being the centre of local trade in Kosa), coal, bauxite and limestone which is mined by big companies in the Surguja area. The area was also rich in forests especially mixed forests of *sal, mahua, amla, sheesham, semul, rohini* and *palas*, to name a few. The Pahadi Korwa, Majhi, Majhwar, Nagesia and many other such tribal groups who practised seasonal gathering and cultivation primarily inhabit the area. Administratively, the area covers the districts of Raigarh, Jashpur, Surguja, and Koriya.

The second ecological zone consists of the Chhattisgarh Plains in southern Bilaspur, Raipur, Durg, Rajnandgaon and Raigarh. This area, forming the Mahanadi Basin, was also the known as the 'rice bowl' of central India. It is particularly rich in indigenous varieties of rice and methods of harvesting water. Apart from this the region also has iron ore, bauxite, limestone, asbestos, and Kosa silk. The area is mostly inhabited by Gonds, Kamars, and cultivators like the Kurmis, Sahus, Kalars, and Satnamis and others.

The third ecological zone in the region is the Bastar or the Dandakaranya Plateau that begins from Kanker and ends in the Dantewada region in the southernmost part of Bastar. This area borders with the East Godavari region of Andhra Pradesh and is drained primarily by the Indravati River. Its main natural wealth consists of forests and minerals. The area is known for its rich *sal* and mixed forests. Bastar is also famous for its minor forest produce like *imli*, *amla*, *chironji*, *mahua*, *harra*, etc., and for minerals like mica, manganese, iron ore, bauxite and limestone. This region includes Abhujmarh, the abode of the Maria Gonds and also has a considerable Kamar and Gond population. It was also one of the oldest Gond feudatory states of the regions due to which its history has acquired significance for scholars of central India.

Although resource-rich, Chhattisgarh is home to large numbers of people who are among the poorest in the country. The gains of development and industrialization have gone to migrants and 'skilled' labour force from outside the state. This has meant that the poorest of the poor were either forced to work as daily wage labourers or look for jobs outside the state. In the plains, in the absence of assured irrigation and second crop over a large area, rural landless can only get part-time seasonal employment within Chhattisgarh. Therefore a large part of the labour force migrates to other parts of the country from this region.

There has been a traditional distinction between the *chatar raj*—the governance of the plains—and the *jangal raj*—the governance of the forests and hills. This distinction has been reinforced by the process of development where the jungle has become the material reserve and hunting ground of the plains. Dams have been constructed in the hills and plains (Gangrel, Madamsilli and Rudri in Raipur on the Mahanadi, Bango on the Hasdeo in Bilaspur) to feed to the industrial process, and a situation has emerged in which the exploitation of mineral reserves under the soil cover is in direct conflict with the preservation of what is above—the forest, agricultural soil, and water.

STATEHOOD AND ITS CONCOMITANTS

In Chhattisgarh, as in the other new states, there was an attempt in the official discourse, to link the event of state formation with the peoples' demand for greater autonomy.[1] However, while a vibrant movement for a new state of Jharkhand and a new state of Uttarakhand existed, the demand for a separate state of Chhattisgarh was relatively weak. This may seem a dichotomy, because there was definitely an articulation for a Chhattisgarhi identity in the various peoples' movements in the region, most notably among workers and peasants owing allegiance to the Chhattisgarh Mukti Morcha (CMM), led by the charismatic Shankar Guha Niyogi. However, this identity articulation did not, as we shall see below, translate necessarily into the demand for a separate state. It was rather an articulation of a deep sense of subjugation, in which the world political economic system in general, and the state of Madhya Pradesh in particular, that treated Chhattisgarh as an internal colony, both played a part. The sense of subjugation and injustice was combined with a strong desire for greater control over their own lives for the toiling people of the region, and with pride in and love for their heritage.

POLITICAL ARTICULATION FOR STATEHOOD

Politically, the demand for a separate state was articulated by the big landowners and traders turned industrialists. This process can be understood if we look at the career of B.R. Jain, an icon of the development process of Chhattisgarh. B.R. Jain's father had a small cycle shop in Bhilai, and Jain himself started a small mechanical repair workshop outside the Bhilai Steel Plant factory gate in the late 1960s. He diversified into rice trade, and with the money made from that, and aided by massive state subsidies that were being handed out to industrialists in the name of development promotion in the late 1970s, started the Bhilai Engineering Corporation. Ironically, this was one of the centres where the late Shankar Guha Niyogi started the CMM-affiliated trade union to demand basic minimum living wage and fair working conditions for workers. B.R. Jain, by then notorious for his involvement in the *hawala* scam,[2] was believed by many to have been involved in the financing of the killers of Niyogi with *hawala* money.

The career of Gurmukh Singh Hora paralleled that of B.R. Jain. Starting with a small scooter repair shop, he graduated to a heavy transport business, to a bar, to a four-star hotel, a MLA's seat and the building of a temple to 'Chhattisgarh Mehtari' (Mother Chhattisgarh) on the highway between Raipur and Jagdalpur to which the devoted throng for blessings during *Navaratri*. It is this industrialist-financier combine that spearheaded the demand for a separate statehood for Chhattisgarh, using the argument for cultural homogeneity of the region, but wanting really to bleed it further, and secure further state subsidies in the process.

Promises Born Out of the Statehood

The new state was launched with much fanfare and glitter on 1 November 2000. At the time of the inaugural ceremonies, Ajit Jogi, the first chief minister of the state, declared that this was the richest state in the country, although inhabited by the poorest people, and that one of the challenges that faced all was that of bridging the many centuries that the people of the state lived in at the same time. Although Jogi's tenure in power ended rather unfortunately,[3] and the events afterwards were even more murky,[4] he did make a sensitive articulation of the challenges faced by the people in the new state. However, if there was any hope that the development vision of the new state would be rooted in any kind of indigenous perspective, this hope was quickly belied. It was soon revealed that the new state had been born in the context of globalization and that the political agenda behind the policy of power devolution was the opening up of the resource bases at the local level to the global market and the MNCs. In this agenda there has been no change in the almost five years since the state has been born, although the government has changed through a process of Vidhan Sabha elections.

Developments since the birth of the state have exemplified and illustrated this trend many times over. Today, the state officially prides itself on its new industrializing and developing face. One of the first institutions to be established by the state of Chhattisgarh was the Chhattisgarh Industrial Development Corporation (CIDC) that got busy immediately upon establishment in negotiating development loans from the Asian Development Bank (ADB) and other international financial institutions. New industrial growth centres were established by 2005 in the districts of Mahasamund, Sarguja, Kawardha, Dhamtari and Raigarh. An industrial policy had been formulated (2004) with the express objective of creating 'an enabling environment for ensuring maximum value addition to the abundant, locally available mineral and other forest-based resources'.[5] The policy also seeks to attract direct investments including investments to 'the most backward tribe dominated areas' and seeks to invite investors including NRI and direct foreign investors with a host of incentives and tariff concessions. The current chief minister of the state, Raman Singh, has gone on an international tour wooing NRI and foreign capital investment and has announced proudly on his return that Texas firms had shown positive interest in investing in the state.

There are many indications that the natural resources of the state are being sold off for very minimal returns—only a few examples will be quoted to substantiate this assertion.

INDIGENOUS ECONOMY ENDANGERED

In the second half of 2002, Chhattisgarh was shaken by the controversy surrounding the proposed transfer of genetic material of indigenous rice varieties from Chhattisgarh to the multinational corporation Syngenta by the Indira Gandhi Krishi Vishwavidyalay (IGKVV) at Raipur. To recapitulate, the seeds of over 19,000 native varieties of rice were collected from farmers by Dr. R.H. Richharia for adaptive research at the then functioning MP Rice Research Institute (MPRRI). This institution, working on native strains of rice germ plasm, was later closed down under pressure from the scientific lobby led by the Manila-based International Rice Research Institute (IRRI) that promoted the strategy of solving India's hunger problem through hybrid and input-intensive imported seeds. This approach was taken up by a section of the agricultural scientists in India and sounded the death-knell for all scientific work with native germ plasma adapted to the soil and eco-systems of India. Through the traumatic period of the shutting down of the MPRRI, and the personal hounding that Dr. Richharia faced for the 'line' he took, the seeds continued to remain in the possession of the successors to the MPRRI, viz., the agriculture college affiliated to what is now the IGKVV. In the early nineties, Dr. Richharia, partially rehabilitated from oblivion, revisited the collection to work on his *magnum opus*, the *Encyclopaedia of Rice in India*. At the time of his death in 1996, this work was authoritatively believed to have been near completion.

The controversy broke in November 2002, when the Raipur edition of the *Dainik Bhaskar*, a local newspaper, reported that the present regime of the IGKVV was negotiating a deal for collaborative research with Syngenta, the corporation that had earlier taken a US patent on the golden rice. In the ensuing climate of TRIPS agreements and perceived bio piracy threat, this expose led to a huge outcry involving scientists, intellectuals, opposition political parties and mass organizations. The deal was stalled under public pressure, although the bureaucracy of the IGKVV was hugely annoyed with the protests and reminded the media that private financing of academic research was an international trend, and the ubiquitous Jogi advised the protesters to emerge from the shell of Chhattisgarh and look at the world.

The Syngenta experience is significant for a number of reasons. Although one attempt at bio piracy may have been defeated, but in the overall legal political climate, other attempts are certain to be made. It is also imperative that we arrive at a proper appreciation of the long-term implications of the conflicting Intellectual Property Rights Regimes (IPR) including that of community rights to biodiversity resources and genetic material. Since Chhattisgarh is the inheritor of enormous forest and agro-bio resources, one can anticipate that this is not the last that one has heard of this debate. In the case of the collection held at the IGKVV, it is possible to argue that the seeds were collected from the farmers under an implicit contract that the MPRRI would conduct adaptive research that would benefit the community. In no way can it be argued that the IGKVV was at any time the owner of the seeds. At best it could be termed a custodian of community property.

The university also violated the letter and intent of the Convention on Bio Diversity (CBD) that insists that academic research on bio resources is contingent on a responsibility for their *in situ* conservation.

Thirdly, the issue reopens the entire concept of 'eminent domain' and its application or misapplication in the matter of community's biodiversity resources. Fourthly and most importantly, it raises the question whether biodiversity conservation is at all possible, *in situ* or *ex situ*, without community ownership and community rights.

TOWARDS PRIVATIZATION OF NATURAL RESOURCES AND BASIC LIVELIHOOD?

The second example to be recalled in this connection is the issue of river privatization. Twenty-two kilometre of the Shivnath River, bordering the Durg and Rajnandgaon districts of Chhattisgarh, was handed over to a private company called Radius Waters Limited. Although the primary objective of the contract was to supply water to the Borsi industrial area, in fact this private ownership of the river caused enormous hardship to river bank villagers and local fishermen whose rights to the use of the river were severely compromised.

Like the seed issue, this issue too became extremely contentious when it was brought into the public domain in 2001–2, and public protest and anger were widespread. The first elected state government was forced to publicly denounce the deed, although owing to technicalities about the actual signatories (the erstwhile state of Madhya Pradesh), the modalities of fixing the compensation in case the deal was unilaterally terminated, etc., the agreement was not ever physically called off. The second elected government preferred to let sleeping dogs continue to sleep, and did not take any kind of position on the case. Most recently, a Public Interest Litigation (PIL) had been filed in the High Court of Chhattisgarh challenging the privatization of a public water resource.

The third example relates to the refusal of the Gram Sabha of Nagarnar village in Bastar to allow their lands to be acquired for the building of a steel plant in 2001. The authorities at the district level proceeded to falsify the Gram Sabha registers, forcibly handing over land to the NMDC for the commencement of land development activities, and when village people protested, they were lathi charged and arrested, allowing release only on the condition of acceptance of compensation cheques for land acquired.

It is a different matter that the technology proposed to be used originally for the plant was developed in Rumania had never got off the experimental stage anywhere in the world, and the NMDC had to subsequently renounce it, and float fresh global tenders for technology transfer. The land acquired from the villagers at the cost of blood and tears stands unproductive today, with only a wall and a signboard proclaiming the existence of the Nagarnar Steel Plant.

In the context of steel, one recalls also the example of the Jindal Steel and Power Limited, a mega project that backs up its steel and captive power plant in the Raigarh district with mines, roads and privileged access to the waters of the Kelo River. Jindal has a long record of hogging the natural resources of the area, of enclosing the people of the area out of accessing the water, forests, and common property resources. Many activists and social workers who have attempted to protest about these practices have been implicated in long and arduous litigation processes in the courts of the Jindal hometown of Hissar in Haryana.

The Jindal group has consolidated its political power along with economic clout. O.P. Jindal, the founder of the group, was a Minister of State in the Haryana government until the time of his death. Navin Jindal, the son, is a Member of Parliament. He has also gained fame through a court verdict upholding individual rights, to fly the National Flag over private premises. Most recently a public hearing in the process of securing environmental clearence for the expansion plans of the Jindal group in January 2005 was attended by some 10,000 people with stories of Jindal's utter disregard for nature, for collective and community rights. Yet, the environmental clearence was obtained, a telling comment on the nature of our polity.

These examples, although dramatic, are merely illustrative. As Chhattisgarh proceeds to 'develop' in the rapid fire mode, one is forced to ask whether opportunities for the poor, for the indigenous people, and for other marginalized groups for a democratic space in the development of the new state have increased or actually shrunk, and whether the choices made of the development paradigm were inevitable. Were there other roads to development in Chhattisgarh? It is our contention that indigenous perspectives do provide alternative routes, and that struggles and movements in Chhattisgarh provide a rich legacy on which alternative models could have been based.

WHAT ARE THE LESSONS FROM INDIGENOUS PERSPECTIVES ON DEVELOPMENT?

CONTRADICTORY POLITICAL TRADITIONS OF CHHATTISGARH: PATRONAGE AND RESISTANCE

We believe that Chhattisgarh has a strong and vibrant tradition of people's movements that has consistently stood for a people-centred perspective of development. The histories of these movements, their articulation and forms of struggle have a lot to teach us about indigenous perspectives on development that are both more equitable and more sustainable than the rapacious perspective we have been discussing above. We have the history of Veer Narayan Singh, who during the drought years of 1856 and 1857, accessed the hoarders' granary and distributed paddy to hungry farmers, laying the argument for the basic entitlement of all people to food. In different ways, Guru Ghasidas' struggle for self-respect and land rights of the Satnamis, and the Mawalibhata Adivasis' refusal to allow a steel plant to come up on their land, are part of the same tradition, a tradition that values equitable development, humanity and social justice. Why is it then that these perspectives have consistently been undervalued? Our contention is that the answer lies in the schism between the 'official' politics of the state and the day-to-day lives and struggles of ordinary people that has been so characteristic of the polity of Chhattisgarh over the last fifty odd years.

It is a paradox that the overarching politics of Chhattisgarh today displays signs of both the politics of patronage and the power of people's movements. The party that has dominated the politics of the region/state has traditionally been the Congress, and the influence of the former royal families in the areas formerly ruled by them has been given legitimacy by the party structures from the time of the reorganization of states. Thus the Congress party political stalwarts have included scions of the royal families of Phuljar, Khairagarh, Surguja and Raigarh. The Bharatiya Janata Party and its previous incarnations have mirrored this process to a limited extent through the patronage of the Raja of Jashpur. In and around Raipur, the long time cultural capital of Chhattisgarh, the political dominance of the Shukla family has continued for generations. This domination has been supported by the economic surplus generated by the powerful rice millers' lobby. The dominance of the Brahmins (from Saryupar or Sarangarh) has been strong in politics, education, cultural life and civil society institutions. Among middle peasant castes, the Kurmis have been the strongest and have dominated Congress politics around Durg through the Chandrakar family for more than two generations. Control of Satnami politics[6] has also been contained within the Congress fold through the patronage of the various branches of the Guru Parivar of the Satnami Sect, powerful in the Bilaspur region.

As against this tendency, the history of people's struggle in what now constitutes the state of Chhattisgarh is extremely rich. Some of these struggles and the issues they highlighted have been mentioned above. We will discuss the example of the CMM in somewhat greater details as this constitutes in some ways the best known, best documented, and most recent of these examples.

THE CMM, A RECENT GRASS ROOT DEMOCRATIC EXPERIENCE

The movement known today as the CMM was born in the mines of Jharan Dalli or Dalli Rajhara, in the southern tip of Durg district, bordering undivided Bastar. In the late 1970s, in the relatively liberal political climate following the lifting of the internal emergency, a trade union, the Chhattisgarh Mines Shramik Sangh (CMSS), grew strong among contractual mine workers in Bhilai Steel Plant's (BSP) captive iron ore mines at Dalli.[7] Many issues led to the birth of the new workers' union. There was a feeling that the mainstream unions which officially represented the workforce until then and had a membership base among both regular and contract workers, were really not sensitive to the issues of the contract workers in the manual mines. These contract workers had no job security, no housing, sanitation, health or welfare facilities unlike the workers in the mechanized mines. There were also certain cultural issues.

Given the history of uneven development in India, the workers in the mechanized mines were those with some technical education, which more or less by definition meant that these workers were recruited from outside the region. The manual mines were given out annual contract leases, and for working these, landless and tribal workers from the surrounding regions were generally employed. There were major cultural differences among the two groups of workers. While workers in the mechanized mines were all male, and the well laid out township where they lived consisted of patriarchal families where the men brought home a family wage, among the manual mine workers, it was common for men and women to work in pairs, with the men and the women bringing home more or less equal wages. The more egalitarian practices of the workers from Chhattisgarh, the relatively more liberal personal and sexual mores of the women were held in contempt by those living in the township who regarded themselves as more advanced, and the Chhattisgarh workers as primitive and backward.

The first struggles of the newly formed CMSS were for housing concessions. Although this met with severe repression from the BSP and the state administration, the struggle achieved its objectives under the dynamic leadership of Shankar Guha Niyogi. Over the next few years, the dominant struggle issue was for parity in work and wages with the regular workers, for the BSP's acceptance of its liability as principal employer and for an ultimate absorption into the regular workforce or 'departmentalization'. The BSP resisted these demands, as in its view, manual working of the mines was only a temporary expedient, and it was ultimately looking at full mechanization of the mines. Realizing that this scheme of things, if successful, would lead to a large number of manual mine workers losing their jobs, the CMSS linked the struggle for departmentalization with a campaign against mechanization. In the process it highlighted the case for a technology option in the mines that recognized labour as a strength and not a liability. The women workers in particular staked their claim to work and recalled the historical experience in which women had been the first to be retrenched whenever mines and industry had been mechanized. The discourse and debates that took place in the light of these positions were among the richest in Indian labour history and confronted issues of women's rights to work, the relationship between labour and technology, and the option of combining mechanized and manual processes in mining so as to eliminate the most hazardous operations while at the same time maximizing employment and human involvement in production.[8]

Development and the Status of Women

In all of this, the role of the women of Dalli Rajhara mines was critical. All participants and witnesses to their struggle between 1977 and 1997 commented on the strength of the women's organization. This has of course to be interpreted in the context of the position of women in the society of Chhattisgarh, which is at the same time so strong and so vulnerable. In many ways, the women of Chhattisgarh enjoy a unique position within the country. The proportion of women in the population (the sex ratio or the number of women per 1,000 men) stands at 990 according to the 2001 census. The sex ratio is universally acknowledged as an indicator of women's well-being, survival and status, and in this the position of Chhattisgarh is second among states in the country (after Kerala's 1,058) and well above the national average.

Unlike women in many other parts of India where the culture of exclusion and seclusion seems to prevail, women in Chhattisgarh are articulate, visible, and play a major role in public production. This can be understood with reference to the role that women play in different areas of livelihood systems. In Chhattisgarh, women are the major agricultural workers. This is so in the production of rice, our main food crop, as well as in pulses, millets and oilseeds. They work in every aspect of crop production, preservation and storage. In certain parts of the state like Abujhmar and Sihawa, women are also known to use the plough, a function that is taboo and prohibited for them in almost all other parts of the country, indeed the world.

The important economic position of women spilled over into the mining sector as this developed in the state and can be seen also among migrant workers from Chhattisgarh who are major contributors to the construction industry nationwide. Many of the metropolitan highways, buildings and national industries have been built by the migrant workers from Chhattisgarh, and the women of Chhattisgarh have been more than equal contributors in these efforts. In the case of mining, the entire operation of manual mining made it necessary for men and women to work in pairs, with one breaking the freshly blasted rock into manageable size nuggets and the other carrying headloads away to the transport point. The most important contribution to both the labour and women's questions by the women of Dalli Rajhara was their insistence on women's equal right to a productive life.[9]

There have been many workers' struggles led by the CMM in the last thirty-five odd years. These have ranged from trade union struggles in the older industries of the region like the Rajnandgaon-based (now defunct) Bengal Nagpur Cotton Mills to the completely unregulated engineering industries around Bhilai and Raipur. The latter developed in the decade of the 1980s and 1990s as ancillary to the Steel Authority of India's Bhilai Steel Plant. The conditions of workers in these industries paralleled those in the Wild West in the nineteenth century, with no limitation to the working hour, no basic facilities, no minimum wage and no continuity in service. The CMM-led struggles in these industries in the decade of the 1980s built-up the first workers' organizations in this sector, and it was the resistance of the industrial mafia to the organization that led to the murder of Shankar Guha Niyogi, leader of the

CMM, in 1991. However, the work of the CMM constitutes an important landmark in the history of peoples' struggles for yet another reason.

CMM AND STRATEGIES FOR DEVELOPMENT

Not only did the CMM-led struggles base their strategy on a critique of the existing models of development, they also are to be remembered for the many experiments and initiatives in alternative development in keeping with the CMMs propagated philosophy of *Sangharsh aur Nirman* (Struggle and Reconstruction). These initiatives covered a large number of issues and were based on the principles of sustainability, ecological wholeness, demystification of technology and the abolition of hierarchies of power. There were important experiments in the areas of health, education and culture. As an example we can quote the experience of the Shaheed Hospital at Dalli Rajhara which based its work on rational health care and medication and, on training health workers to a high level of competence and responsibility.

The efforts of the CMM also dug up from oblivion the history of Veer Narayan Singh, a Chhattisgarhi in the 1857 struggle who earned the wrath of the British administration by distributing grain from a hoarder's store to hungry people in a famine situation. In the struggle of the CMM, Veer Narayan Singh and his movement became an important icon for a development model that would be more equitable, sharing and caring. Through its praxis CMM established the dialectical relationship between its visions of *Sangharsh* and *Nirman* in which each lived for and sustained the other (*Sangharsh ke liye Nirman; Nirman ke liye Sangharsh*).[10] Of course, the initiatives and their outcomes never achieved copy book perfection given the fact that they had to struggle for survival in an overall hostile environment, yet they demonstrated that it was possible to do things differently and gave to the toiling people a concrete glimpse of hope in a way of life that would perhaps one day be theirs.

CHALLENGES BEFORE ALTERNATIVE VISION

The experience of Chhattisgarh raises several questions about the choice of development paradigms, about the logic of political decentralization in a world spiralling into the bottomless pit of the unified global village, and about mainstreaming of the indigenous way of life.

The hollowness of the argument for local autonomy given by the political establishment is borne out when we see that the new state gave almost no space for the development vision of organizations like the CMM, and instead opened the state to an army of external (sometimes international) consultants who descended upon us with Vision Documents, Strategy Papers and Turnkey Proposals. Those who had argued for a pro-people development strategy or for regional articulation of aspirations were quickly marginalized.

The Chhattisgarhi language, not to mention the several other tribal languages spoken in the state found no place in the world of education or governance. Promises made about decentralizing authority were broken. Large areas of Chhattisgarh are currently governed by the Panchayat Extension to the Scheduled Areas Act (PESA) which is supposed to introduce significant space for village-level decision-making. However, we have seen from the example of the Nagarnar case that there are major problems with regard to the actual operationalization of the provisions of the Act. It is also a pertinent question whether political devolution can happen without economic devolution. In the current socio-political climate, what are really the possibilities for decentralized governance opened up through the PESA is a question deserving serious thought.

There are also serious problems with the so-called efforts to integrate the 'backward' region of Chhattisgarh into the socio-political mainstream. We can understand this with reference to the changes in the position of women. We have spoken earlier of the central position of women in the production systems of Chhattisgarh. It is not as if derogatory practices like witch hunting (*Tonhi Pratha*) did not exist in Chhattisgarh. But despite this, women enjoyed certain freedoms and social spaces in terms of relationships and normative behaviour in the region. The image of the strong woman is not historically or sociologically unfamiliar in Chhattisgarh. However, in recent years we find that not only are crimes against women on the rise, the traditional society's attitude towards women is also changing for the worse. Caste/tribe panchayats have emerged as severely patriarchal bodies of *siyans* (elders) and in several cases have meted out severe punishments to women transgressing what are perceived to be customary laws. These trends are in keeping with hardening attitudes to female morality among male-dominated groups of community elders in many parts of the country. Dowry at the time of marriage was an almost unknown phenomenon twenty years ago, but with the coming of sections of the indigenous population into the service sector, with the money inflow for government servants following the implementation of the Fifth Pay Commission, it has become standard for the lower middle and middle classes to hand out and receive the customary dowry package of refrigerator, TV set, motorcycle at the wedding of a daughter or a son. Certain provisions of customary law like the *Churhi Pratha* which once gave women the freedom to end an unpleasant relationship and contract another that is more compatible, are today being used by men to throw out economically dependent and vulnerable wives and children and contract subsequent relationships. The cultural creation of the 'dependent' wife is itself a product of the cultural integration of Chhattisgarh into mainstream India. Whatever have been women's rights and entitlements in indigenous society; processes responsible for their interpretation and codification are not working today in the interests of women.

The experience of Chhattisgarh outlined above raises several issues that are important for the development discourse in the state and beyond. The nature of the federal process in India can itself be called into question in some ways. The organization of the territory of India into states is supposedly meant to take into account regional aspirations and interests. The experience of Chhattisgarh shows that there are serious fissures in the definition and interpretation of such aspirations. In this context, the comparative experience of the other new states of India, of regions aspiring to statehood, as well as of the European experience of federalism can be extremely illuminating. There is definitely a tension between the visions of development demanded by the global and indigenous villages, and the tension continues to this day. Chhattisgarh's future course will, it appears, be determined to a large extent on the way this tension is worked out, resolved, or contained.

NOTES

1. See 'Seeds of Protests and Change: Guru Ghasidas and the Satnam Panth', 'Tribal Protest and Rebellions: Bhumkal in Bastar (1910)', 'Emerging Identity and Socio-cultural Spaces: New Chhattisgarh in a New India', from Sanket Bhopal *Chhattisgarh—A State is Born* in the official website of Government of Chhattisgarh (www.chhattisgarh.nic.in). The formula 'New Chhattisgarh in a New India' directly refers to one of the Chhattisgarh Mukti Morcha slogans.
2. Regarding the hawala scandal, journalist Vineet Narain broke the story and it was reported in 1998 in *Frontline* following the judgement. Also see Sudha Mahalingam 'Jain Hawala Case: Diaries as Evidence', *Frontline* magazine, vol. 15, no. 6, 21 March–3 April 1998, accessed on [2] 2 November 2006. The *hawala kand* expose linked the black money racket with the activities of crime syndicates in India and the Middle East.
3. Ajit Jogi's party lost the Assembly elections in 2004, and the former chief minister was captured on tape in a sting operation trying to bribe newly elected opposition members to support him.
4. During Jogi's stewardship of the state, a major opposition leader was murdered, and investigations by the Central Bureau of Investigation have implicated Jogi's son as a leading organizer of the conspiracy that led to the murder.
5. For a critique of the Chhattisgarh Industrial Policy, see Sanjeev Ghotge's analysis in NCAS papers, 2005.
6. The Satnamis were converted to the monotheistic 'Satnam' faith from depressed positions in the hierarchical caste structure through the work of the nineteenth-century social reformer, Guru Ghasidas. In Chhattisgarh, Satnami politics bears the closest resemblance to what is termed Dalit politics elsewhere. See 'Guru Ghasidas and the Satnami Panth' op. cit.
7. The old name for the settlement now called Dalli Rajhara was Jharan Dalli, after a *jharan* or stream between the low hills of Dalli and Rajhara on the traditional road from Rajnandgaon into Bastar. Rich reserves of iron ore were discovered in both hills. Once mining began in 1957, the Dalli hill

was reserved for manual mining and the reserves on Rajhara hill were exploited for a fully mechanized mine. While the mechanized mines were worked by the regular employees of the BSP, the workers in the manual mines were contract workers.

8. For a more comprehensive analysis of the question of women and technology as it surfaced in Dalli Rajhara, see Ilina Sen's article in *Labour and Capital* (1995).
9. See Ilina Sen's article in Ilina Sen (ed.), *A Space Within the Struggle*, 1990. Also see Anil Sadgopal, and Shyam Bahadur Namra (eds.), *Sangharsh aur Nirman* (Hindi), Delhi: Radhakrishna Prakashan, 1996.
10. The philosophy of integrating struggle and reconstruction owed its ideological roots to the articulation of an independent Jharkhand by Marxist leader, A.K. Roy, and his efforts to achieve this relationship within the larger struggles of the Jharkhand Mukti Morcha. See A.K. Roy, 'Jharkhand se Lalkhand' (Hindi, mimeo), 1984.

REFERENCES

Ghotge, Sanjeev, 2005: *A Critique of the Chhattisgarh Industrial Policy*, National Centre for Advocacy Studies.

Sanket Information Group. 'Chhattisgarh: A State is Born', Bhopal, 2000.

Sen, Ilina (ed.) 1990: *A Space Within the Struggle: Women's Participation in People's Movements*, Delhi: Kali for Women.

——— 1995: *Sukhvasin: Migrant Women of Chhattisgarh*, FES.

——— 1992: *Les Femmes, Le Travail Et La Mine Au Chhattisgarh* in Gerard Heuze (ed.), *Travailler En Inde, The Context of Work in India*, Collection *Purusartha*.

——— 1996: 'Technology and Women: "A Case Study from the Mining Sector in India" in Women and Work in South Asia Contemporary Perspectives, Labor, Capital and Society, vol. 29, nos. 1 & 2.

——— 1996: 'Industrial Restructuring and Women Workers: A Case Study' in N. Rao, et al. (eds.), *Sites of Change: The Structural Context for Empowering Women in India*, FES and UNDP.

Sundar, Nandini, 1997: *Subalterns and Sovereigns: An Anthropological History of Bastar*, Delhi: Oxford University Press.

Shukla, H.L. 2000: *Chhattisgarh Rediscovered*, Delhi: Aryan Books International.

CHAPTER SEVEN

Tribal Movements and the Articulation of Autonomy

VIRGINIUS XAXA

As observed earlier, the Jharkhand movement has been the only tribal autonomy movement which could transform itself into an organized and sustained struggle in mainland India. In other autonomy articulations, this was conspicuous by its absence. An interesting question that emerges is as to why other autonomy articulations could not transform themselves into organized and sustained movements. An equally interesting question is why autonomy demands in the north-east region, even though their articulation excepting for Nagaland were made much later, were relatively more swiftly conceded to than the demand of the separate state of Jharkhand. For an answer to this question, howsoever sketchy it may be, it is necessary to look not only into the structural settings but also the pattern and process of mobilization of Jharkhand and the north-east.

The issue of autonomy at the level of region, community or ethnicity assumes a place of critical importance as it has implications for stability, integrity and unity of India. Region, language and ethnicity though distinct as concepts and categories more often than not, overlap or coincide with each other, at least in the context of India. Indeed states as they exist today are all carved out around a language or related consideration. The regional autonomy has hence tended to be invariably autonomy for a linguistic or ethnic group and vice versa. This is most evident in case of north-eastern states. As to whether the autonomy is to be described as regional or ethnic depends on the character of its mobilization and participation. Ethnic as a generic term has multi-dimensional bases and in India it covers such dimensions as language, religion, nationality, race, caste, tribe and so on. The present paper confines itself to the issue of autonomy raised and articulated by the groups described in India as tribes.

The tribe as a category towards understanding of the complex Indian society was added during the colonial period. Hence many scholars describe it as a colonial construction (Beteille, 1995, Singh, 1993). Though tribe as a category and as a point of reference may be treated as a colonial construction, the image and meaning underlying the term tribe was far from being a colonial construction. There had been much affinity and resemblance between the connotation implied in the term tribe and the image and idea that the larger Indian society had constructed of groups and communities that came to be later described as tribes. There has been no agreement among scholars over the use of the term tribe in the Indian context. They oscillate in their position between the textbook definitions of tribes (i.e. the 'universal' cliché of tribes as introduced in the textbooks in most of the countries) on the one hand, and the recognition of the groups and communities as Scheduled Tribes (ST) under the Constitution for purpose of administrative and political concession on the other. Further it is one thing to use the term and category 'tribe' and another as to determine which groups and communities to be included into it. Since there has been increasing pressures from groups and communities for their inclusion into the category because it is tagged with administrative and political concessions, adoption of uniform and consistent criteria has been compromised.

At the turn of the twentieth century, the term 'tribe' was generally used to identify people who lived in isolation from the dominant community of the region. The dominant communities varied linguistically and culturally from one region/territory to another. Yet they had one thing in common. That is, they were all part of civilizations and shared social organizations (social, economic and political) that were markedly similar. Since tribes in India were conceived primarily as those outside of the civilization, they were invariably represented as primitive or backward even when they were the ruling community in the region. Further, civilizations in India being primarily infused by religions, the colonial authorities conceived tribes as also those falling outside the major religions.

The Indian constitution has enshrined special provisions for the welfare and protection of the tribes. Accordingly, under the constitution the president of the country is authorized to specify tribes or tribal communities or parts within those communities, which shall be identified as STs in relation to a given state. Under the provision the constitutional order of 1950 declared 212 tribes in 14 provinces to be STs. The number of communities so declared stood at over 550 as per the constitutional amendment order of 1976 (Khubchandani, 1992). Interestingly, the Anthropological Survey of India in a recent survey conducted under the People of India Project identified 461 tribal communities in India out of which 174 were subgroups (Singh, 1993). It may be noted that communities scheduled in one state may not necessarily be scheduled in another state. That is, one may belong to the same ethnicity or share the same language, yet one may not necessarily be recognized as a ST in another state.

The STs as per the 2001 census (provisional) account for 84.32 million or 8.2 per cent of the country's total population. Of tribes so identified there are wide ranging diversities among them in respect to their modes of livelihood, ecological features, language and linguistic traits, economic conditions, cultural characteristics, demographic and biological traits, besides of course the regions inhabited. In view of this a lot of dissatisfaction has been shown over the use of the term tribe. In fact, in changed social situations it becomes more appropriate to talk of them as ethnic entities rather than as tribes. Notwithstanding such differences they share features that are similar to each other in many respects, especially in relation to the dominant communities. They resemble each other in respect of their values, belief systems and above all their social structure. They are also similar in another sense. That is, despite the post-independent phase of economic development, they have remained the most stricken by poverty, illiteracy, ill health and other similar features. There has also been increasing erosion of their control over land and other resources.

ADMINISTRATIVE AND ECONOMIC INTEGRATION OF TRIBES

As noted earlier tribes in India are dispersed over the length and breadth of the country. They occupy distinct territory or sub-territory within a given region. By virtue of the fact that they lived in relative isolation from the dominant community they enjoyed autonomy of governance over the territory they lived. Indeed the autonomy of their economic, social and cultural dimensions was built into the very definition of the tribe. The advent of British rule however drew and incorporated them into the larger economic, political and social framework. It is not that tribes did not have such encounters earlier. Many tribes in different parts lived under alien political suzerainty at some point or other. The suzerainty ranged from symbolic gesture of loyalty to the payment of tribute/tax to the political authority. The extension of the British rule was however different. They introduced new and uniform civil and criminal laws. They set-up an administrative structure that was alien. They took control of land and forest and introduced new land and revenue settlements as well as forest laws and administration. They facilitated trade and commerce in the tribal areas and encouraged non-tribes from elsewhere to move on a large scale and settle down in the tribal areas. They imposed various kinds of taxes as well as put restrictions on their social and cultural systems. All these led to the curtailment of autonomy that tribes had so far cherished. A series of outbreaks broke out in the event in the different parts of the country. The fact that these resistances against the alien authority and its collaborators were described in the administrative reports as revolts, rebellions or insurrections is a pointer to the fact that the autonomy question was central in these resistances.

REGIME OF EXCLUSION OF TRIBES UNDER THE BRITISH ADMINISTRATION

In response to resistance, the British administration toyed with the idea of a suitable administrative set-up for the tribes. After much experimenting they came up with arrangements, which were different from those in the non-tribal areas. The distinct legislative and executive measures adopted for tribes aimed primarily at protecting and safeguarding the interests and welfare of the tribes. Since 1874, tribes or tribal areas came to be governed by the Scheduled District Act. As per this Act, the government was required to notify as to what laws were to be enforced in the Scheduled Areas/Districts. Such provision continued under the Government of India Act 1919, which gave power to Indians of self-governance on certain subjects. It may be noted that enactment made by legislature/legislatures were not directly applicable in tribal areas unless so desired by the executive authority. Even under the Government of India Act 1935, tribal areas declared as Excluded and Partially Excluded were not brought under the purview of federal or provincial legislatures (Roy-Burman, 1983; Verma, 1990).

Within this broad framework of administration of the tribal areas, there have however been variations. Broadly, they were of two kinds, which were dependent upon the kind of experience and perception the British had of tribes, on the one hand, and their strategic location in the colonial scheme of administration on the other. For tribes or regions to which the British had an easy access or tribes that were less troublesome, the British adopted one kind of strategy and for the remaining another. The British tried to protect the former through legislative measures, the latter through a combination of legislative and special administrative arrangements. The latter included such arrangements as regulation of movement of people from outside and little tinkering with the existing social arrangement. In the process, the latter came to have an arrangement that gave tribes some kind of autonomy over their life and their resources even after they had become incorporated into the larger political system. The non-tribes were not only restricted from moving into these areas but also tribes were allowed to govern themselves as per their customary laws to a limited extent. That is, the presence of the state through its agencies such as revenue, police or forest department was almost tenuous.

Whereas the former was the case with mainland India, the latter were in vogue in the frontiers of the north-east region. Whether legislative or legislative-cum-administrative, the arrangements were products of strategic considerations of the British coupled with their paternalistic orientation to tribes, especially in the wake of increasing conflict between tribes and non-tribes. It needs hardly any mention that the incorporation of tribes and tribal areas into the colonial state opened up the floodgate for influx of people from the plains leading to massive appropriation of their land and other resources by force, fraud and deceit. The tribal revolt and rebellion that began with the onset of colonial rule and saw unprecedented increase in their occurrences all through the nineteenth century had their genesis in these relations between tribes and non-tribes. The early revolts were the revolt of Pahariya Sirdars (1778), Tamar revolt (1789, 1794–5), tribal revolt (1807–8), agrarian tribal revolts (1811, 1817, 1820). However, it is the revolts that took place after the Great Kol Insurrection of 1831–2 that have received wide attention. The prominent among these revolts are the Bhumij revolt (1832–3), the Santhal rebellion (1855–7), the kherwar/sardari movement (1858–95), the Birsa Munda movement (1895–1900), and so on (Raghavaiah, 1978; Bosu Mullick, 1993).

All these revolts/rebellion had in fact their main roots in their grievances against loss of land by the tribals. The grievances however did not acquire the form of land- or forest-based movement as the issues were intricately connected with over all destabilization of society brought about by the colonial rule and alien administration. Since those who usurped tribal land were outsiders including the British administration, the movement took the form of a revolt against the British rule and the aliens especially the landlords, moneylenders, and traders. Discontent during the period was over the whole system of rule and administration, which besides bringing them under alien authority caused havoc in their lives that they had never experienced before.

THE INDIAN CONSTITUTION AND THE ADMINISTRATION OF TRIBES

The arrangements made for the administration of the tribal areas during the British period were continued within some form in the post-Independent era. Nowhere is this better reflected than in the provisions made in the Indian Constitution for administration of areas inhabited by the tribes. It may be mentioned here that there are various kinds of provisions in the Indian Constitution for the welfare, protection and development of the tribes. There are provisions for representation of tribes in the parliament and state legislatures and in government and semi-government services in proportion to their population. There is provision for protection of their language and culture and for special care towards their social, economic and cultural development. The latter are in important ways tied up with the nature of the administration of areas inhabited by the tribes.

The Indian Constitution makes reference of two areas in this context, viz., the Scheduled Areas and Tribal Areas. The Scheduled Areas, marked on the basis of majority population of the Scheduled Tribes in the district, had provisions for special legislative powers of the governor, governor's report to the president and constitution of the Tribal Advisory Council. The governor for example had the power to stop the extension of the Act of the parliament or the state legislatures to the Scheduled Areas or allow it only with certain modification as deemed fit by him, of course in consultation with the council.

It may be noted that the Act, unlike in the British period, is generally applicable in the Scheduled Areas unless specified otherwise by the governor.

The governors have also been empowered to make regulations for peace and good governance of the tribal people. The regulations centred mainly around prohibition of transfer of land from tribes to non-tribes and restriction of moneylenders' activities in the Scheduled Areas. The provisions so made were however hardly effective [ibid.]. To begin with, tribes were no doubt given rights but they were given these rights without any corresponding powers to enforce them. There were no doubt executive and judicial agencies of the government to enforce it but the enforcement was tardy mainly due to the lack of will on the part of the enforcement agencies. Both the executive and judicial authorities were indifferent and insensitive to the rights of the tribal people. On the other hand, tribes themselves had very little say or hold in these institutions. They continued to be dependent on the benevolence and radical zeal of the sympathetic officials. Not only that but there have also been occasions when the rights so conferred have been withdrawn due to the pressures from the non-tribes. The legislatures that conferred such rights also made it a point to take away such rights when it found it to be inconvenient. The Andhra Pradesh (Scheduled Areas) Land Transfer Regulation 1959, and as amended in 1970, for example, aimed at prevention of transfer of land from tribe to non-tribes. Any transfer of land under the regulation was to be considered null and void. However this provision was withdrawn through a government notification in 1979 mainly due to pressure from the non-tribes. As per this notification all non-tribals who were in occupation of lands—up to 5 acres of wet land or 10 acres of dry land—in the Scheduled Areas should not be evicted under the regulation of 1959. Thus in spite of the Act of restoration in vogue since 1959, as much as 7,51,435.66 acres of land were still in the hands of non-tribals by 1995. Similarly the Kerala Scheduled Tribe (Restriction on Transfer of Lands and Restoration of Alienated Lands) Act was included in the Ninth Schedule of the Constitution for fear of being challenged by a court of law. Yet the act did not go unchallenged. The act as we know was repealed by the Kerala Restriction on Transfer by and Restoration of Lands to Scheduled Tribes Bill 1999 (Bijoy, 1999; Rao, 1996; Verma, 1990).

The tribal areas governed by the Sixth Schedule of the Constitution have been considered as those that formed the erstwhile excluded areas within the state of Assam. Today, most of these areas have been carved out into separate states of their own. While this has been so, the provision under the tribal areas has been extended to some other areas in the north-east, as well such as Tripura. The provisions under the Sixth Schedule purport to provide for a self-contained code for the governance of the tribes living in those areas. Its avowed objective is to ensure considerable extent of autonomy and self-management rights to the tribes so that they may be able to follow their traditional way of life and practices and introduce changes that they themselves desire. In short, the act makes provision for the institutions of the autonomous district and region councils.

This scheme of administration was accepted on three considerations. The social customs and social organizations of the tribal people were distinct from those of the non-tribal people. There was the fear of exploitation of the tribal people by the non-tribal people on account of the latter's superior organization and experience in business. There was also another fear that unless suitable financial provisions were made or powers conferred on local committee themselves, the provincial government might not, due to pressure of the plains people, set apart adequate fund for the development of the tribal areas (JHADC, 1997).

The council has thus been given power as that of a state or union. It has the legislative wing, executive and the judicial wing. The councils have been given power to make laws in matters connected with social customs, land and forest, and so on. They have also been given judicial and regulatory powers in such matters as control of money-lending and trade by non-tribals, establishment of village and town committee, and so on. They also enjoy executive powers in such matters as establishing and managing primary schools, dispensaries, markets, fisheries, ferries, village roads, bridges footpaths, playgrounds, community halls, and so on. It has also initiated measures towards ensuring better health, medicine and sanitation facilities for the inhabitants that come under its jurisdiction (Roy-Burman, 1997; JHADC, 1997).

In view of the powers so vested in the councils, tribes in the north-east have been able to protect themselves from the exploitation of non-tribals to a far greater extent than the tribes of other regions. One of the criteria in terms of which this point could be made is the size of agricultural labourer population among the tribal population in India. Such size has been many times higher in mainland India as compared to the north-eastern region. In fact, the percentage of tribal agricultural labourers in north-eastern states like Mizoram, Nagaland, Manipur, and Meghalaya was mere 3.3, 0.5, 2.3, 13.1, respectively. In contrast, it was as high as 46.6 per cent in Andhra Pradesh, 25.5 in erstwhile Bihar, 38.3 in Orissa, 29.5 in Madhya Pradesh, 39.4 in Gujarat and 55.5 in Kerala (Planning Commission, 2000).

ARTICULATION OF THE DEMAND FOR AUTONOMY

Although organized movements for autonomy either within Indian Union or outside were on the whole absent in the early years after Independence, the articulation to this effect by certain tribal leadership had not altogether been absent. Jharkhand in contrast did not get autonomy and the movement continued. The autonomy demand meanwhile had begun to be aired in other places as well. Such articulation was far and few in mainland India. Other than the demand of Bhilisthan (state for the Bhil tribes), Gondwana (state for the Gond tribes) and Jharkhand (state for the people of Jharkhand), there was hardly any such voice heard. There had also been a separate state demand for south Gujarat tribes in the 1970s. However, with the exception of Jharkhand, others failed to take the form of a sustained movement.[1]

The stirring of autonomy movement by tribes in the form of separate state could be traced to the period preceding the end of the British rule. However, in its nascent form it had already begun to be articulated in the 1920s. The tribal leadership in Jharkhand as well as Nagaland had already made reference to it at the visit of the Simon Commission to India in 1929. The difference was that while tribal leadership in Jharkhand was articulating separate state *within* India, the Naga leadership was referring to a *sovereign* state. After India became independent, the movement for a separate state, both in Jharkhand and Nagaland assumed intense mobilization and mass participation.

Unlike in mainland India, the movements for autonomy have been widespread in the north-eastern region. The movement in Nagaland turned out to be violent and the Indian government has to deploy the army. Soon as a part of the strategy to contain the movement, the Nagas in 1963 were granted a separate state within the Indian Union. The Nagas were however unhappy with the autonomy and the struggle for sovereign autonomy continued. It has also been most fiercely fought. However, by the 1960s the movement for a separate state began to gain wide currency among the tribes living in the hill districts of Assam. These comprised the Khasi Hills, Jaintia Hills and Garo Hills, which now form the state of Meghalaya; Lushai Hills, which constitutes the state of Mizoram; and the districts of North Cachar Hill and Mikir Hill in the present state of Assam which are still agitating for a separate state.[2] Paradoxically enough, these regions/districts already had certain degree of autonomy, which was hitherto not enjoyed by tribes including hill tribes in other states of the region such as Tripura, Manipur, Arunachal Pradesh, viz., the erstwhile NEFA.

The autonomy that the hill tribes of Assam enjoyed was contingent upon the special system of administration that was introduced there. The areas coming under such administration was known as the Sixth Schedule Areas. They were governed by the Sixth Schedule provisions of the Constitution. Under the schedule there was a provision for the constitution of autonomous district/regional councils as per the rules laid down for its constitution. The council enjoyed legislative, executive and judicial powers. There were matters such as land, inheritance, marriage and divorce, forest (other than reserved forest), on which it could enact laws. It could impose and collect taxes, establish schools and dispensaries, construct roads, canals, and so on. Under the provisions, the tribes thus enjoyed autonomy in respect of matters falling under their jurisdiction. They had the power of self-managing their economy, society and culture. Even an act of the parliament or state legislature could not apply automatically unless it was specifically extended by the governor.

Notwithstanding the autonomy enjoyed by the tribes of the hill districts, the demand for further autonomy in the form of a separate state came to the surface. The demand soon got transformed into a strong movement. There was intense mobilization and widescale participation of the people in the movement. In Mizoram, the erstwhile Lushai Hills district, the movement moved in the direction of cession from India. The demand for a separate state was eventually conceded and the state of Meghalaya and the Union Territory of Mizoram were created. In Mizoram even after the grant of larger autonomy, the struggle for cession from India continued. Indeed the movement came to be marked by widespread armed struggle, which came to an end with the signing of an accord in 1986.

How does one explain the autonomy movement that took place

in the hill districts of Assam, which already enjoyed autonomy under the Sixth Schedule of the Constitution? The answer lies in the fact that the autonomy they were provided with had in practice many limitations. To begin with, though the autonomous district councils gave some powers to the tribes in respect of determining many aspects of their life, the powers provided suffered from limitations.[3] The limits to power came from two sources. One was the limited power given to the institution of the district council. Law-making power in general was constrained by the fact that until the governor gave assent, the law promulgated by the council would have no effect. That is, a law enacted by the council had no effect unless given assent by the governor. At the same time, while the district councils expected the governor to exercise his discretion in the matter, the judicial pronouncement expected the governor to be guided by the advice of the Council of Ministers. Hence, although the governor had absolute power *vis-à-vis* the district councils, he invariably exercised it at the advice of the Council of Ministers. Thus the district council could be dissolved at will, as and when it was inconvenient to the state government. Even its acts or regulations could be annulled or suspended. Such doings by the governor had its root in the politics of the state, which was invariably dominated and dictated by the community that was numerically, economically and politically dominant. Needless to say that the political competition at the state level, especially along ethnic lines, acted as an obstacle to the functioning of the autonomy at the district level.

The district councils had provisions for executive function in respect of several matters listed in the Sixth Schedule but without any mandatory development function. At best, the concerned state governments, with the consent of the council, assigned development functions to them (Chaube, 1973; Roy-Burman, 1997). The sources of revenue of the district councils or of the regional councils were and have been specified in the Constitution itself, but some of the major sources of revenue were under the control the state government. And the latter was expected to pass on the share of the council after due computation which sometimes took years. An important fact to note is that some of the revenue raising powers of the autonomous councils in the Sixth Schedule Areas were less than the powers envisaged for Gram Panchayats in non-tribal areas in some states (Roy-Burman, 1997). Since funds collected through tax, license and other means by the council were meagre, the council had to depend on state government for funds for carrying out administrative and development activities. Along the years, the disbursement of funds by the state governments to the district councils revealed to be far from smooth and adequate.

The second and the main source of the limit to the power of the district councils came from the actual politics of the state of which the tribal regions were a part. One of the major aspects of politics at the state level was the deep divide between the tribes and non-tribes or the plains people and the hill people. The roots of this divide besides being geographical were also social, cultural, linguistic and even economic. Whereas the people in the plains practised settled agriculture and represented the Hindu social structure and culture, the same was not the case in the hills. The predominant form of agriculture was shifting cultivation and their religious practices were characterized either by animism or Christianity which the missionaries actively spread from the nineteenth century onwards. As noted above, non-tribes who were numerically dominant and socially and economically powerful dominated the state-level politics. Not only was their tendency to dominate the tribes, but the politics was also to thwart and scuttle the functioning of the institution by blocking grants and creating other impediments (Chaube, 1973; Roy-Burman, 1997). In the hill districts of Assam, the demand and movement of the tribal communities for a separate state emerged out of a situation where the district councils failed to cater to the needs and aspirations of the tribal people.

With the grant of separate states to erstwhile hill districts of Assam, the autonomy demand and movement did not come to a halt in the region. Rather it opened up the space for such articulation in new areas/groups of the region. Of these areas, the movement has been more intense, violent and widespread in tribal inhabited hill areas of Tripura and Bodo inhabited areas of Assam. It is interesting to note that the Bodos and Tripura tribes, though situated in the north-east, did not have the provision of the autonomous district councils as the case had been with the other hill tribes of the region. This had historical root. The historical process which the Bodos and Tripura tribes went through differed from those of the hill tribes of Assam. The tribes in Tripura who until Independence constituted a numerical majority became numerical minority after the Independence due to exodus of the Bengali population from erstwhile Pakistan, now Bangladesh. This unprecedented demographic change also led to erosion of control over land, forest and other resources. In Bodo-inhabited areas of Assam too, migration of the Assamese as well as the Bengali population had been going on since the British rule. As a result large-scale alienation of lands from tribes to non-tribes had gone on for near about a century. This not only affected the demographic but also the cultural pattern of the region. There was much acculturation to Assamese and Bengali languages as well as to Hindu religion and the corresponding social structure.

Whereas the hill tribes of erstwhile Assam came to be governed by the Sixth Schedule provisions, it was not so in the case of the Bodos and Tripura tribes. They did not even enjoy the provision of the Fifth Schedule that had been applicable to the tribal people in mainland India, where they constitute majority population. Rather, general laws and regulations applicable to the population at large governed them, even though being areas predominantly inhabited by tribals. Like in the erstwhile hill districts of Assam, here too there was widespread participation of the people in the separatist movement. The movement is popularly known as Bodoland Movement in case of the Bodos. The separate state movement articulated by the tribal people in Tripura was not known by a distinctive name. The participation in the movement included road blockade ranging from 24 to 100 hours, demonstration in front of government offices, processions and rallies in which participation of men and women especially youth was most pronounced. In response, the government came out with extension of certain autonomy to the people in the form of autonomous regional councils (ibid.).[4] Notwithstanding the government's response, the demand and agitation for the creation of a separate state has not come to a halt in the two areas. Autonomy so granted has fallen far short of their demand for a separate state. And hence the movement is still on. Of course, the kind of support and participation the people have lent to the movement has been on the wane. The movement has passed into the hands of small group or groups of people who have taken recourse to armed struggle and have been demanding cessation from India.

With this, there has now even been a charge in the form of articulation. That is, there is now an articulation for cessation from India. In Tripura this had its genesis in late 1970s; in Bodoland this began with the signing of the Bodo accord in 1993. The movement for a separate state is still going on in the hill districts of present-day Assam, which have the provision of the Sixth Schedule areas. Hence the districts already enjoy some autonomy in the form of autonomous district councils. These districts had the option of being part of Meghalaya when Meghalaya and Mizoram were formed. However, the option was not acceptable to the people. The long-standing demand for a separate state thus continues in these districts.

Autonomy has overwhelmingly marked the tribal movements in north-east India. Other types of movements in the region, though not altogether absent, have been few and less striking. In contrast, movements other than autonomy have been the characterizing features of tribal movements in other parts of India.

FAILED AUTONOMIST MOVEMENTS IN TRIBAL-DOMINATED REGIONS OF PENINSULAR INDIA

The demand for a separate state for Gonds, the major ST community in central India, came to be more sharply articulated after Independence although echoes of it were there even before Independence. In a memorandum submitted to the States Reorganization Commission in May 1963, the Gond leaders had made demand for the formation of a separate state for the Adivasis, to be carved out of the tribal areas of Chhattisgarh and contiguous districts of the Rewa region and Vidarbh (Singh, 1983). A number of organizations had reiterated the demand. However, the demand remained merely at the level of articulation. It failed to translate itself into a sustained and an organized movement. The reasons have been referred to later in the discussion.

The same could be said about the demand for autonomous Adivasi states in south Gujarat, which was voiced for the first time by an Adivasi MLA in the State Legislative Assembly in 1969. A conference too was held and a demand was made, but an organized movement did not follow. The demand here was primarily employed as a strategy to gain some benefits or concessions for the tribal people (Desai, 1983). The main divide between tribal political movements in India is that in the north-east, they tend to move in the direction of creating greater space in the form of autonomy, even to the extent of being secessionist, whereas in peninsular India they are instrumental in the sense that they aim at betterment of the ST community's status by ensuring access to livelihood and other related issues.

THE JHARKHAND MOVEMENT

The only autonomy movement worth the name in these parts of India has been that for Jharkhand. In fact, this movement has been one of the longest struggles for autonomy in India. The echo of a separate state for the tribals was already in the air in the late 1920s. By the late 1930s, an organization by name of Adivasi Mahasabha had already been formed to spearhead the movement for a separate state. In the years after Independence, an intense mobilization started to support the demand. In fact, in the very first legislative assembly election held after Independence, the Jharkhand Party bagged as many as 30 seats in the Bihar assembly.[5] In fact, it was the major opposition party. This spectacular success in the assembly election was largely due to the demand of a separate state for the tribals. There was also a massive participation of the people when the States Reorganisation Committee visited Ranchi. The committee however found the demand untenable on the ground that tribals spoke different languages and they comprised only a little over one-third of the population. The demand was accordingly rejected. There was a lull in the movement but the demand was kept alive.

The Jharkhand Party formed to spearhead the movement got

disintegrated into a number of splinter groups. Soon, other organizations emerged and began to aggressively articulate the demand for separate state of Jharkhand. Prominent among these organizations have been the Jharkhand Mukti Morcha (JMM) and All Jharkhand Students Union (AJSU).[6] The demand was partly conceded when Jharkhand was granted autonomous regional council status with some legislative as well as executive functions.[7] By this time the separate state of Jharkhand had become an important electoral issue and national political parties just could not ignore it. In a sense, it was the constraints of electoral politics, which set into motion the formation of the separate state of Jharkhand. The constraint itself was the result of a long-drawn struggle carried out by the tribals and, at a later phase, also by the Jharkhandi non-tribals.

One of the important commonalities that Jharkhand movement shared with the Nagas is that the groups involved in the movement represented heterogeneous tribal groups in the sense that they spoke different languages and occupied different territories. In Nagaland there were about 13 tribal groups. Similarly in Jharkhand there were about 29 tribal groups. The movement was, however, principally spearheaded by a small number of tribal groups.

In Jharkhand, the tribes that have been the backbone of the movement have been the Santhals, Mundas, Oraons, Hos, and Kharias. In Nagaland the moving force behind the movement have been the Angamis, Aos, Semas, Lothas, and so on. The societal feature in reference was valid to a great extent in the case of hill districts of Assam as well. But excepting this feature, there have been striking differences, especially in respect of structural features.

To begin with, Jharkhand was marked by a large influx of people from outside since the onset of the British rule. At the same time the tribal people had been squeezed out of their territory to fill in the need for cheap labour required by the British capital. This had serious impact on the demographic structure of the tribal population in the region. Alongside these processes, there was large-scale alienation of land from tribes to non-tribes, a process, which has continued to this day. Thus tribes have lost very substantively their control over land and other resources. Nagaland had to witness none of these features. The features described in reference to Jharkhand were also markedly absent in the Sixth Schedule Areas in the state of Assam. The policy adopted by the British towards these tribes to begin with, and later by the Indian state, had made this possible. The absence of a large presence of non-tribals, coupled with control over land, forest and other resources gave the tribes strength to fight the government, which was hostile to the tribals and their interests. Equally important was the strong articulation of their cultural distinctiveness *vis-à-vis* the non-tribals, in which the place of language was very important.

In fact, it was the issue of the imposition of Assamese—the language spoken by the Hindu and caste population in Brahmaputra Valley of Assam—as the medium of instruction in schools even for tribals, which provided the immediate spark for the demand for a separate state in the hill districts of Assam. There were however a few autonomy movements in north-east which shared much of the structural features of Jharkhand. This has been the case with tribal autonomy movements in Tripura and Bodo autonomy movement. Like in Jharkhand tribes in Tripura and Bodos have gone though the similar demographic and social processes.

This has not only affected the demographic but also the cultural pattern of the region. Acculturation to Assamese and Bengali languages as well as to Hindu religion and its social structure has also been quite marked, as has been the case with Jharkhandi tribals as well. Again, the relation of the Bodos and tribals in Tripura, in respect of the state government, has been similar to those in Jharkhand. Despite these commonalities, there has been one striking difference, especially with the Bodos. Whereas, the Bodo movement is solely waged by the Bodos and for the Bodos, the Jharkhand movement was spearheaded by a number of tribal groups.

The mobilization in the north-east has been on the whole more focused on the issue of autonomy. As far as the pattern of mobilization is concerned, it has ranged from peoples' peaceful participation in programmes such as rallies, *bandhs* and public meetings to use of violence of one form or another against the non-tribals and, more importantly, against the armed forces. It has also taken the form of violence against police and other armed forces. Generally mobilization has been peaceful in the early phase of the movement.

It has also been characterized by wide participation of the people. However, with the passage of time most of the autonomy movements have turned out to be violent. They have even acquired the form of armed struggle by organized bands or groups.

In the case of Jharkhand movement, however, while the use of violence has not altogether been absent, its use has been sporadic in comparison to north-east India. Further, in the Jharkhand movement, often the issues of separate state got entangled with the issue of land, forest, displacement from development projects, and discrimination in employment in government and public sector undertakings. Mobilization in Jharkhand, unlike in the north-east was less sharply focused on the issue of autonomy.

As for the question as to why other autonomy demands in the non-north-east India could not be translated into organized and sustained movements, there could be many answers. However, what seems to be most glaring is the absence of a dynamic middle class howsoever tiny it may be. The size of employment of tribals in the tertiary/service sector could be taken as a pointer. This in case of tribes is contingent on advantages that tribes have been able to take of the reservation facilities. The sad fact is that tribes on the whole have not been able to take advantage of it. As per the report of the National Commission for Scheduled Castes and Scheduled Tribes, tribals represented only 2.89 per cent in Group A, 2.68 per cent in Group B, 5.69 per cent in Group C and 6.48 per cent in Group D in the central ministries at the beginning of 1995. As regards public sector enterprises, their representation at the beginning of 1996 was 2.27 per cent in Group A and 3.52 per cent in Group B services (National Commission for SC&ST, 1996). This has much to do with the lack of literacy and hence the lack of critical educational attainment (ibid.). Equally important is the lack of sharp cultural boundary between tribes and non-tribes (Bose, 1975; Sinha, 1965; Bailey, 1961). Loss of tribal language coupled with high level of Hinduization has weakened the cultural boundaries. The mark of identification of tribes as Adivasis was surely an important and necessary factor for articulation of a distinct identity but this was not sufficient to translate it into an actual political mobilization process.

So we can conclude that where tribes have gone through increasing marginalization in the sense of loss of control over land, forest and other resources and where there has been no provision of autonomy whatsoever, the articulation of autonomy movements has been on the whole weak. The tribal situations in central, western and southern India bear witness to this. The only exception has been the case of Jharkhand in eastern India. This means that pauperization and expropriation do not necessarily lead to autonomy movements. They are important but not sufficient as one can see from cases other than that of Jharkhand.

It is equally interesting to ask here as to what made the autonomy movement in Jharkhand sustainable whereas the same could not be sustained in other parts of mainland India. One can identify a number of factors, which were present in the case of Jharkhand but were marked by absence elsewhere in the region. One of them is that the tribes in Jharkhand had a long history of struggle against the colonial rule and outside exploiters. This helped them forge a shared identity despite differences of language and region occupied by them. The exploitation and domination that continued in the post-Independence era only reinforced the shared historical identity. In sharpening this identity the role of a tiny but an articulate middle class has been very crucial. It is the middle class which felt the most intense sense of discrimination and domination that they and their fellow tribesmen were subjected to in respect of the benefits of development, employment, trade, commerce, and so on. Indeed their position in independent India is almost the same as those of the Indian middle class under the colonial rule. What also helped to keep the struggle alive was the intense communication among the middle class, which was facilitated by the growth of towns in the tribal region. The middle class initially moved in the direction of acculturation but halted the process once social mobility become possible through political mobilization (Orans 1965).

Equally important has been the strong sense of identification with their language and culture. This identification sharpened the difference between tribes and non-tribes. This sense of identity was also marked off by identity of distinct religion, especially Christianity. Indeed in many ways Christianity contributed to the vitality and vibrancy of tribal language and culture. It were the Christian missionaries who gave new lease of life to tribal languages by giving them scripts, introducing them as medium of instruction, codifying tribal customs, traditions, songs and music. This of course does not mean that they did not cause any damage to tribal culture. The damage was most pronounced in areas that were thought as non-conducive to the promotion of the Christian ethics and values. The movement for autonomy in Jharkhand was thus rooted in cultural differences between tribes and non-tribes on the one hand and the uneven character of development between them on the other.

Unlike in central, western and southern India, the movements for autonomy have been widespread in the north-eastern region. They have also been most fiercely fought out there. Interestingly the articulation of autonomy in the north-east has its genesis not so much in marginalization as in fear of losing their distinct language, culture, customs and traditions on account of domination by an alien language and culture. In short, the basis of autonomy in the north-east was the issue of distinct identity. The social origin of autonomy movements and the degree of their mobilization thus lay not so much in pauperization and marginalization as in other factors. Sinha's formulation in the case becomes quite pertinent. In his view tribal solidarity is positively correlated to convergence of the following factors. These range from ecological and socio-cultural isolation *vis-à-vis* the core peasantry and a certain level of numerical strength to provide striking power, on the one hand, to location near international border and a certain level of literacy and education to provide elite leadership on the other. The historical experience of conflict and opportunity for political rank combined with limited scope for economic rewards are also adduced to the above factors (Sinha, 1972). At the root of such movement lies the strong sense of identity politics, which in the context under reference has primarily been articulated in opposition to the dominant regional community. There is, of course, an identity politics in peninsular India as well but it has assumed forms other than that of autonomy movement. Rather one of the dominant forms of identity politics here has been the divide between Christians and Hindus in which the role of agencies like the VHP and other outfits has been critical. Identity politics in terms of political autonomy as noted earlier in the discussion has been on the whole weak.

To conclude the autonomy movements by the tribals in India have not all been of the same nature, level and character. Broadly they have been articulated in the form of demand for separate states within the Indian union. It is when these have not been forthcoming that the demand has been raised for cessation from India. This is not to deny movements that have been secessionist in character from the outset, but such movements have, however, been few.

NOTES

1. For details of these movements refer relevant articles in K.S. Singh (ed.), *Tribal Movements in India*, vol. 1.
2. For accounts of the movements among different tribes of the region see the articles contained in K.S. Singh (ed.), *Tribal Movements in India*, vol. 2; also *Hill Politics in North-East India* by S.K. Chaube.
3. The power conferred on the district council has already been referred to earlier.
4. For details on movements among the Bodos and Tripura tribes, refer to the relevant articles in K.S. Singh (ed.), *Tribal Movements in India*, vol. 1.
5. See in this volume Cyril Robin, 'The Creation of Vananchal: Reassessment of the Jharkhand State'.
6. For a comprehensive account of the history of the movement and organizations involved see *Jharkhand Movement* by A. Tirkey, also K.S. Singh, 'Tribal Autonomy Movements in Jharkhand', in K.S. Singh (ed.), *Tribal Movements in India*, vol. 2.
7. Refer Tirkey's work for provisions granted under the regional council.

REFERENCES

Bailey, F.G., 1961: '"Tribe" and "Caste" in India', *Contributions to Indian Sociology*, 5.

Beteille, A., 1995: 'Construction of Tribes', *The Times of India*, 19 June.

Bijoy, C.R., 1999: 'Adivasis Betrayed: Adivasi Land Rights in Kerala', *Economic and Political Weekly*, 34 (22).

Bose, N.K., 1975: *The Structure of the Hindu Society*, tr. Andre Beteille, Delhi: Orient Longman.

Bosu Mullick, S. 1993: 'Jharkhand Movement: A Historical Analysis', in M. Miri (ed.), *Continuity and Change in Tribal Society*, Shimla: IIAS.

Chaube, S.K., 1973: Delhi: Hill Politics in North-East India, Delhi: Orient Longman.

Desai, I.P., 1983: 'The Tribal Autonomy Movement in South Gujarat', in K.S. Singh (ed.), *Tribal Movements in India*, vol. 2, Delhi: Manohar.

Jaintia Hills Autonomous District Council (JHDC), Meghalaya (1997): Seminar Paper on Autonomy of Self-Governance (Mimeograph), DCRC, University of Delhi.

Khubchandani, L.M., 1992: *Tribal Identity: A Language and Communication Perspective*, Shimla: IIAS.

Orans, M., 1965, *The Santhal: A Tribe in Search of Great Tradition*, Detroit: Wayne State University Press.

Planning Commission, 2000: *Tribes in India* (*A Data Sheet*), Govt. of India.

Raghavaiah, V.R., 1978: 'Tribal Revolts in Chronological Order: 1778–1971', in A.R. Desai (ed.), *Peasant struggles in India*, Bombay: Oxford University Press.

Rao, B. Janardhan, 1996: 'Tribal Land Rights, Government Action and Socio-Political Movements' (Mimeograph), Rajiv Gandhi Institute for Contemporary Studies.

Ray, Niharranjan, 1972: Introductory Address in K.S. Singh (ed.), *Tribal Situation in India*, Shimla: IIAS.

Report of the National Commission for Scheduled Castes and Scheduled Tribes, 1996.

Roy-Burman, B.K., 1983: 'State and Tribes in India', *Mainstream*, 26 November.

——— (1997): 'Sixth Schedule and Seventy Third and Seventy Fourth Amendments of the Constitution', Keynote Address at Workshop on Decentralisation and Self-Governance: Experience of a District Council in Northeast India (Mimeograph), DCRC, University of Delhi.

Singh, K.S., 1993: 'The Problem', in 'Marginalized Tribals', *Seminar* (412).

——— 1983: 'Tribal Autonomy Movements in Chotanagpur', in K.S. Singh (ed.), op. cit.

——— 1983: 'The Gond Movements', in K.S. Singh (ed.), op. cit.

Sinha, S., 1972: 'Tribal Solidarity Movements in India: A Review', in K.S. Singh (ed.), *Tribal Situation in India*, Shimla: IIAS.

Sinha, S., 1965: 'Tribe-Caste and Tribe–Peasant Continua in Central India', *Man in India* 42(1).

Tirkey, Agapit, 2002: 'Jharkhand Movement: A Study of its Dynamics', AICFAIP & Other Media Communications, Delhi.

Verma, R.C., 1990: *Indian Tribes through the Ages*, Delhi: Govt. of India.

CHAPTER EIGHT

Mapping the Scheduled Tribes: Questioning the Creation of New States in India

BERTRAND LEFEBVRE

INTRODUCTION

Some of the latest debates surrounding tribal population can be apprehended with census data and methods of geography. The creation in 2000 of the new so-called tribal states (Chhattisgarh and Jharkhand) is clearly a question where geography matters. Such *modus operandi* is not new in the Indian tribal policy. The creation of Nagaland in 1963, and Mizoram, Meghalaya and Arunachal Pradesh in 1972 wished to offer new administrative and political territories to channellize the independence and autonomy aspirations of the tribal populations. These creations were often a tool facilitating the implementation of development programmes and offering a more direct support from the central government to the tribal populations. As noted by Saha and Srivastava (1983), the tribals from these states received much more subsidies from the central government than their counterparts from central India. Such policy has partly explained the good performance of these states in social development (e.g. literacy) and the weakening of political movements calling for Independence. The creation of Chhattisgarh and Jharkhand was often introduced as a second wave of tribal states. One of the main arguments for the creation of these new states was to give the tribal population from central India new territories to improve their political representation and to accelerate their development, thanks to decentralization and tools of governance.

We wish to analyse how such agenda was translated into the territorial formation of two new administrative and political entities. Confronting these new states with the spatial distribution of Scheduled Tribes (ST) we wish to question their legitimacy and their relevance as new territories for better political representation of tribal populations. Mapping census data can help us to have a rejuvenated look on this debate. Being more like an exploratory technique, spatial analysis can rarely confirm theories but it at least can deny false ones or truncated discourses (Goodchild and Janelle, 2004: 7). By focusing on the geography of ST population, our objective is to offer a critical perspective on the concept of tribal state. In this paper, we wish also to present general facts about the tribal population in India as others contributions from this collective volume are focused on particular cases or questions.

This chapter is organized into three sections. The following section discusses the relevance of census data to approach ST population and its geography. The next section introduces the present spatial distribution of ST population in India with regard to the formation of Chhattisgarh and Jharkhand. The third section discusses the territorial formation of Chhattisgarh and the delineation of new borders along the process.

SCHEDULED TRIBES, CENSUS AND GEOGRAPHY: STORY OF A MISSED ENCOUNTER

There is a long tradition of statistical production in India dating back from the British Raj period. An exhaustive census gathering social and demographic information on population has been regularly held since 1870. Such amount of information allows us not only to study long-term trends but also to make comparison between territories or to focus on a particular population, in our case, the tribal population.

Before proceeding any further, it is of great interest to understand how the tribal population has been defined by the Census of India through time. The definition has shifted from a religious basis to an 'origins' base in 1941. The Constitution of 1950 gave birth to a list of STs and a list of Scheduled Areas mainly based on the 1936 list of Backward Tribes promulgated by the colonial administration (Maharatna, 2005: 13). A few decades later, this system was dropped because of its limitations. Tribal communities living outside the Scheduled Areas could not be recognized as STs, leaving them out of the reservation policy and development programmes of the central and state governments. In 1976, the area restriction on tribal identity was cancelled, the list of STs becoming applicable on every part of the state. As the restrictions to the definition have been removed, the recognition of STs has become wider and the question of their representation a matter of greater concern. Some states and union territories like Punjab, Haryana and Delhi do not have any list. The state-wise character of the lists makes it difficult to follow the widespread of certain tribal groups or migrations.

According to the last Census (2001) the STs population is 84 million, that is 8.33 per cent of the Indian population (Table 8.1). The ST population has risen by 25.37 per cent between 1991 and 2001 (Indian population: 21.34 per cent). In fact, the growth of the tribal population during the past century has broadly followed the general demographic trends in India. As mentioned before, the increase of ST share in the Indian population is mainly due to a wider recognition of the tribal population and less restrictive norms for the definition of STs. If the number of STs is increasing at the national level, some states have been more active in their recognition policy, particularly when tribal local-level activism has met state support like in Maharashtra and Karnataka (Maharatna, 2005: 23).

As pointed out by Arup Maharatna (2005), the data coming from the Census of India have remained untapped by researchers interested in Indian tribal population. The study of tribes in India has for long been a matter of interest for anthropologists who pay little attention to aggregative data. Their methodology, usually based on a micro-level perspective, has often led them to be sceptical of approaches observing tribal population as an aggregated population. This kind of opposition is broadly an artefact. The geographers for instance, are quite familiar with the multilevel approach and the need to understand a phenomenon either geophysical or social, at different scales. The unity of the STs as a category should not overshadow the diversity existing within this population. There have been some attempts in the past decades to

TABLE 8.1: STATE-WISE DISTRIBUTION OF SCHEDULED TRIBES IN INDIA (2001)

State	ST pop 2001	% ST India	% ST	Group	% ST India
Jammu & Kashmir	1,105,979	1.32	10.90		
Himachal Pradesh	244,587	0.29	4.02		
Uttaranchal	256,129	0.30	3.02		
Uttar Pradesh	107,963	0.13	0.06		
Bihar	758,351	0.90	0.91	G.1	4.20
Daman & Diu	13,997	0.02	8.85		
Goa	566	0.00	0.04		
Kerala	364,189	0.43	1.14		
Tamil Nadu	651,321	0.77	1.04		
Andaman & Nicobar	29,469	0.04	8.27		
Sikkim	111,405	0.13	20.60		
Manipur	741,141	0.88	31.00	G.2	2.17
Tripura	972.301	1.16	34.37		
Arunachal Pradesh	705,158	0.84	64.22		
Nagaland	1,748,779	2.08	89.28		
Mizoram	839,310	1.00	94.46		
Meghalaya	1,992,862	2.37	85.94	G3	6.52
Dadra & Nagar Haveli	137,255	0.16	62.24		
Lakshadweep	57,321	0.07	94.51		
Assam	3,308,570	3.94	12.41		
West Bengal	4,262,884	5.07	6.42		
Andhra Pradesh	5,024,104	5.98	6.59	G.4	19.02
Karnataka	3,390,819	4.03	7.13		

Rajasthan	7,097,706	8.44	12.56		
Jharkhand	7,087,068	8.43	26.30		
Orissa	8,145,081	9.69	22.13		
Chhattisgarh	6,616,596	7.87	31.76	G.5	53.54
Gujarat	7,481,160	8.90	14.76		
Maharashtra	8,577,276	10.20	8.85		
Madhya Pradesh	12,233,474	14.55	20.27	M.P.	14.55
India	84,062,791	100.00	8.33		
Madhya Pradesh (b. 2001)	18,850,070	22.42	23.22		
Bihar (b. 2001)	7,845,419	9.33	7.14		

Source: Census of India, 2001.

use the census data related to STs, particularly through mapping the results. A map can offer a powerful angle to explain a process or to reveal correlation between areas or populations. The map is indeed the most simple and intuitive way to shed light on the spatial context in any data analysis (Goodchild and Janelle, 2004). *An Atlas of Tribal India* (Raza and Ahmad, 1990) was at the beginning of the 1990s an outstanding publication. Including 188 plates and many detailed tables, this book offered an exhaustive view on the demographic, social and economic situation of STs. Even if most of the data was sourced from the 1971 and 1961 censuses and thus somewhat dated, the authors tried to study the tribes in a historical and comparative perspective. Unfortunately after this project, no major publication has come out. It is surprising in comparison of the incredible development of Geographic Information System (GIS) and mapping software during the same period. The *India: An Illustrated Atlas of Tribal World* (Mandal et al., 2002) offers very poor information regarding tribal populations and their geography. Published in 2002, but using the 1981 census data, the text is mostly descriptive, offering very little analytical scope. The district-wise maps, lost in the middle of pictures of tribals, and geophysical maps are here only as a poor illustration of the ST settlements. The Census of India has published an atlas on STs using district-wise data from the last two censuses that aims at reviving the use of maps in social sciences (Census of India, 2005). The number of variables is impressive, covering a large range of fields from the demographic to social and economic features in 1991 and 2001. The maps and their commentary are presented in a very rigorous manner but leaving very few space for in-depth analysis. Data produced by the Census of India can be used in a more analytical perspective and thus can offer an instructive scope on debates surrounding the Indian tribal population.

THE GEOGRAPHY OF ST POPULATION AND THE NEW STATES: A GEOGRAPHICAL DISCREPANCY

In this section, we will present the ST population's spatial distribution in India with regard to the formation of the new states of

Chhattisgarh and Jharkhand. The tribal population has of course a specific geography. It is often the practice to present this geography by gathering state-wise (Table 8.1) results on a so-called regional basis (north, east, south, west). It is also pointed out that due to the different sizes of the states, the state-wise share of ST must be analysed in relation to the total tribal population in India. In our opinion and keeping in mind the idea of questioning the creation of new tribal states, we thought it better to build our analysis not on a regional basis but using this absence of statistical correlation at the state level. The lack of statistical correlation between the share of ST and the total number of ST is indeed very instructive on the various situations faced by tribal population in each state. The political representation of tribes or their integration into the mainstream may not have the same significance and impact from one state to another according to their share or their number. Obviously, there is no question of integration into the mainstream when tribal population is the majority of the state's population.

Creating a chart based on the share of ST in each state population and the contribution of each state to the Indian tribal population, we built an instructive typology of five groups on the various situations that exist across India (Fig. 8.1). The list of states can be read from Table 8.1. This typology will allow us to question the impact of the creation Chhattisgarh and Jharkhand on the shifting balance of ST population between these states and their originating states. But using only state-wise data would be far from being satisfactory as it doesn't inform us on the sharp local contrasts that exist within states such as Madhya Pradesh or Maharashtra in term of tribal presence. For instance around 40 per cent of the ST households in Maharashtra are concentrated in five districts out of thirty-five. Mapping the share of ST population in the total population for 2001 at a sub-district level (5,459 subdistricts, Map 8.1) will give us a deeper understanding of the changes in the ST spatial distribution.

The first group of states (G.1) is marked by negligible ST presence either by their share or in number. All these states together host only 4.2 per cent of the total ST population in India. We find some of the smallest union territories (Daman & Diu, Andaman

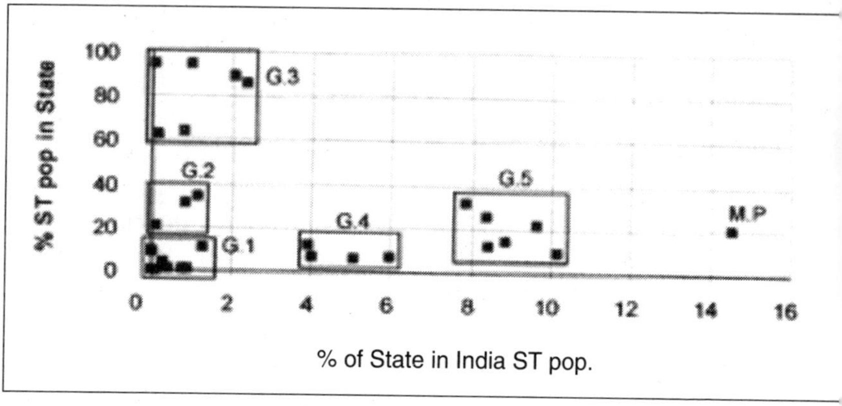

Fig. 8.1: Classification of Indian States according to ST Population (2001).

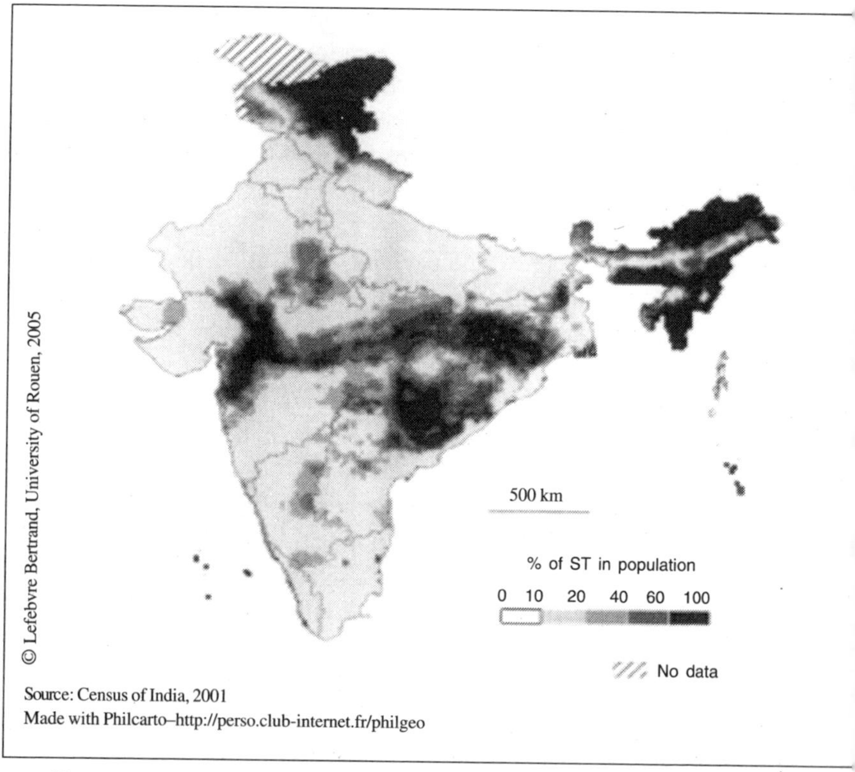

Map 8.1: The Spatial Distribution of ST Population in Sub-districts (2001)

& Nicobar) and some of the most populated states in India like Uttar Pradesh, Tamil Nadu or Bihar. Historically most of these plain areas have never hosted important tribal groups. It is only in some of the mountainous parts (e.g. Jammu & Kashmir) that some tribal clusters can still be found.

The second group (G.2) is characterized by a small number of ST (<1 million pop.) but their presence can be seen as much more significant with a ST share exceeding 20 per cent of the total state population. The states of Sikkim, Manipur and Tripura are all located in north-east India and were princely states at the time of British colonization. The tribal presence has been eroded for long now. In Tripura the migrations of Bengali workers are dated back from nineteenth century and were part of the British Raj strategy to control and develop the colonial economy. In 1874, 64 per cent of the population was ST. In 1911, the share felt sharply to 36 per cent of the population. In 2001, the share of ST had now stabilized around 34 per cent. In Manipur, the formation of a Hindu kingdom during the seventeenth century and the following 'Hinduization' of the population from the valley left the ST population in the hilly parts of the state. A sheer contrast can be read from Map 8.1 between the Hindu valley and the tribal hills.

In the third group (G.3) the tribal population represents the majority of the state population (always > 60 per cent). Like the second group, most of the states are located in north-east India. Contrary to Tripura and Manipur, detribalization and Hinduization did not occur in these remote areas. As no feudal administration was effectively controlling these tribal areas, the British administration drew an inner-line to exclude these remote tribal margins from Assam (Saha, 1988: 257). Thus, no massive labour migrations were enforced. It is only at the time of Independence that some migrations from Assam and eastern India started to gain impetus. In Arunachal Pradesh the share of ST population declined from 89 per cent of the total population in 1961 to 64 per cent in 2001. The migrants mainly settled in the valley areas of Arunachal Pradesh (e.g. Dibang Valley, Lohit) just across the former inner-line.

The fourth group (G.4) presents a completely different profile from the previous group. Apart from Assam the share of ST in this group is always below the national average. This trend is balanced by a significant number of ST, always exceeding 3 million of ST population. These four states altogether host almost one fifth of the total ST population in India. Assam and West Bengal are welcoming some of the most populated tribes like Santhals and Mundas. With Andhra Pradesh they are on the margins of the main tribal population clusters (north-east and central India). Interestingly Andhra Pradesh and Karnataka are also known for their recognition policy for the past decades. Some secondary isolated tribal pockets can be seen from the map in these two states.

The fifth group (G.5) corresponds to more than the half of the total tribal population in India. In all the states composing this group, the share of the ST is largely exceeding the national average and the total number of ST in each state is more than 6 million. We could attach Madhya Pradesh (MP) to this group even if the great number of ST (more than 14 million) put this state in a distinct position compared to the others. The tribal belt that runs through central India crosses all these states. While Moguls and Marathas claimed their rights over these tribal areas, their suzerainty was rarely enforced, keeping tribals on the margins (Saha, 1988: 256). This tribal stronghold came under rapid erosion only in the colonial era (Sinha, 1962: 71 cited in Saha, 1988). The enforcement of land property rights and the development of moneylending turned tribesmen into a cheap workforce, forced to leave their lands and to migrate (e.g. to tea plantations in Assam). Hindu and Muslim migrants from the plains following the steps of the colonial administration outnumbered the remaining tribesmen in many parts of the tribal belt. Such shift in the balance of population can be seen on the map. Saha describes such movement as 'the territorial collapse of the tribal social formation' (Saha, 1986: 63, cited in Saha, 1988). We can picture the gradual erosion of ST presence on the fringes of the tribal belt like in Rajasthan and Madhya Pradesh. We can even spot the formation of isolated pockets where the share of ST is now under 20 per cent of the total population like in Orissa and Chhattisgarh.

Another major learning from Map 8.1 is the trans-state character of the ST population geography. High concentration of STs can be found on both sides of many state borders, for instance along the Gujarat-Madhya Pradesh-Maharashtra border. This is mainly the consequence of the States Reorganisation Commission (SRC) that reshaped interstate boundaries of India in 1955 according to the main regional linguistic areas. The continuous tribal territory was fragmented into several parts which became districts on the margins of the newly created states. Tribals became demographically marginalized in many big states like Maharashtra and Gujarat while their territory became fragmented. In the north-east, the tribal margins of Nagaland, Mizoram, Meghalaya and Arunachal Pradesh were merged with the Assam state. The upsurge of insurgent tribal movements fighting for Independence, or for better recognition of their identity has led to the creation of new states or union territories in the north-east. This first wave of new-born tribal states in the 1960s and 1970s was reshaping the boundaries of the 1955 SRC. The tribals were granted territories where they represented the large majority of the population. Map 8.1 shows clearly the remaining perfect match between these state boundaries and the ST population geography from the north-east.

Keeping in mind this experience and all the main features from Map 8.1 and the Table 8.1 and Fig. 8.1, scepticism prevails about the relevance of the new tribal states and their boundaries. The creation of these new states was supposed to improve the representation of ST in the population and thus in the state apparatus. The creation of Chhattisgarh and Jharkhand had a different impact on the repartition of tribal population between them and their former state (MP and Bihar). While 90 per cent of the ST population from former Bihar are now living in Jharkhand, only 35 per cent of the ST population from former MP are living in Chhattisgarh (Table 8.1). The new Bihar is now a state with a very low presence of STs (G.1) while Madhya Pradesh remains the leading state in terms of the number of tribal population. The creation of Jharkhand has improved the representation of tribals: while the STs were representing only 7 per cent of the total population in former Bihar, they count now in Jharkhand for 26 per cent of the total population.

Compared to this new situation, the 'gain' appears to be very poor in MP. Before the creation of Chhattisgarh the share of ST in MP was around 23 per cent of the total population. In the truncated MP the share has fallen to 20.27 per cent and in Chhattisgarh it has risen up to 31 per cent. In any case, the ST populations in both states are far from representing the majority of the population, contrary to most of the north-eastern states. The delineation of the new boundaries has a lot to explain for the weak tribal presence in the new states. Chhattisgarh offers a good example of such mismatch.

IN SEARCH OF CHHATTISGARH: A TRIBAL STATE WITHOUT TRIBALS?

During the debates in the Lok Sabha on the Madhya Pradesh Bill (2000) geography was been often mobilized to justify the creation of Chhattisgarh (Lok Sabha, 2000). Going through the minutes of the debates is particularly insightful on the agenda behind the territorial formation of Chhattisgarh.

> Chhattisgarh is itself a culturally and geo-graphically complete State. There is no controversy over borders, over survey numbers. [. . .] Chhattisgarh has natural resources in abundance. It has the best diamond mine and other mineral areas. This Chhattisgarh region is integrated from the viewpoint of language, geographically and culturally. (*Shri Vikram Verma*)

> The Chhattisgarh was known earlier as Dandakaranya, Gondvana, Dakshin Kaushal or a zone of 36 forts. [. . .] Chhattisgarh is enriched with mineral like iron ore and other valuable minerals and has 46 per cent forest cover. [. . .] Out of twelve thousand varieties of rice in the world nearly ten thousand varieties are found in this area alone. (*Shri Suresh Pachouri*)

> Chhattisgarh has been a well-organized State from geographical and cultural point of view since thousands of years. [. . .] Chhattisgarh has got immense natural and archeological wealth. About 45 per cent of its land area is covered with forests. Its forest produce include Tendu leaves, Gond, Green Amla, Bahera, Mahua, Chiraunji, etc. which are in plenty. Coal, diamond, limestone, uranium, tin, etc. are found in abundance in this area. Maximum species of paddy are produced there and therefore, this area is called, 'the rice bowl. (*Shri Bhagatram Manhar*)

Geographically, Chhattisgarh is bigger than Punjab, Assam and Haryana. Chattisgarh is covered with lush green forest. Tendu patta of the area is of a good quality and the bamboo forests are very famous. There are plenty of herbal plants which are yet to be exploited. If the rivers of Chhattisgarh are exploited in future a huge quantity of electricity will be generated. Hundred per cent of diamond, tin ore and quartz ore are in Chhattisgarh. I would like to assure the house that the Chhattisgarh State though small, will be a prosperous state. (*Dr. Charan Das Mahant*)

On reading these quotes, geography is indeed more conceived as a nomenclature (bigger than Punjab) or in a naturalist (natural abundance, from mines to rice and forests) and ecological (how to exploit the natural resources?) sense. The enumeration of the geo-physical or environmental features is supposed to show the unity of Chhattisgarh so as to prove its supposed geographical equilibrium. These so-called geographical features were used to 'naturalize' the birth and the existence of a constructed political entity that lacked long-lasting political and social demand, contrary to the case of Jharkhand. Reading the Lok Sabha minutes on the Madhya Pradesh Bill (2000), the tribal populations are never a matter of great interest, except to explain that along with SC and OBC they represent the majority of the population. The ST population and their geography are never used as an argument to justify the creation of Chhattisgarh, which has to be created more because of its great natural resources potential, than the great improvement it will provide for ST population in terms of local development and political representation.

Such debates may explain why the borders dividing Chhattisgarh from Madhya Pradesh do not find any grounds, just considering the geography of ST population. Many eastern sub-districts from Madhya Pradesh have share of ST in their population equivalent to the sub-districts from the northern area of Chhattisgarh (Map 8.2). There was some discussion in the Lok Sabha during the Madhya Pradesh Bill (2000) to include six more districts from Madhya Pradesh to Chhattisgarh (Umaria, Shahdol, Sidhi, Dindori, Mangla and Balaghat). This demand has remained unsatisfied even if four of these districts have a ST population exceeding 44 per cent of the total population (Map 8.2). Including these districts would have added 2.7 millions of STs to Chhattisgarh and improved by two points the share of tribals in the newborn state. Many districts or sub-districts in Orissa, Maharashtra and Andhra Pradesh neighbouring Chhattisgarh could have been added in this respect. While in the 1960s the tribal states were built on a very homogeneous basis giving birth to new political and administrative entities with a majority of tribals, the latest interpretation of 'tribal state' is creating new territories where the tribal population is a relative majority and is spatially marginalized. The geography of ST population in Chhattisgarh refers to the same centre-periphery model that prevailed in the Assam previous to 1963 (Map 8.2). The three north-eastern districts and the two southern districts from Chhattisgarh host 52 per cent of ST population of the state. In the heart of Chhattisgarh and particularly around its capital Raipur, the ST hardly represent 10 per cent of the total population. Such contrast raises a lot of questions in terms of development objectives and territorial segregation. Being so far from, or so few, in the new political and administrative set-up of the state how are tribals expected to influence decisions? We can even consider that new tribal states could be created from Chhattisgarh. The three northern-eastern districts host around 1.5 million tribal population representing 53 per cent of the total population of these districts. The southern districts host around 1.4 million tribal population representing 71 per cent of the total population of these districts. These demographic figures are very similar with the profile of the north-east Indian states (Fig. 8.1, G.3). In fact, these two areas are inherited from the princely states of Bastar in south Chhattisgarh and Surguja, Oodeypore, Jushpore in north Chhattisgarh.

CONCLUSION

Twenty years ago, Suranjit Kumar Saha stated that 'without secure territorial bases of political power, it is unlikely that the tribals of middle India will ever have an equitable share of the economic development' (Saha, 1988: 267). He further added:

> A more appropriate and mature political response to these expressions of legitimate grievance of the tribals would be to carve two, or possibly three states, out of the

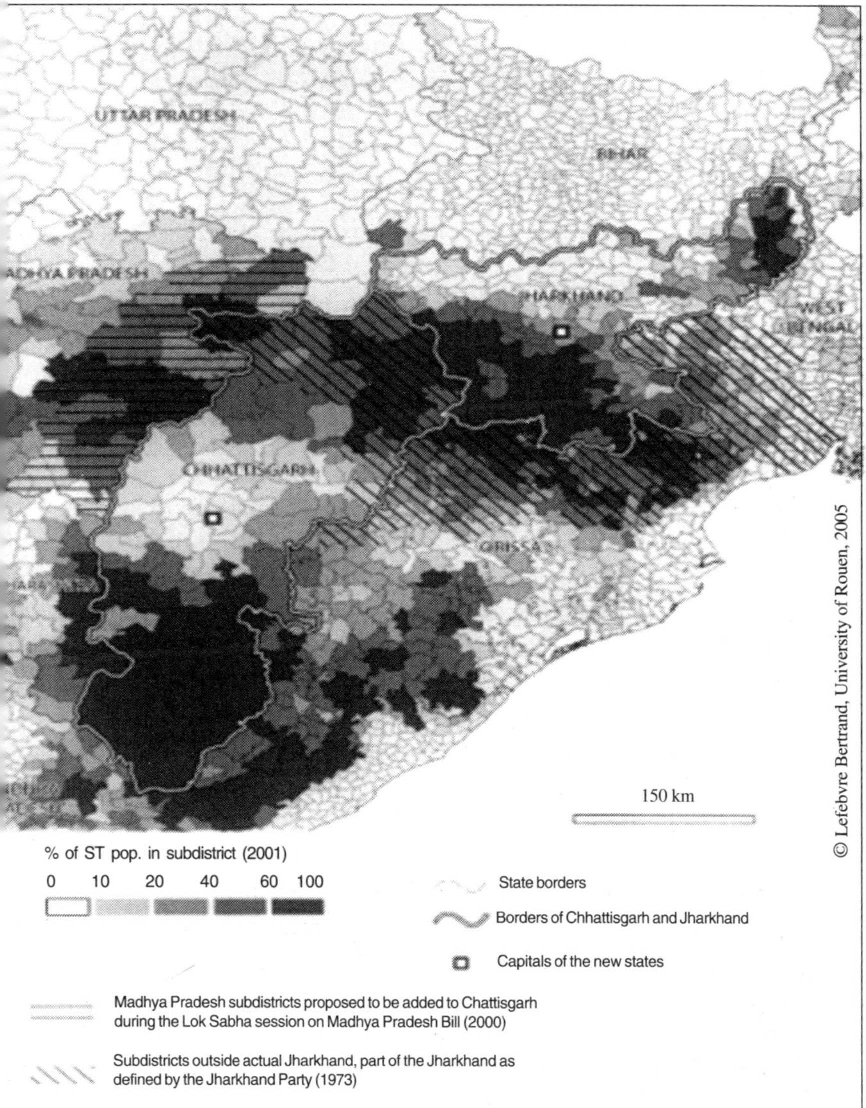

Source: Census of India, 2001

Made with Philcarto–http://perso.club-internet.fr/philgeo

Map 8.2: The Formaiton of Chhattisgarh and Jharkhand

contiguous tribal districts of middle India. [. . .] Creation of these new states will enable the tribals of the region to control the apparatus of State power in their own home territories. Such tribal control on State power is an essential precondition for effective implementation of tribal development programmes and loosening the stranglehold of the forces of exploitation currently operating in the tribal area. (ibid.: 268)

The creation of Chhattisgarh and Jharkhand are answering the request of S.K. Saha. At first glance, it seems a mature political decision and a much awaited tool to give better political representation and economic power to the tribals. But something went missing on the way. Chhattisgarh and Jharkhand are dividing the biggest tribal pockets from the tribal belt without offering to the tribal population new political territories where they are representing the majority of the population. Keeping in mind the necessary homogeneity of tribal population's presence in the new states, the delineation of the Chhattisgarh and Jharkhand boundaries is far from being satisfactory. On Map 8.2 we can see the area once claimed to be part of Jharkhand by the Jharkhand Party in 1973. The area covers large parts of Orissa and Chhattisgarh. It could have been another possible territorial formation for Jharkhand state. Following S.K. Saha's suggestion, it would have been more relevant not to create only one tribal state but probably two out of the former Madhya Pradesh. The western part of Madhya Pradesh hosts a large tribal population but it has not benefited from the reshaping of Madhya Pradesh (Map 8.1). The major western tribal cluster remains divided between Gujarat, Madhya Pradesh and Maharashtra. The absence of any important natural resources, contrary to Chhattisgarh or Jharkhand, may have been seen as a major obstacle for improving local democracy and tribal political representation in western Madhya Pradesh.

Indeed, the real issue may lie in the relevance of the state as the best political tool to improve local democracy and encourage decentralization towards tribal population. S.K. Saha assumed that following the north-east tribal states cases, the creation of new states in central India should tackle most of the social, political and economic challenges faced by the tribal population. Looking at the first years of Chhattisgarh and Jharkhand, the non-tribal social and economic elites brought by Hinduization and colonization in the tribal belt of central India seem to have hijacked the concept of tribal state to their own profits. While colonization meant the training and inclusion of tribal elites in the British administrative system in areas like Nagaland, the same meant the displacement of tribal populations and the arrival of new administrative elites in central India. The historical dimension should not be overshadowed by spatial and territorial considerations in the making of new administrative and political territories. We have to keep in mind the spatialism's risk that leads to focus on maps and forget about the composite and dynamic aspect of an area and a society. A high level of ST presence does not necessarily mean that strong political claims do really exist for state creation. The diversity in terms of ST presence all over India should not be underestimated; leading us to state that there is only one way to improve political representation of tribal communities. Different tools were already implemented at the time of creation of new tribal states: the policy of seats reservation in local and national assemblies, the Sixth Schedule of the Indian Constitution that gives more autonomy to tribal areas, the existence of tribal councils. At the national and state levels, different programmes exist to help the tribal population to improve its political and socio-economic status. The Census of India produces a wide range of data on social and economic issues that could help improve the efficiency of such programmes with a more territory-sensitive approach. As we tried to demonstrate in this paper, geography as a science has much to offer to political and social debates in present India.

ACKNOWLEDGEMENTS

I would like to thank Samuel Berthet and Rémy Delage for their comments on this paper.

NOTE

1. Excluding Punjab, Haryana, Chandigarh, Delhi and Pondicherry where no STs are registered.

REFERENCES

Census of India, *Scheduled Tribe Atlas of India*, Census of India, 2005.

Goodchild, M.F. and D.G. Janelle, 2004: 'Thinking Spatially in the Social Sciences', in M.F. Goodchild and D.G. Janelle (eds.), *Spatially Integrated Social Science*, Delhi: Oxford University Press, pp. 3–17.

Maharatna, A., 2005: *Demographic Perspectives on India's Tribes*, Delhi: Oxford University Press.

Mandal, R., S. Mukherjee and A. Datta, 2002: *India: An Illustrated Atlas of Tribal World*, Delhi: Anthropological Survey of India.

Raza, M., and A. Ahmad, 1990: *An Atlas of Tribal India*, Delhi: Concept Publishing Company.

Saha, S.K. and K. Srivastava, 1983: 'Federalism and Inter-regional Resource Allocation Policy in India', *Third World Planning Review*, 1983, vol. 5, no. 1, pp. 37–56.

Saha, S.K., 1986: 'Historical Premises of India's Tribal Problem', *Journal of Contemporary Asia*, vol. 16, nos. 3–4, pp. 274–319.

———, 1988: 'The Territorial Dimension of India's Tribal Problem', in M. Shepperdson and C. Simmons (eds.), *The Indian National Congress and the Political Economy of India, 1885–1985*, London: Gower Press, pp. 253–69.

Sinha, S., 1962: 'State Formation and Rajput Myth in Tribal Central India', *Man in India*, vol. 42, no. 1, pp. 35–80.

Synopsis of debates (Proceedings other than Questions & Answers), Lok Sabha, 31 July, n.p., http://parliamentofindia.nic.in/lsdeb/ls13/ses4/31072k.htm [accessed on 4 March 2009].

CHAPTER NINE

PESA: De-centering the Political Economy Tribal Empowerment in the Global Context

SAVYASAACHI

It is now over ten years since the 'Panchayat Raj (Extension to Scheduled Areas) Act 1996' (PESA) has been in the political arena (for details see Appendix 1).

It was expected that this Act would be a useful tool for tribal self-rule. Today in 2009 we can ask how PESA has fared on the ground. There are several organizations and researchers who are currently taking stock through empirical, consultative and participatory processes. The result of their research is awaited. In the meantime, there are several questions that need attention.

Some of these questions are: What are the provisions in PESA relating to the objective living conditions of the people (tribal and non-tribal) in the Fifth Scheduled Areas? Do the provisions enable the struggle for tribal self-rule? Do its provisions realign political forces (tribal and non-tribal) to hold back forces of destructive development? Do its legal provisions create adequate conditions and appropriate spaces for the enrichment of tribal traditions and customary practices? Do these provisions also create opportunity for traditions to respond to contemporary questions of conservation and development?

I have tried in this paper to look at PESA in the global-national context, at all level of states and with reference to the village context.

In the conditions created by WTO-Sponsored neo-liberalization of the economies across the world with special emphasis on the countries of the south (the so-called developing countries), India is a financial hot spot and all policy measures have been designed to welcome with open arms outside investors. The government tries to put in place adequate policies and programmes for this purpose. PESA is one such example. It is interesting that the language of PESA nowhere suggests this. However, if we read PESA in the global context and alongside other concurrent legislations, we can get a sense of the underlying design. This aspect is discussed in the first section of this essay.

In 1996 PESA was acclaimed as a progressive legislation that gave constitutional recognition to tribal customary rights, and also empowered the tribals to take decisions in accordance with these rights. This was seen as a progressive step towards self-rule. There are three sets of questions related to this issue.

What is the impact of this empowerment on the relations between the tribal and the non-tribal people? For instance, PESA started off a political process (Hindu reaction) of 'bringing back the tribal to the Hindu social fold from Christianity'. From this it is obvious that such empowerment was threatening to a section of non-tribal people. How did this affect the empowerment process? This aspect is discussed in the second section of this paper.

How effective is PESA in preventing these corporate players from subverting the customary tribal traditions and rights? This question is addressed in the third section of this paper.

Is this empowerment of customary rights sufficient in the global context, to equip the tribal people adequately and appropriately for self-rule, to meet on equal terms these corporate international players? This question is addressed in the fourth section.

PESA: INDIAN POLITICAL ECONOMY IN THE GLOBAL CONTEXT

There is resonance across the changes in the global context, in the legal regime in India and the enactment of PESA.

The crisis in world economy in the latter half of the twentieth century (1970s and 1980s) on account of an alarming depletion of natural resource base, amongst other things, led to a paradigmatic transformation of production lines. National boundaries were opened up for speedy movement of factors of production. Faster technologies were introduced and transnational commodity chains governed by the market started to determine relations of production. The state gradually began to function in accordance with the market and created new commensurate legal regimes.

The years 1986 and 1989 are significant. In 1986 India opposed the framing of a new GATT arrangement at the Uruguay Round of GATT negotiation.[1] In 1989 however the Government of India had to agree[2] to the new GATT arrangement. This new arrangement was to include agriculture and intellectual property rights, amongst other things. In 1989 the smashing of the Berlin Wall turned the war between the economies of free market and state-planned communist economies in favour of the former. This sped up the Uruguay Round[3] of talks which then moved on to the formation of the WTO in 1995.

In India, simultaneously, in 1986 the L.M. Singhvi Committee submitted its report recommending constitutional status for panchayats. In 1988 the Parliament Consultative Committee appointed a sub-committee under the chairmanship of P.K. Thungan to consider constitutional amendment. On 15 May 1989 the Constitution (64th Amendment) Bill was introduced in Parliament.[4] Though the Constitution Bill won a two-thirds majority in the Lok Sabha, it failed in the Rajya Sabha.

In 1991 the Indian government formulated its New Economic Policy and the Congress party government introduced the 72nd (Panchayats) and 73rd (Municipalities) Constitutional Amendment Bills, which were passed in both chambers in December 1992 as the 73rd and 74th Amendment Acts, and came into force in 1993. In 1995 four years after the New Economic Policy, India became a founder-member of the WTO.

These changes launched the Indian economy on the path of neo-liberalization.[5] This was the global backdrop of PESA.

PESA was enacted in 1996 (within the frame of the 73rd Amendment), only a year after India, along with other founding members, ushered in the WTO.

The national context of PESA is the long history of tribal movements that have struggled for autonomy and self-rule. It goes back as far as the revolt of the Pahariyas in 1778. This was followed by the Koli disturbance (1784–5) and the revolt in Tamar of Chhotanagpur (1789; 1794–5). Thereafter records show at least eighty recorded events of confrontation—acts of minor protest and major revolts—by tribal people in different parts of India until 1971.[6]

The enactment of PESA in 1996 was viewed as a cumulative success of these struggles. The greater success was the formation in 2000 of two new tribal states Jharkhand and Chhattisgarh four years after PESA.

The provisions of PESA empower the Gram Sabha and gives constitutional legitimacy to tribal traditions.[7] For instance, 'A State legislation on the Panchayats that may be made shall be in consonance with the customary law, social and religious practices and traditional management practices of community resources.'

At the same time, the provisions also open the way for land acquisition and rehabilitation. The significant point here is that this cannot be without consultation of the Gram Sabha. This is clear from the following clause:

> The Gram Sabha or the Panchayats at the appropriate level shall be consulted before making the acquisition of land in the Scheduled Areas for development projects and before re-settling or rehabilitating persons affected by such projects in the Scheduled Areas; the actual planning and implementation of the projects in the Scheduled Areas shall be coordinated at the State level.

This clause clearly affirms that the state can acquire land for development (neo-liberalization). This is in agreement with other legislations undertaken by the Government of India that prepared the ground for new factors of production introduced by the WTO. Two years after PESA, in 1998[8] the Government of India drafted the 'National Policy, Package and Guidelines for Resettlement and Rehabilitation', and also the Land Acquisition (Amendment) Bill. In 2007, yet another policy on both was tabled for public debate. This latest version detailed the process of rehabilitation and land acquisition and came in the wake of acquisition of land for Special Economic Zones.

The provision for land acquisition and rehabilitation open the way for multiple industrial players (regional, national and international) and for speedy movement of all factors of production (human resource, commodities, finance, information, technology) across national, regional and local boundaries. These provisions give constitutional legitimacy to the private sector to work in tribal areas with corporate projects and displace large number of people.

Thus under PESA there is opportunity to use natural resources (in consonance with traditions) only where tribal people are fortunate to not be displaced by development projects. In other areas, the tribal people have to now compete for these natural resources. For this they can participate, in principle, at different platforms at the local, regional, national and global levels, where the local and regional can sit alongside the national and global stakeholders to negotiate development agendas. For instance a Maria tribal from Bastar could come to Delhi to attend a UNDP meeting and sit on the table along with representatives of the Government of India, the World Bank and NGOs. Such a meet can also happen in Bastar.

PESA, CENTRE AND THE STATE

Does the PESA Act empower the Gram Sabha adequately and appropriately to meet and negotiate with the private corporate stakeholder? An important aspect here is the impact of PESA on the relation between the tribal and the non-tribal people.

PESA is a central legislation. Its impact in the nine states[9] where PESA has to be extended to the Panchayats (Andhra Pradesh, Bihar, Gujarat, Himachal Pradesh, Maharashtra, Madhya Pradesh, Orissa and Rajasthan, Chhattisgarh and Jharkhand) is not yet fully understood.

All the states have to adopt PESA as required by the law within one year of its passing by the centre or else PESA would be automatically applicable. Madhya Pradesh has made rules but has failed to notify them. Chhattisgarh adopted MP's rules after bifurcation but also has not notified the rules. Maharashtra made an amendment to its Gram Panchayat (GP) Act in 2003 but it is still unknown in most circles. Not notifying means that the law cannot be implemented and by inference that it is not adopted. It is clear that in several states the governments are reluctant to operationalize the PESA mandate.[10]

In a detailed analysis of PESA, Upadhyay[11] (2004) 'delves in some detail into the manner in which the States' have subverted the mandate of the central legislation through carefully using the wordings in law to make the implementation vague and ineffective, especially in the context of 'community resources' in Scheduled Areas.

In Jharkhand the *Times of India* of 21 September 2005 reported:

The Jharkhand State Assembly, on 29 March, adopted a resolution that the union government should be requested to amend the Panchayat (Extension to Scheduled Areas) Act of 1996 to facilitate the de-reservation of the post of panchayat heads in the areas where the Scheduled Tribe population is below 40 per cent.[12] Agitations and counter-agitations have been going on intermittently . . . over PESA, and the momentum picked up after the High Court on September 2 termed a provision in the PESA as unconstitutional. The second provision of clause (g) of section 4 of PESA that gives hundred per cent reservation to tribals to head all the three levels of the local self-governance bodies in scheduled areas was termed by the court as excessive, unreasonable and against the principles of equality as prescribed under Article 14 of the Constitution.[13]

Further,

The landmark judgment against the Central Act (PESA[14]) passed by Parliament after deliberating on Bhuria committee report has triggered resentment among tribals who accused the Arjun Munda government of failing to put up the case in a proper perspective during hearing of a bunch of Public Interest Litigation (PIL) filed for and against the act.[15]

PESA seems to have provided the opportunity to the ruling class to consolidate its position to not let PESA become operational. There is more-willful violation,

The Panchayat Extension to Scheduled Areas or PESA Act of 1996 requires gram sabhas to be consulted for land acquisition. And yet, in Jharkhand, and in Orissa, this has either been systematically ignored or, as a recent report from the field documents, the police surrounds the gram sabha meetings and threatens the ordinary members, forcing them to agree to the proposal of giving up their lands at throwaway prices (*Down to Earth*, 31 October 2006).[16]

The interests of the ruling class lie with corporate industrial development which is in agreement with the agenda for the globalization of the economy.

Corporate players are interested in the rural market for consumer goods and large-scale development projects related to land, water, forest and minerals such as, building of dams, hydroelectric power plants, mining, and commercialization of agriculture. These projects are insensitive not only to the fragile ecosystem but also to tribal customary practices.

For instance, the Rs. 300 crore state-of-the-art project in Chhattisgarh is another effort of the National Mineral Development Corporation (NMDC) in eco-friendly mining. The unique Romelet technology developed by Moscow Institute of Steel and Alloys (MISA), Russia, will be used for the first time in the world to extract iron from iron ore slimes. With the plant, this backward area of Bastar district will soon appear on the industrial map of India.[17] The plant is likely to be commissioned by May 2005.[18] The construction of the proposed Romelet Steel Plant at Hiranar was abandoned because of the opposition of the people in early 2000. Now the Chhattisgarh government has planned to shift it to the Nagarnar.[19] According to recent updates Steel Minister Ram Vilas Paswan and Chhattisgarh chief minister jointly laid down the foundation stone of this NDMC initiated steel plant in Nagarnar village. It is expected that production would begin by August 2011, Paswan informed. (http://www.bombaynews.net/story/402478). Similarly in Jharkhand,

> To the dismay and disillusionment of mass movements in Jharkhand, newly elected government officials plan to uphold agreements struck by the previous State government with leading steel and mining companies. In return for 169,198 crore Rupees (app. US $3.8 billion) of investment, these agreements promise companies massive land acquisition for their mines and steel plants, which will deforest no less than 57,000 hectares of forest and displace 9,615 families, many of them located in legally protected Scheduled Areas set aside for indigenous Adivasi peoples in the State.[20]

Why this reluctance?

The demographic structure is in favour of the non-tribal population. The census of 2001 shows that in states to which PESA is extended the tribal population is in a minority. It ranges from 6.6 per cent of the total population in Andhra Pradesh to 26.3 per cent in Jharkhand (see Appendix 2).

The amendments necessary for PESA to become effective will undermine the interests of the ruling class which is predominantly non-tribal people either by birth or in their thinking. There is need for appropriate amendments in state laws/acts which impinge on specific provisions contained in the Central Act namely (i) Land Acquisition Act; (ii) Excise Act; (iii) State Irrigation Act; (iv) Minor Forest Produce Act; (v) Mines and Minerals Acts; (vi) Land Revenue Code/Act; (vii) SC/ST Land Alienation Act; (viii) Moneylenders Act; and (ix) Regulated Market Act. No doubt, some state governments (MP) have already amended some of the relevant acts, while others are yet to follow suit.[21]

These amendments will legally strengthen the Gram Sabha to have control over prospecting of minor minerals, planning and management of water bodies, management of minor forest produce,[22] and prevent alienation of land (including the power to restore any alienated land of a ST).

PESA AS INSTRUMENT FOR STRUGGLE FOR TRIBAL RIGHTS

To what extent can PESA be instrumental for struggles for people friendly agenda for development and hold back forces of destructive development?

Some significant facts about the Nagarnar Steel Plant in Bastar, as reported, are as follows:

> National Mineral Development Cooperation decided to establish a steel plant at Nagarnar in May 2001. The NMDC in collusion with the state officials contrived acquisition of land. People resisted. . . . Chhattisgarh State PUCL went to the area for a fact finding mission and found out that the district administration along with the police had lathi charged and fired upon the people in order to make them abide by the unlawful intention of the state.

The National Scheduled Caste and Scheduled Tribe Commission on the basis of inquiry conducted under Article 338(5) of the Constitution came to the conclusion that the acquisition process was violative of the Constitutional mandate for the Scheduled Areas.

The advice of the National Commission was totally ignored and pressure was mounted for taking over the law wrongfully. The people insisted that they can have a dialogue only after the NMDC and the state government restart the process on the basis of the recommendations of the National Commission. The concerned Gram Sabha also decided to have a joint assembly on 2–3 March 2002 in which the concerned officials of the state and NMDC were also invited. The invitation was also extended to a number of National Dignitaries to come and advice on the issues, which concern the democratic governance at the village level in Scheduled Areas. The concerned officials of the Government did not respond, the police did not allow the high dignitaries like Siddhraj Dhadda, Vandana Shiva, Dada Geetacharya and senior journalist Manimala. Nevertheless the joint assembly was held on 2nd but was adjourned on 3rd because of the unseemly restrictions and honoured guests being returned.

As it seems, the state government, under the pressure of inviting foreign capital, is hell bent on suppressing the people's right over livelihood resources, throwing their constitutional provisions and legality of its own action to the wind. The state is behaving in such a way in its hunger for foreign capital that it can go to any extent suppressing and butchering the people and their democratic voice.

The joint assembly of Gram Sabha in its resolution made it clear that they were not opposed to the establishment of steel plant. However, the Assembly resolved that the guidelines must be followed and complete rehabilitation package including land for land should be prepared for all directly and indirectly affected in the likely zone of influence of the steel plant. It was also resolved that the agreement must also provide safeguards against privatization as in Balco in the form of shareholding for the community. The local officers conveyed to the people that all but two of their demands were acceptable. The people asked for a formal response which could be placed before the Joint Assembly of Gram Sabhas for their consideration.[23]

PESA helped the struggle. Its utility is perhaps not more than compelling the state to follow the provisions of the act with regard to land acquisition and rehabilitation.

At least in this case PESA has not been useful to critique the design of development programmes from the perspective of tribal traditions and customary practices.

It is not possible to make generalizations on the basis of this example. There could be other instances where PESA has been used differently.

PESA AND TRIBAL TRADITIONS

In the global context to confront corporate international players does PESA and the Forest Right Act, 2007 equip the tribal people adequately and appropriately for self-rule, and to meet these players on equal terms?

The PESA empowerment of customary rights extends only to MFP and the entire forest (see Appendix 1). Studies show that even this is far from being realized. It has been argued that the rights over MFP cannot be de-linked from rights over the forest. This limitation was sought to be overcome with the Scheduled Tribes (Recognition of Forest Rights) Bill, 2005. This forest bill seeks to extend tribal people's right to the forest.

It would benefit the forest-dwelling STs in all the states. Besides recognizing their traditional rights over the forest land under their occupation and their habitat for self-cultivation for their livelihood and providing them access to, use or disposal of minor forest produce, it will also remove from their psyche the threat of eviction or removal from the forest land under their occupation. They will also be entitled to the benefits of various schemes of the government after vesting of clear-cut title of land in their favour.[24]

What is the relation between these institutions and the legal Panchayat institutions?

For instance, in Abujhmarh, Bastar, and Chhattisgarh, the Sarpanch (head, legal Panchayat institution) and the Kasar Gayata (head of the customary institution) are two different people. The former is accountable to the district magistrate and the latter is the caretaker of the village on behalf of Mother Earth. The former can be from any clan, while the latter is from the clan that first settled the village. Before PESA was enacted the Sarpanch was more powerful than the Kasar Gayata because he had the power to use money for specific development programmes, such as digging bore wells and making roads.[25] Will the Kesar Gayata recover his power and prestige under PESA?

According to Vasavi, an activist press correspondent, 'Munda, Oraon, Kharia, Ho and Santhal continue to respect their tradition of social and political practices'. Their political system is the foundation of a cultural notion of *consensual democracy* and collective community lifestyle. It defines and regulates social rights over resources, which is based on the collaboration of men and women. Among the Mundas, this system is called Parha Raja. It is based on the exogamous sub-division of a clan. The Parha does all the work. The orders of the Parha Raja prevail over the whole clan and the villages where the Mundas live. The *Khuntkatti* land of the Mundas is sacred for all the villagers. This land is taken care of and worshipped under the authority of the Parha Raja.

In the Kolhan area, which is called Ho Dishum, the Munda-Manki system prevails. In the ancient traditional land system, the king's land was called *maanjhihas*, the queen's personal land was called *devri*, the land given for worship by the tribal kings was called *devottar*, and the social and cultural land of the Sarna was called *sarna-asthal*.

Among the Santhals and Pahariya in Santhal Pargana, there is a system of Manjhi-Haram, Manjhi-Pargana and Dishum Pargana. Among the Pahariya there is the system of the chief or the head. These systems settle the socio-cultural and political matters and undertake administrative and judicial work. Historically, these systems were relatively safe during the Mughal period than during British rule. The colonial process of destruction of the traditional system increased at a sharp rate after Independence.

Vasavi observes that today there is a clash between the people's political-social systems and the legal rational system of the government. The government compelled by the 73rd Constitutional Amendment passed the PESA. This generated enthusiasm amongst the people who expected that the Act would create space for tribal ancestral systems. As a result the system of tradition was gradually revived and started to work in many areas. In other areas, such as in the Oraon region, the Parha system has been destroyed. In most of the areas, Gram Sabhas that derive legitimacy from the legal rational system have been formed. Vasavi strongly feels that it is necessary to revive peoples' systems. The formation of Gram Sabhas is linked to the gradual undermining of peoples' political systems.

An important observation made by some activists is that PESA is supported by those who hold the de-colonized view, that the dynamic and progressive aspects of customary practices and traditions of governance need to become integral to a development vision. However the question remains, are custom and law miscible? What happens to the dynamic aspect of customary practices when they become customary law?

Customary law is a contradiction in terms—custom and laws are fundamentally different because their respective legitimacy is grounded in different world-views. Custom is grounded in the everyday experience accumulated in oral traditions, and law is grounded in the deductive processes of legal-rational written tradition. In custom, religion and politics are organically related, and their separation is the basis of law.

B.K. Roy-Burman has classified the relation between customary practices and statutory law under four categories:

1. In the first category the state gives place within its legal system to rules pertaining to institutions like marriage, inheritance and adoption. These are then classified as personal law. Some of these may be codified in the written form, some may not be.
2. In the second category are rules pertaining to the use of community resources amongst several forest dwelling communities. Irrespective of their status in state law, the forest dwellers generally recognize the jurisdiction of specific communities over specific hill ranges, waterways and so on.
3. In the third category are included tribals who were declared criminal, overlooking the fact that what the British saw as crime they saw as guerrilla warfare against the barbarism perpetuated by 'civilization'. These people lost their livelihood.
4. The fourth category includes customary practices that are parallel to behavioural norms prescribed by non-state establishments. For example, the Totos of West Bengal, a small tribe, perform an annual festival involving the sacrifice of nine cows, but claim to be Hindus. When some Nepali migrants tried to protest, the Totos complained of interference with religion.[26]

The provisions of PESA and the Forest Bill include all these.

However, they do not include material culture. The customary practices in legal-rational system of governance do not allow forest-based livelihoods such as shifting cultivation. Thus without the material culture what is left of customary practices are social institutions, rituals, myths, and folklores. PESA thus disempowers—it legitimizes customary practices on the one hand and de-legitimizes customary spaces, ways of knowing linked with forest based livelihoods, on the other. In other words, it destroys the space for customary governance.

PESA functions to fulfil the objectives of the centre (state). For instance, there is no way in which the centre can be questioned on the land acquisition act. The problem with this Act is not only the procedures for obtaining permission from the people to acquire land for 'public good', but also the definition of what constitutes the notion of 'public good'. The legal system is based on a notion of public good that gives priority to issues of national military-industrial security and it privileges the laboratory sciences that contribute to the making of the military-industrial regime. In contrast, the customary practices give priority to questions of livelihood, education and privilege and indigenous experiential learning.

It is clear that this process of codification has its political economy—it brings communities and their practices within the preview of the modern legal system. This de-centering is an aspect of the political economy of PESA. Further, it inadequately equips the tribals, for this legal instrument is inappropriate for participation in the global-free competition over natural resources. For instance, within the framework of PESA there is little possibility of questioning the centre with regard to globalization.

THE EXPERIENCE SO FAR

What emerges is that PESA was enacted in keeping with India's commitment to the WTO—to open the way for international players. The developments so far suggest that it has added to the antagonism between the tribal and the non-tribal peoples. Traditions and customary rights are in contradiction with the neo-liberal material culture of large dams, steel plants and intellectual patent regimes.

PESA and the Scheduled Tribes (Recognition of Forest Rights) Bill, 2005 do not adequately and appropriately equip the tribal people to withstand this onslaught.

The provisions in both legislations lose their strength on account of the Land Acquisition Act and the rehabilitation policy. The amendments in both these undermine the material conditions for the creative enrichment of traditions and customary practices. Certain kinds of land-forest-natural resource-human relations are inviolate and need to be protected by the Land Acquisition Act. These land-forest-natural resource ensure people's subsistence, restore nature's capacity for regeneration, restore biodiversity in nature and pluralism in social life. The land acquisition needs to be reoriented to the economy of nature, that is, principles of conservation.

APPENDIX 1

THE PROVISIONS OF THE PANCHAYATS (EXTENSION TO THE SCHEDULED AREAS) ACT, 1996 NO. 40 OF 1996

(24 December 1996)

An Act to provide for the extension of the provisions of Part IX of the Constitution relating to the Panchayats to the Scheduled Areas.

Be it enacted by Parliament in the Forty-seventh Year of the Republic of India as follows:

Short title

1. This Act may be called the Provisions of the Panchayats (Extension to the Scheduled Areas) Act, 1996.

Definition

2. In this Act, unless the context otherwise requires, 'Scheduled Areas' means the Scheduled Areas as referred to in Clause (1) of Article 244 of the Constitution.

Extension of Part IX of the Constitution

3. The provision of Part IX of the Constitution relating to Panchayats are hereby extended to the Scheduled Areas subject to such exceptions and modifications as are provided in section 4.

Exceptions and modifications to Part IX of the Constitution

4. Notwithstanding anything contained under Part IX of the Constitution, the Legislature of a State shall not make any law under that Part which is inconsistent with any of the following features, namely:
   (a) A State legislation on the Panchayats that may be made shall be in consonance with the customary law, social and religious practices and traditional management practices of community resources;
   (b) A village shall ordinarily consist of a habitation or a group of habitations or a hamlet or a group of hamlets comprising a community and managing its affairs in accordance with traditions and customs;
   (c) Every village shall have a Gram Sabha consisting of persons whose names are included in the electoral rolls for the Panchayat at the village level;
   (d) Every Gram Sabha shall be competent to safeguard and preserve the traditions and customs of the people, their cultural identity, community resources and the customary mode of dispute resolution;

(e) Every Gram Sabha shall—
  i. approve of the plans, programmes and projects for social and economic development before such plans, programmes and projects are taken up for implementation by the Panchayat at the village level;
  ii. be responsible for the identification or selection of persons as beneficiaries under the poverty alleviation and other programmes;

(f) Every Panchayat at the village level shall be required to obtain from the Gram Sabha a certification of utilisation of funds by that Panchayat for the plans, programmes and projects referred to in clause (e);

(g) The reservation of seats in the Scheduled Areas at every Panchayat shall be in proportion to the population of the communities in that Panchayat for whom reservation is sought to be given under Part IX of the Constitution:
Provided that the reservation for the Scheduled Tribes shall not be less than one-half of the total number of seats:
Provided further that all seats of Chairpersons of Panchayats at all levels shall be reserved for the Scheduled Tribes;

(h) The State Government may nominate persons belonging to such Scheduled Tribes as have no representation in the Panchayat at the intermediate level or the Panchayat at the district level:
Provided that such nomination shall not exceed one-tenth of the total members to be elected in that Panchayat;

(i) The Gram Sabha or the Panchayats at the appropriate level shall be consulted before making the acquisition of land in the Scheduled Areas for development projects and before re-settling or rehabilitating persons affected by such projects in the Scheduled Areas; the actual planning and implementation of the projects in the Scheduled Areas shall be coordinated at the State level;

(j) Planning and management of minor water bodies in the Scheduled Areas shall be entrusted to Panchayats at the appropriate level;

(k) The recommendations of the Gram Sabha or the Panchayats at the appropriate level shall be made mandatory prior to grant of prospecting licence or mining lease for minor minerals in the Scheduled Areas;

(l) The prior recommendation of the Gram Sabha or the Panchayats at the appropriate level shall be made mandatory for grant of concession for the exploitation of minor minerals by auction;

(m) While endowing Panchayats in the Scheduled Areas with such powers and authority as may be necessary to enable them to function as institutions of self-government, a State Legislature shall ensure that the

Panchayats at the appropriate level and the Gram Sabha are endowed specifically with

(i) The power to enforce prohibition or to regulate or restrict the sale and consumption of any intoxicant;
(ii) The ownership of minor forest produce;
(iii) The power to prevent alienation of land in the Scheduled Areas and to take appropriate action to restore any unlawfully alienated land of a Scheduled Tribe;
(iv) The power to manage village markets by whatever name called;
(v) The power to exercise control over money lending to the Scheduled Tribes;
(vi) The power to exercise control over institutions and functionaries in all social sectors;
(vii) The power to control over local plans and resources for such plans including tribal sub-plans;

(n) The State Legislations that may endow Panchayats with powers and authority as may be necessary to enable them to function as institutions of self-government shall contain safeguards to ensure that Panchayats at the higher level do not assume the powers and authority of any Panchayat at the lower level or of the Gram Sabha;

(o) The State Legislature shall endeavour to follow the pattern of the Sixth Schedule to the Constitution while designing the administrative arrangements in the Panchayats at district levels in the Scheduled Areas.

Continuance of existing laws on panchayats

5. Notwithstanding anything in Part IX of the Constitution with exceptions and modifications made by this Act, any provision of any law relating to Panchayats in force in the Scheduled Areas, immediately before the date on which this Act receives the assent of the President, which is inconsistent with the provisions of Part IX with such exceptions and modifications shall continue to be in force until amended or repealed by a competent Legislature or other competent authority or until the expiration of one year from the date on which this Act receives the assent of the President:

Provided that all the Panchayats existing immediately before such date shall continue till the expiration of their duration unless sooner dissolved by a resolution passed to that effect by the Legislative Assembly of that State or, in the case of a State having Legislative Council, by each House of the Legislature of that State.

K.L. MOHANPURIA,
Secretary to the Government of India

APPENDIX 2

TOTAL POPULATION, POPULATION OF SCHEDULED CASTES AND SCHEDULED TRIBES AND THEIR PROPORTIONS TO THE TOTAL POPULATION

State Code	India/State/UT	Population			Proportion of SC Population	Proportion of ST Population
		Total Population	Scheduled Castes (SC) Population	Scheduled Tribes (ST) Population		
	India[@]	1,028,610,328	166,635,700	84,326,240	16.2	8.2
02	Himachal Pradesh	6,077,900	1,502,170	244,587	24.7	4.0
08	Rajasthan	56,507,188	9,694,462	7,097,706	17.2	12.6
10	Bihar	82,998,509	13,048,608	758,351	15.7	0.9
20	Jharkhand	26,945,829	3,189,320	7,087,068	11.8	26.3
21	Orissa	36,804,660	6,082,063	8,145,081	16.5	22.1
22	Chhattisgarh	20,833,803	2,418,722	6,616,596	11.6	31.8
23	Madhya Pradesh	60,348,023	9,155,177	12,233,474	15.2	20.3
24	Gujarat	50,671,017	3,592,715	7,481,160	7.1	14.8
27	Maharashtra	96,878,627	9,881,656	8,577,276	10.2	8.9
28	Andhra Pradesh	76,210,007	12,339,496	5,024,104	16.2	6.6

Source: Primary Census Abstract, Census of India, 2001.

NOTES

1. Devdutt, *WTO: A Challenge for Swadeshi Swaraj*, Delhi: Pragya Sansthan, 2002, pp. 74–5.
2. Ibid.
3. These talks were initiated in the 1980s jointly by the USA, the European Union and Japan to promote free trade and economic globalization.
4. Information Centre on Local Governance in India, see http://www.localgovernmentindia.org/local-government-india.asp?id=1
5. Baldev Raj Nayar, 'Political Structure and India Economic Reforms of the 1990s', in *Pacific Affairs*, vol. 71, no. 3, Autum, 1998, pp. 335–58.
6. Shachi Arya, *Tribal Activism: Voices of Protest*, Jaipur and Delhi: Rawat Publications, 1998, pp. 216–20.
7. The enactment of PESA comes only after the panchayat in the mainstream (non-Scheduled Areas) was constitutionally empowered. Past experience with elected panchayats which supplanted traditional tribal systems, however, led to a legal challenge in the Andhra, Bihar, Maharashtra and Orissa High Courts. The Andhra Pradesh High Court ruled in 1995 that such a routine extension would be ultra vires of the Constitution, and that Part IX could only be extended to Scheduled Areas through an Act of Parliament. In 1994, the Government of India constituted a committee of MPs and experts under Dilip Singh Bhuria to frame such a law (Nandini Sundar, '"Custom" and "Democracy" in Jharkhand', *EPW*, 8 October 2005; also see 'Laws, Policies and Practices in Jharkhand', *EPW*, 8 October 2005.
8. The rural development ministry came up with the first draft of a rehabilitation policy way back in 1993. The draft clearly stated that it had been drawn up in view of the new economic policy and the expected rise in demand for more land, hence displacement. In 1994 this draft was revised, but it did not include rehabilitation as a right of those displaced. The draft was widely debated and an alternative draft was proposed. Civil society came up with an alternative draft endorsed by more than 1,500 people.

   In 1998, the ministry for rural development proposed a draft Land Acquisition Bill as well as a draft National Rehabilitation and Resettlement Policy for displaced persons. This met with severe opposition from affected people and voluntary groups, and another set of meetings was organized to discuss the draft. In 2000, after several consultations, an alternative civil society draft, the Land Acquisition, Rehabilitation and Resettlement Bill was formulated.

   The biggest problem with the policy was that it ignored the issue of land acquisition and the problems therein. These have been discussed widely at consultations of people's groups and CSOs, which gave their inputs to the National Advisory Council of the UPA government on the proposed policy. In March 2006, the National Advisory Council put up the draft National Development, Displacement and Rehabilitation Policy (December 2005) on its website.

The draft NRP 2006, which has now been introduced by the ministry of rural development, is not even close to the NAC draft. While some ideas and concepts have been borrowed, the current proposed policy appears to have discarded the key principles and components that were repeatedly raised in drafts laid down by social action groups and the NAC in 2006. for discussion see Manshi Asher and Rifat Mumtaz, *Displacement in the Time of Development*, 2006. http://www.infochangeindia.org/analysis143.jsp

9. See *Fact Sheet On Ministry Of Panchayati Raj*, http://pib.nic.in/archieve/factsheet/2005/panchayatiraj20051219.pdf
10. According to *Social Watch*, 2004: 'The PESA Act is one of the most potent legislative measures of the recent times, which recognizes the tribal peoples' mode of living, aspirations, their culture and traditions. But the fact that in most of the state the enabling rules are not in place more than eight years after the adoption of the Act suggests that the state governments are reluctant to operationalize the PESA mandate. The state legislations have omitted some of the fundamental principles without which the spirit of PESA can never be realized. For instance, the premise in PESA that state legislations on Panchayats shall be in consonance with customary laws and among other things traditional management practices of community resources are ignored by most of the state laws. . . . However, the state legislations, perhaps by design, through a twist of legal language have taken away powers from the Gram Sabhas'. The Second Citizen's Report in *Social Watch*, 2004, at http://www.socialwatchindia.com/institutions.htm
11. S. Upadhyay, 2004, 'Tribal Self-rule Law and Common Property Resources in Scheduled Areas of India: A New Paradigm Shift or Another Ineffective Sop?', paper presented at the Commons in an Age of Global Transition: Challenges, Risks and Opportunities: 10th Biennial Conference of IASCP, organized by International Association for the Study of Common Property at Oaxaca, Mexico, during 9–13 August.
12. *Panchayati Raj Update*, vol. XII, no. 3 (135), March 2005.
13. http://timesofindia.indiatimes.com/articleshow/1237584.cms
14. This insertion is mine.
15. The landmark judgement against the Central Act passed by Parliament after deliberating on the Bhuria Committee report has triggered resentment among tribals who accused the Arjun Munda government of failing

to put up the case in a proper perspective during hearing of a bunch of Public Interest Litigations (PIL) filed for and against the Act.

'The Government deliberately put up a weak defence during the hearing, I am afraid, the High Court judgement could neither maintain the spirit of the Central Act nor the scheduled areas spirit,' Adivasi Adhikar Morcha's Chief Convenor and former Bharatiya Janata Party (BJP) MP Salkhan Murmu contends.

The morcha is a conglomeration of several adivasi groups championing their rights and have threatened to announce economic blockade any day. Significantly the morcha boasts tribal political leaders cutting across party lines.

Murmu alleges the domination of non-tribals, particularly Mahto Kurmis, in the NDA cabinet has prevented the government from moving the Supreme Court against the High Court directive to annual reservation of heads in Scheduled Areas.

'Even the Government dragged its feet after BJP's national Vice-President and former Jharkhand Chief Minister Babulal Marandi asked the Arjun Munda regime to move the Supreme Court', says Jharkhand People's Party president Surya Singh Besra.

Setting 31 October as the deadline for the completion of Panchayat polls, the High Court has given two options to the government to complete the exercise—either come out with appropriate amendment of law immediately or follow the principles of reservation.

Moments after the judgement Chief Minister Arjun Munda cancelled the 22 August notification issued to conduct Panchayat polls in five phases from 26 September, citing it would take legal opinion following the High Court directive.

The Munda cabinet had already urged the centre for a suitable amendment to the Act saying controlling it is necessary to maintain social harmony.

On 29 March, the Jharkhand assembly also unanimously passed a resolution recommending de-reservation of posts of mukhias, pramukhs and presidents at the respective levels of the three-tier system in those Scheduled Areas where the tribals constitute less than 40 per cent of the population. As the tribals cutting across party lines held *adivasi adhikar morchas*, the non-tribals also set up a conglomeration of different organization under the umbrella of Jharkhand Pradesh Panchayati Raj Adhikar Manch with BJP leader and former MP Ramtahal Choudhury as its convener.

Another non-tribal outfit, Yuva Chatra Sangharsh Samiti, which came into prominence as an anti-domicile outfit countering the *adivasi/moolvasis*, is also spearheading the anti-Panchayat provision in the Scheduled Areas.

'The tribals who constitute only 27 per cent should keep in mind the rights of the rest 73 per cent of the population staying in Jharkhand', reminds Samiti Convener and LJP's state unit vice-president Uday Shankar Ojha.

'Three years ago, they wanted to throw us out of Jharkhand, and now they want us to be deprived of panchayat participation', claims Ojha. See *Jharkhand Faces Panchyat Raj Act Controversy*, Wednesday, 21 September 2005, PTI post on Indiainfo.com

16. Amit Bhaduri, 'Economic Growth a Meaningless Obsession', in *Seminar*, no. 569, January 2007.
17. 'Dy PM to Lay Foundation Stone of NDMC Romelt Steel Plant at Nagarnar Tomorrow'. PIB Press Release, 22 September 2003.
18. International Research and Technological Cooperation of MISA-TU (Moscow State Institute of Steel and Alloys Technological University) in 2002, see http://www.ir.misis.ru/english/about/general.htm
19. Nirmal, 'Nagarnar Steel Plant: A Plan for Destruction', in *Peoples March: Voice of the Indian Revolution*, vol. 3, no. 11, November 2002.
20. Tom Griffiths, 'Save Our Sacred Forests! Indigenous Movement in Jharkhand Challenges Plans for Industrial Development that Threaten Adivasi Forest, Farmlands and Way of Life', see Forests, farmlands and Way of life and see http://www.forestpeoples.org/documents/asia_pacific/india_jharkhand_feb07_eng.pdf
21. N.C. Saxena 'Issues in Panchayats'. See http://www.panchayats. org/downloads/Panchayats%20NC% 20Sax.PDF
22. 'UPA National Common Minimum Programme—Recommendations on Tribal Welfare and Development', National Advisory Council, Government of India, and Second Bhuria Committee report.
23. Samatha, *Update on Nagarnar*, 19 March 2002, Kisan Sangharsh Samiti, Nagarnar Bastar, Chhattisgarh [mail to: Samatha@satyam.net.in].
24. Forest Bill: A Historic Step, 24 January 2006, News@indlaw.com
25. Based on information from the field.
26. B.K. Roy-Burman, 'Persistence of Folk Law in India with Particular Reference to Tribal Communities', in Budhadeb Chaudhuri (ed.), *Ethnopolitics and Identity Crisis*, Tribal Studies of India Series, T 149, Delhi: Inter-India Publications, 1992.

CHAPTER TEN

Smaller States, Federalism and Decentralization: Implications for Governance in Chhattisgarh

GIRISH KUMAR

The creation of Chhattisgarh as an independent state was one of the biggest surprises of the year 2000. All the more perhaps since it was created along with two more new states, namely, Jharkhand and Uttaranchal, though the demand for the latter was not as longstanding and tortuous as that of the former. This is not to deny, however, that lately the Uttaranchal region had witnessed movements to this effect and also had to bear the wrath of the most populous state of Uttar Pradesh to which it was then a part of. Yet to see the birth of these three states together was a puzzle, if not bewilderment, to political watchers as well as scholars of Indian federalism. What was, after all, the rationale? How could one justify the creation of this new state? There was no demand *per se*. What prompted the NDA government to take this decision?

'To accommodate the aspirations of the rising middle class, the new entrepreneurs coming from among both tribal and non-tribal groups', the apologists argued. They went on, 'the detractors of the then Congress leadership in Madhya Pradesh would gain an opportunity; likewise, there would be more room at the apex level for the bureaucrats in a new state and, the lesser mortals in a vast officialdom, originally from Chhattisgarh region would happily go back home and vice versa. Above all, the people will not have to go all the way to distant Bhopal; now with a government closer to them at Raipur their grievances would be speedily redressed. Of course, there would be losers', they hastily added, 'such as hoteliers in Bhopal and the owners of the fleet of buses earlier used to ferry people from Raipur to Bhopal and back along with hundreds of others associated with the trade of serving the short duration visitors'.

The message was loud and clear that the creation of a new state is the only way to take the government closer to the people. Arguably, if that was the sole objective, it could have been achieved by following the route of decentralization. This is not to say that decentralization is panacea for all ills. Yet this is recognized the world over as the most potent and cost effective way to serve the people than under a centralized structure of authority and power.

Viewed from this perspective, the creation of Chhattisgarh was clearly a reflection of the crisis of representative democracy. The people and society have suffered from this malady of democracy for quite long. It has distorted the meaning and scope of politics *per se.* In continuation, let it also be admitted, this has led to all sorts of distortions in the functioning of the political system, including the reversal of the role of the pillars of the system—legislature, bureaucracy and judiciary. Yet the political class as a whole does not seem to accept the bitter truth. That what forms the core of the problem of mal-governance is the ever-increasing distance between the electors and the elected. The creation of yet another state was certainly not the answer to this growing chasm between the representatives and their constituencies.

THE PERFECT DIAGNOSIS AND THE WRONG TREATMENT

'Democracy at the centre and at the level of states but at the district level and below is the bureaucracy. This is the essence of the Indian democracy.' That is how E.M.S. Namboodiripad had summed up the Indian representative democratic system. That was the late 1970s. Prior to that, it should be noted, and in due recognition of the constitutionally recognized federal structure, the Indian states had already been twice reorganized. For the first time the exercise, however, was carried out on linguistic lines during the mid-1950s (e.g. Andhra Pradesh, Mysore, Madhya Pradesh et al.) and in the early 1960s (Maharashtra and Gujarat, for instance). One can, therefore, safely argue that the creation of Haryana and Himachal Pradesh were the first attempts to implement the idea of smaller states. There are claims and counter-claims for and against the imperatives of smaller states and the evidence can be culled out from the experiences of these two smaller states, leaving aside the odds associated with hilly topography of Himachal Pradesh.

The 1970s saw the birth of as many as five smaller states in the troubled north-eastern part of the country. Within a decade autonomous district councils were created in the Sixth Schedule Areas and a specially designed package was also introduced to administer the areas falling under the jurisdiction of the Fifth Schedule. Undoubtedly, there may have been little gains here and there. But it is equally true that essentially all these had been ad hoc arrangements to meet the exigencies of the time. They were never designed to tide over the crisis once and for all and quite naturally, they have failed to yield the desired results. The prolonged crisis due largely to the unresolved question of Nagas/Meetees and Kukis and the intermittent insurgency in the areas as well as the heavy deployment of the army to prevent unrest would bear testimony to this fact. Above all, there are larger states (in terms of their territorial dimensions) in the country that are better governed and also, there are tiny states with poor track record of administration. Is it any wonder then that people look askance and question the motive behind the creation of Chhattisgarh?

OVERLOOKING HISTORICAL LEGACY

The unfolding of Chhattisgarh did not begin with the reorganizaton of Madhya Pradesh in 1956 when the principalities and the small kingdoms spread in the tribal tract of sprawling Chhattisgarh were clubbed with the state of Madhya Bharat, the princely states of Vindhya Pradesh and Bhopal. Rather, the historical paradox of this geographical region goes back to 1860 when the boundaries of Central Province were drawn up by the then British colonial power. Indeed, the British had created the previous three coastal presidencies (Calcutta, Bombay and Madras, later giving way to provinces following the changes in their administrative set up) largely for the purpose of expanding and strengthening their empire in India. Development was not on their agenda. In fact, it was the dismay, distrust and devastation of the 1857 uprising that prompted the British Crown and its trusted viceroy to give a serious thought to their continuation and hence redefining their role in India. The end result was a new script for a new province, befitting its geographical location, which was aptly named as the Central Provinces. And for the first time development was put on the agenda of British rule in India.[1]

Undoubtedly, the earlier provinces had large chunks of sea-coast and since the rise of mercantile trade these areas had been in regular touch with traders of foreign origin. Along with the exchangeable commodities, these unannounced visits of traders also brought new ideas to these parts. In short, the rulers and, most significantly, the people had obtained an opportunity to come out of the shell of their traditional thinking and learn/imbibe entrepreneurial skills. Is it any wonder that as compared to the present western, southern states and, to some extent, West Bengal, the states belonging to the hinterland (the so-called heart of the country), an euphemism of the stagnant cow belt, are backward? Politically it may not be true, but from the development indices the Hindi belt states are far behind the developed west and south. It bears repetition that if from 1857 onwards people were deceived by their colonial masters, their indigenous rulers behaved no differently in the post-Independence era.

FAILED REORGANISATION

The fact is that, it was a multi-ethnic, heterogeneous, highly complex part that came into being as a modern Madhya Pradesh in 1956. The state of Madhya Pradesh, from which the present state of Chhattisgarh was carved out, had borders with as many as seven states. In most of the neighbouring states the reorganization process evolved as a concerted effort whereas in the absence of a unified language and also a unified political community the state could not reap the advantages of an opportunity to mobilize people for a collective goal. On the contrary the reorganization had negative impact on the politics and society of the state. In fact, following the reordering of the boundaries of the neighbouring states whatever was left out was merged together to give shape to Madhya Pradesh. Therefore, notwithstanding the reorganization, there remained an apparent political and social disjunct between the regions glued together. It had several negative consequences.

First of all, the administrative machineries of the different regions were so varied[2] in their orientation, perception and skills that they found themselves unable to cope with their territorial boundaries. Second, their level of political consciousness and exposure to political institutions were equally varied than in any other reorganized state. Third, the social composition of the two broadly different zones was also quite heterogeneous. In the princely states of Bhopal, Madhya Bharat and Vindhya Pradesh, for instance, the presence of upper caste was the highest (nearly one-fifth as compared to 12.9 per cent state average, as per the 1931 census) with very low level of tribal population. It was almost reverse in Mahakoshal and the Chhattisgarh regions. The point to be noted here is that parts of the Chhattisgarh region, prior to reorganization had relatively better administrative machinery. It is also true that with Raipur, Durg and Bhilai, the Chhattisgarh region (then part of Madhya Bharat) was also bestowed with a handful of cities catching up fast with thriving commerce and big industry in Indore, Gwalior, Bhopal and Ujjain (all in Madhya Bharat) and Jabalpur (Mahakoshal). Although the share of industrial output to the state GDP was not much, the presence of these modern industrial towns was indicative of the relatively developed network of roads and transport infrastructure (Jaffrelot, 1996: 135). But for all practical purposes the hinterland of Chhattisgarh was rural with very low level of urbanization and scanty transport and communication network. In terms of educational attainments and health care services this region was poorly endowed.

ABSENCE OF POPULAR LOCAL LEADERSHIP AND FRACTURED POLITY

Among the Congress leaders, the most influential, Pandit Ravi Shankar Shukla belonged to Raipur. Prior to the reorganization of Madhya Pradesh he was the chief minister of CP and Berar for a decade. In appreciation of his long governing experience, and being more suave and politically astute among the first generation of the Congress leaders of the region, he was logically elected as the first chief minister of Madhya Pradesh after its reorganization. His untimely demise within a couple of months created a void in the state. Given the intense factionalism (more appropriate to say both inter- and intra-regional) in the state, the centre had to intervene. And perhaps for the first time a centrally-imposed politician, Katju (then a union cabinet minister) took the reins of power in Madhya Pradesh. Rivalry, party feud, internal dissension all reached an alarming proportion. So much so that the centre had to 'intervene frequently to save its endangered magistrate and to maintain stability in the state' (Wilcox, 1968: 148). The Congress party won the assembly elections both in 1957 and 1962, but its social base did not expand. In fact, the voter turnout was very low.[3] Ironically, the Congress won the 1967 election too, but with a slender margin, leading to the government's downfall in six months. The next five years were marked by political instability.[4] The return of Congress in 1972 did not salvage the situation. For by then Indira Gandhi had emerged as the most powerful leader of both the party and the government and over-centralization of power became her tool to rule the roost. Thereafter paying attention to regional imbalances was not on the agenda of the government. All these things reached their zenith during Emergency and the Congress lost in the 1977 election. The second return of the Congress to power in 1980 and its continuation till 1989 brought no relief to a backward region like Chhattisgarh. During this period, however, Motilal Vora with Raipur as his base (like that of Pandit Ravi Shankar Shukla and his son Shyama Charan Shukla who was also the chief minister of the state in the late 1980s) was put at the helm of affairs, but largely because of the blessings of Rajiv Gandhi. The 1989 election brought the BJP to power. Again, this government was dismissed in 1992 in the wake of the demolition of the Babri Masjid.

It was only under the Digvijay Singh-led government that fresh initiatives were taken to empower local tribal communities.[5] Thus, in the four decades starting from 1956, three chief ministers from the Chhattisgarh region ruled the state. But the tribal population did not find favour even during their rule. The reason was two-fold. First, the near absence of local tribal leadership; second, both the chief ministers were Brahmins, not the original inhabitants of Chhattisgarh, and who essentially represented the relatively developed pocket of the region, Raipur and the industrial belt of Durg and Bhilai.

The 1980s also witnessed the emergence of Chhattisgarh Shramik Sangathan led by an immensely popular trade union leader, Shankar Guha Niyogi. Niyogi launched a successful campaign against the exploitation of largely tribal labourers by a combined trio of moneylenders, contractors and traders. As a result, he became a sworn enemy of both the Congress and the BJP. The assassination of Niyogi and the subsequent spread of RSS cadres even in remote tribal villages eventually provided a stronghold to the BJP in the region. Slowly, but gradually, the BJP emerged as a popular political force in the region.

CONVERGENCE OF INTERESTS

It also deserves mention that the first lot of Hindu refugees (displaced from Pakistan) had settled down in this region. And since the birth of the Jan Sangh (the first incarnation of the BJP) these refugees had formed the core of this party. Over the years, they had grown up, comprising a sizeable political community. Being in control of the trade and commerce in the area, they had the surplus to generously finance the activities of the party of their choice, i.e. the BJP. However, being confined to a region, their contribution to the state politics and to the distribution of state resources was negligible. Thus the stakes of both the party and its regional loyalists were interdependent. And the party was looking for an opportunity to pay back to its faithful followers. The creation of Chhattisgarh was going to serve the party interest in more ways than one. It was this confidence that prompted the BJP-led NDA government to set-up a new state.

First of all, the BJP knew that as long as the Chhattisgarh region was a part of larger Madhya Pradesh they could not have one more state government in their command. Second, it was in accordance with their ideological pursuit that the pan-Hindu identity could gain the upper hand only at the cost of weakening diverse regional identities. This could be achieved only by creating a large number of smaller states. In the long run, this strategy, the BJP ideologue strongly believed, would overshadow regional identities. Interestingly, included amongst the NDA allies of the BJP were the parties championing the cause of regional identities. Either they did not realize the game plan of their biggest ally or they were swayed away with the illusion that the fulcrum of coalition politics had taken a new turn. Indeed, for the first time this gave more voice to regional satraps in cobbling the union ministry and in resource allocation to its allies, they believed. Perhaps they did not have any option either. It is equally true that the BJP provided enough indication to its prospective allies that it was ready to create more space for them. As a proof it even expressed its willingness to have political compromise on its core agenda (dropping its demand to scrap the special status for Kashmir, a uniform religious code, etc.). Be that as it may, the same BJP, in spite of coming to power, stood alone in 1996 and lost the gamble. Two years later in 1998 it changed the strategy and reaped handsome rewards. It was the continuation of this arrangement that inter alia culminated in the formation of three new states.

WHAT HAVE BEEN THE EXPERIENCES OF OTHER STATES?

Taking administration proximate to the people has been an engaging theme in several states. If there was no justification for the creation of a new state, at least the political elite will call for the creation of new districts. Let us consider the case of the Vidarbha region in Maharashtra, for instance. There has been a persistent demand for the creation of a separate state for this region. This is the state where the Congress had a relatively long stint in power. And, apart from Gujarat, Maharashtra is the only state where Panchayat elections have been regularly held since 1962 though they were not mandatory. Yet in spite of decentralization at work, the Vidarbha region remained relatively backward. Hence, the demand for a new state came up again in the early 1980s. Their ire was directed against the leaders of the western part of Maharashtra which had become the most prosperous region in the state. It was not that the detractors of the then Congress leadership, who had risen to political prominence not because of their hard work but had climbed up because of the split in the Congress and with the blessings of Indira Gandhi, were not aware of this fact. But as late-comers they were impatient and looking for a quick way to gain power. They raised this issue which was eventually turned down. The Committee of Regional Imbalance (CORI), set-up to look into the causes of regional imbalances in the state, had reiterated that it was the prolonged nurturing of local-level institutions including decentralized panchayati institutions that led to the prosperity of western Maharashtra.

There is yet another instance from West Bengal. Since 1978 when elections to three-tier Panchayati Raj Institutions became a regular feature in the state, local development gradually fractured the demand for Jharkhand state comprising its south-west districts. So much so that for a little over a quarter of a century, the Left Front managed to govern one of its most populous districts of Medinipur without resorting to its split. Till the late-1990s when the population of this district had already touched the nine million count (but through effective decentralization of power with enough space for local-level leadership, of course under the guidance of the local unit of the CPI-M), the state had managed to reach out to the people. And without any clamouring for a new district it was doing well. In January 2002, Medinipur was split into two districts.

The case of Bihar is an example in clear contrast. For years the successive state leadership evaded panchayat elections (Kumar, 2001). On the other hand, it went on redrawing district boundaries by setting up a number of new districts. This process was accelerated during the combined regime of Laloo Yadav-Rabri Devi (1990–2005). They repeated the same argument—taking administration closer to the people. But the avowed objective of this exercise (setting up new districts) was to oblige the faithful loyalists so that they could run the new districts as their personal fiefdoms.

CHALLENGES BEFORE CHHATTISGARH

Years of isolation and neglect have led to a big gulf among Chhattisgarh's different regions, some of which are still at the primitive stage of development.[6] 'The villages, small upcoming townships or *kasbas*, which have witnessed induced developments, have over the decades been largely marginalized by a ruthless band of traders, middlemen and moneylenders. The latter have all along enjoyed the patronage of politicians and police combine. The ruthless exploitation drew the attention of ultra-leftists who stepped in on behalf the hapless populace. In fact, besides Andhra Pradesh, Bihar, Jharkhand, Madhya Pradesh, and Orissa, Chhattisgarh is the sixth state where the Naxal movement is fairly strong.

The spread of education has also contributed to the state's paradox. Despite reservation for tribal population in government jobs, all educated tribal boys and girls could not be absorbed into the public sector. In fact, their tryst with the so-called modern educational system has rendered them all the more useless. Being formally educated did not mean acquiring all the skills required for entering a competitive job market. On the other hand, they find it equally odd to settle back in their traditional occupations. Therefore the people have long been subjected to multi-layered deprivation. In one part of the region people are still living at a primitive stage whereas the other part has a sizeable population of educated unemployed. No doubt, the region has suffered from extreme disparities. In fact, it would be difficult to say the Chhattisgarh paradox is akin to classical intra-regional diversities noticeable in other states of this continent-size country.

Again, this is not to argue that the case of Chhattisgarh is unique or unparalleled in India. Remote areas in other states that have also remained isolated for quite long have suffered from neglect, stagnation and subsequent relative backwardness. In fact, to a large extent, this is equally true of Jharkhand. In any case, the living paradox of this state is likely to be accentuated in the coming years. For, the new state would find it extremely difficult to fulfil the two sets of contradictory demands.

Those who champion the cause of the tribal self-rule would look back to a tranquil, if not primitive, life not mediated by the coercive instruments of the state. That means restoring the communitarian way of life, with emphasis on direct democracy than strengthening the representative democracy whereas the latter has been the logical outcome of the formation of the new state. Addressing demands of the great majority of people would call for measures from the government in order to nurture the forest and natural resources with investment in small irrigational schemes, smooth supply of organic fertilizer to make the semi-arid land fertile. Some of these issues could have been handled by effective devolution of functions with matching powers and finances to panchayati institutions. This does not seem to be happening, though, unlike Jharkhand, the new state leadership of Chhattisgarh had quickly conducted elections to panchayati bodies. This would also necessitate steps for eliminating the layers of middlemen who thrive at the cost of unorganized tribal population, the producers of the primary produce or engaged in gathering and selling of raw produce like tamarind—one of the primary means of sustenance of people for numerous villages dotting the districts of Bastar, Dantewada and so on.

Whereas the growing middle class would like state intervention for the sake of creating jobs to earn more and enjoy more comforts, this would call for opening the area for huge investments, along with unhindered access to mineral deposits—the twin preconditions for creating jobs for the middle class. It is not clear how the political elite would reconcile the emerging contradictions between modernist agenda of faster economic growth without incorporating the concerns of equity. Besides, the existence of primitive tribes and the middle class at the distance of a few hours could be a sheer delight for anthropologists, but for impatient development planners it would be sheer bewilderment.

These problems having strong roots in the anthropology of this region would have persisted even in undivided Madhya Pradesh. Deep-rooted inequalities (having strong cultural and economic base) aggravated by deprivation and widespread poverty had for long prohibited the evolving of shared concerns for the common cause. There is no short-cut solution to this century-old structural problem of underdevelopment. Rather, this would entail a painstaking, prolonged process of skill formation, preceded by access to formal education to the people who are placed at the lowest level of the socio-economic ladder. It would also call for a strong political will and commitment to change the *status quo*. Surely, the new state would take time. It also deserves the benefit of doubt before its intentions are questioned. Yet if one looks at the choice of strategy of economic development and growth adopted in Chhattisgarh, it would confirm the abject surrender of the instruments of the state in serving the interest of narrow urban middle class. Will it be any surprise if the poor, neglected tribal populace, particularly those living in villages, ultimately find themselves cheated by the political elite of this new state?

NOTES

1. This is not to deny that Bengal was partitioned on the grounds of development way back in 1905 and later, on the same considerations, Bihar and Orissa combined were carved out of Bengal in 1911.
2. The reorganized state had five distinct regions, having varying administrative and political orientation and experiences. The Vindhya Pradesh was itself an amalgamation of as many as 38 princely states. Likewise, Madhya Bharat was composed of 25 native states earlier administered under the thumb of hereditary rulers and most of them were essentially politically backward. This was equally true of the princely state of Bhopal. The remaining two regions were Mahakoshal and the Hindi-speaking areas of Chhattisgarh and Sironj (carved out of Rajasthan, a state known for its entrenched feudal moorings). Prior to Independence, the last two, Mahakoshal

and Chhattisgarh, were governed under the provisions of the British-India acts, whereas the rest—Bhopal, Madhya Bharat and Vindhya Pradesh—were under the exclusive control of princely states. Therefore, the level of economic and political developments, including their exposure to village-level institutions was at variance. Above all, the Mahakoshal region, being part and parcel of CP and Berar, had earlier experienced various political and administrative reforms.

3. The voter turn out in Madhya Pradesh was found lowest among all the 15 states in the 1962 Assembly elections. 'The low levels of political participation (i.e. voting) are generally accompanied by high levels of power concentration at the local level in rural India. The states that were high on the participation list were among those most active in the state reorganization movement,' observed Weiner. Ironically, the state of Madhya Pradesh also underwent the process of reorganization but it was 'not the result of a political movement by culturally conscious groups for a state of their own. . . . Though Hindi is the lingua franca, there is in fact, little communication from one part of the state to another and from one social group to another. There are few interest associations linking regions of the state along functional lines' (Weiner and Osgood, 1975: 345-6).
4. During 1967–72, the state was ruled by an amalgamation of several political parties, including the dissidence of the Congress under the banner of Sanyukta Vidhayak Dal but all along this interregnum the political actors remained busy in cobbling ministries and performing a balancing act to ensure their survival in power than paying attention to effective governance.
5. Following the passage of the Parliament Act 1996 (to extend the provisions of the 73rd Constitutional Amendment with enhanced power for the village assembly), the district administration led by a genuinely concerned district magistrate helped the tribal population to form cooperatives to run the tamarind trade in the region. The twin objective of this campaign was to empower tribal collectives and to oust the middlemen from this trade. See *Tamarind Route to Gram Swaraj* (1999).
6. The *Abhujmadh* (literally means unknown or perhaps unsettled/unresolved habitation of wildlife) region, for instance, is still inhabited by people to whom 'clothing' is an alien conception. The entire *Abujhmadh* region is spread over 4,000 sq. km. area now falling under the territorial jurisdiction of Bastar and Dantewara district administration. This thinly/sparsely populated region is dotted with 237 villages. This includes 32 villages abandoned on account of shifting cultivation. See, Aarti Dhar 'In the Wild Woods', *The Hindu* (Sunday Magazine, 7 July 2002).

REFERENCES

Dhar, Aarti, 2002: ' In the Wild Woods', *The Hindu* (Sunday Magazine), 7 July.

Jafferelot, Christophe, 1996: *The Hindu Nationalist Movement and Indian Politics, 1925 to the 1990s,* Delhi: Viking.

Kumar, Girish, 2001: 'Overcoming State Resistance: Panchayat Elections in Bihar', *Economic and Political Weekly,* vol. 6, no. 20, 19 May, pp. 1681–4.

The Tamarind Route to Gram Swaraj (1999), Rajiv Gandhi Development Mission, District Collectorate, Jagdalpur (Bastar).

Weiner, Myron and John Osgood (eds.), 1975: *Electoral Politics in the Indian States: Party System and Cleavages,* vol. IV (*Studies in Electoral Politics in the Indian States*), Delhi: Manohar.

Wilcox, Wayne, 1968: 'Madhya Pradesh', in Mynor Weiner (ed.), *State Politics in India,* New Jersey: Princeton University Press.

Contributors

SAMUEL BERTHET received his Ph.D in history and his work focuses on the social and cultural dynamics of the subcontinent with reference to the development of the modern state, education, representation and the transmission of knowledge. He has also worked on maritime history, taught at Visva Bharati (Santiniketan), and JNU (New Delhi), and has been scientific coordinator of two European projects on Maritime History between Europe and South Asia. He is currently director of Alliance française de Chittagong (Bangladesh). He has authored and co-authored many books and has contributed to volumes—including the recent *Dictionnaire de l'Inde contemporaine*—besides curating seven exhibitions.

GIRISH KUMAR is Senior Fellow, Indian Institute of Public Administration, New Delhi. Previously, he was Senior Fellow and Head, Political Science division, Centre de Sciences Humaines, New Delhi, and also had a brief stint in France as Visiting Professor at the Université de Picardie, Amiens. He has worked at the Lal Bahadur Shastri National Academy of Administration, Mussoorie, as Senior Research Officer. Prior to that, he was Senior Coordinator at the Institute of Social Sciences, New Delhi, and Visiting Fellow at the European Institute for Asian Studies, Brussels. Dr. Kumar has previously published *Health Sector Reforms in India* (ed., 2009), *Local Democracy in India: Interpreting Decentralization* (2006), *State Politics and Panchayats in India* (co-authored, 2003) and *West Bengal Panchayat Election 1993: A Study in Participation* (co-authored, 1996).

BERTRAND LEFEBVRE is a Ph.D student in geography at the University of Rouen. He is a specialist in spatial analysis and geomatics.

AMIT PRAKASH is Associate Professor at the Centre for the Study of Law and Governance, Jawaharlal Nehru University, New Delhi. Earlier, he has also served as Assistant Research Professor at the Centre for

Policy Research, New Delhi. He has a doctoral degree from the School of Oriental and African Studies, University of London. He is the author of several articles in national and international journals in the area of political analysis, discursive structures of the Indian state, electoral patterns and trends in India and some of its units, etc., and of the books, *Jharkhand: Politics of Development of Identity* (2001) and *Politics and Internal Security* (2004). He is also co-editor (along with Niraja Gopal Jayal and Pradeep K. Sharma) of *Local Governance in India: Decentralisation and Beyond* (2006).

CYRIL ROBIN is currently lecturer in 'Geopolitics and Economy in South Asia' at the Institute of Political Studies, Paris. He was previously Research Fellow, Centre de Sciences Humaines, New Delhi between 2004 and 2009. He received his Ph.D from the Institute of Political Studies, Paris. His dissertation deals with the rise of the Other Backward Classes on the political scene in Bihar (1952–2005).

SAVYASAACHI teaches sociology at the Department of Sociology, Jamia Millia Islamia. He is the author of *Between the Earth and the Sky: The Penguin Book of Forest Writings.*

ILINA SEN is a well-known feminist scholar and human rights activist. She is Professor and Head, Department of Gender Studies, Mahatma Gandhi Antarrashtriya Hindi Vishwavidyalaya in Wardha.

DIPANKAR SENGUPTA is Professor of Economics at the Department of Economics, University of Jammu. Prior to this, he has taught Economics at the Jawaharlal Nehru University and has been a researcher in the Centre de Sciences Humaines, New Delhi. He publishes in the areas of International Political Economy and Development Economics.

VIRGINIUS XAXA is Professor of Sociology at Delhi School of Economics, Delhi University. He is the author of *State, Society, and Tribes: Issues in Post-Colonial India* (2008), *Economic Dualism and Structure of Class: A Study in Plantation and Peasant Settings in North Bengal* (1997) and co-author of *Plantation Labour in India* (1996).

Index